Frank Raymond III
Leon Ginsberg
Debra Gohagan
Editors

Information Technologies: Teaching to Use– Using to Teach

Information Technologies: Teaching to Use–Using to Teach has been co-published simultaneously as *Computers in Human Services*, Volume 15, Number 2/3 1998.

*Pre-publication
REVIEWS,
COMMENTARIES,
EVALUATIONS . . .*

"**A** most useful volume. . . Displays the current diversity in the use of technology in social work education. The entries range from interactive TV, web-based courses to computer applications in the class."

Elbert Siegel
*Department of Social Work
Southern Connecticut State University*

More pre-publication
REVIEWS, COMMENTARIES, EVALUATIONS . . .

"Information Technologies: Teaching to Use–Using to Teach*, edited by Frank B. Raymond, Leon Ginsberg, and Debra Gohagan, is a collection of papers from the historic first conference of the same name, held in September, 1997. Both undergraduate and graduate social work faculty have contributed to this benchmark book. The two subtitles, *Teaching to Use* and *Using to Teach* form the two subsections of the book and serve to organize the respective papers.

Using to Teach includes several articles which address the use of interactive television (ITV) for the delivery of distance education. Social work faculty will find much useful information on the designing of ITV courses and on what to expect in students' reactions to this technology.

The *Teaching to Use* section approaches the social work curriculum by examining the future of information technology and the issues we all must face in incorporating it into our teaching. Butterfield's important and thoughtful paper on the future of human services and the emerging information economy should be a required reading for all social workers. It is a road map of the issues we will encounter in the next five to ten years.

Social work educators, students, practitioners and managers will find this collection of papers from the historic first conference on social work education and information technologies to be invaluable in establishing a fix on our current position in these uncharted waters and for plotting courses into the early twenty-first century."

Marshall L. Smith, PhD, MSW
Professor of Social Work
Rochester Institute of Technology

The Haworth Press, Inc.

Information Technologies: Teaching to Use– Using to Teach

Information Technologies: Teaching to Use–Using to Teach has been co-published simultaneously as *Computers in Human Services*, Volume 15, Numbers 2/3 1998.

The *Computers in Human Services* Monographic "Separates"

Below is a list of "separates," which in serials librarianship means a special issue simultaneously published as a special journal issue or double-issue *and* as a "separate" hardbound monograph. (This is a format which we also call a "DocuSerial.")

"Separates" are published because specialized libraries or professionals may wish to purchase a specific thematic issue by itself in a format which can be separately cataloged and shelved, as opposed to purchasing the journal on an on-going basis. Faculty members may also more easily consider a "separate" for classroom adoption.

"Separates" are carefully classified separately with the major book jobbers so that the journal tie-in can be noted on new book order slips to avoid duplicate purchasing.

You may wish to visit Haworth's website at . . .

http://www.haworthpressinc.com

. . . to search our online catalog for complete tables of contents of these separates and related publications.

You may also call 1-800-HAWORTH (outside US/Canada: 607-722-5857), or Fax 1-800-895-0582 (outside US/Canada: 607-771-0012), or e-mail at:

getinfo@haworthpressinc.com

Jeremy Shapiro, PhD (CHS 8(1), 1991). *"This landmark volume presents an original and–until now–unavailable perspective on the uses of computers for community- and social-change-based organizations."*

Computer Literacy in Human Services Education, edited by Richard L. Reinoehl and B. Jeanne Mueller (CHS 7(1/2/3/4), 1990). *"This volume provides a unique and notable contribution to the investigation and exemplification of computer literacy in human services education."*

Computer Literacy in Human Services, edited by Richard L. Reinoehl and Thomas Hanna (CHS 6(1/2/3/4), 1990). *"Includes a diversity of articles on many of the most important practical and conceptual issues associated with the use of computer technology in the human services." (Adult Residential Care)*

The Impact of Information Technology on Social Work Practice, edited by Ram A. Cnaan, PhD, and Phyllida Parsloe, PhD (CHS 5(1/2), 1989). *"International experts confront the urgent need for social work practice to move into the computer age."*

A Casebook of Computer Applications in the Social and Human Services, edited by Walter LaMendola, PhD, Bryan Glastonbury, and Stuart Toole (CHS 4(1/2/3/4), 1989). *"Makes for engaging and enlightening reading in the rapidly expanding field of information technology in the human services." (Wallace Gingerich, PhD, Associate Professor, School of Social Welfare, University of Wisconsin-Milwaukee)*

Technology and Human Service Delivery: Challenges and a Critical Perspective, edited by John W. Murphy, PhD, and John T. Pardeck, PhD, MSW (CHS 3(1/2), 1988). *"A much-needed, critical examination of whether and how computers can improve social services. . . . Essential reading for social workers in the field and for scholars interested in how computers alter social systems." (Charles Ess, PhD, Assistant Professor of Philosophy, Morningside College)*

Research in Mental Health Computing: The Next Five Years, edited by John H. Greist, MD, Judith A. Carroll, MSW, Harold P. Erdman, PhD, Marjorie H. Klein, PhD, and Cecil R. Wurster, MA (CHS 2(3/4), 1988). *"Provides a clear and lucid perspective on the state of research in mental health computing." (David Servan-Schreiber, MD, Western Psychiatric Institute & Clinic and Department of Computer Science, Carnegie Mellon University)*

Information Technologies: Teaching to Use–Using to Teach has been co-published simultaneously as *Computers in Human Services*, Volume 15, Numbers 2/3 1998.

Cover design by Thomas J. Mayshock Jr.

The Haworth Press, Inc., 10 Alice Street, Binghamton, NY 13904-1580 USA

Library of Congress Cataloging-in-Publication Data

Information technologies : teaching to use–using to teach / Frank B. Raymond III, Leon Ginsberg, Debra Gohagan, editors.
     p. cm.
     Includes bibliographical references.
     ISBN 0-7890-0679-0 (alk. paper)
     1. Social work education. 2. Social work–Computer-assisted instruction. I. Raymond, Frank B. II. Ginsberg, Leon. III. Gohagan, Debra.
HV11.I46 1998
361.3'2'071–dc21   99-10046
                                                        CIP

Information Technologies: Teaching to Use– Using to Teach

Frank B. Raymond III
Leon Ginsberg
Debra Gohagan
Editors

Information Technologies: Teaching to Use–Using to Teach has been co-published simultaneously as *Computers in Human Services*, Volume 15, Numbers 2/3 1998.

The Haworth Press, Inc.
New York · London

INDEXING & ABSTRACTING

Contributions to this publication are selectively indexed or abstracted in print, electronic, online, or CD-ROM version(s) of the reference tools and information services listed below. This list is current as of the copyright date of this publication. See the end of this section for additional notes.

- *Abstracts of Research in Pastoral Care & Counseling*
- *ACM Guide to Computer Literature*
- *Applied Social Sciences Index & Abstracts (ASSIA) (Online: ASSI via Data-Star) (CDRom: ASSIA Plus)*
- *Behavioral Medicine Abstracts*
- *caredata CD: the social & community care database*
- *CNPIEC Reference Guide: Chinese National Directory of Foreign Periodicals*
- *Computer Abstracts*
- *Computer Literature Index*
- *Computing Reviews*
- *Current Contents: Clinical Medicine/Life Sciences (CC:CM/LS) (weekly Table of Contents Service), and Social Science Citation Index. Articles also searchable through Social SciSearch, ISI's online database and in ISI's Research Alert current awareness service.*
- *Engineering Information (PAGE ONE)*
- *IBZ International Bibliography of Periodical Literature*
- *Information Science Abstracts*
- *INSPEC Information Services*
- *INTERNET ACCESS (& additional networks) Bulletin Board for Libraries ("BUBL"), coverage of information resources on INTERNET, JANET, and other networks.*

(continued)

- *Library & Information Science Abstracts (LISA)*

- *Microcomputer Abstracts*

- *National Clearinghouse on Child Abuse & Neglect*

- *Periodica Islamica*

- *Psychological Abstracts (PsycINFO)*

- *Referativnyi Zhurnal (Abstracts Journal of the All-Russian Institute of Scientific and Technical Information)*

- *Sage Public Administration Abstracts (SPAA)*

- *Social Planning/Policy & Development Abstracts (SOPODA)*

- *Social Work Abstracts*

- *Sociological Abstracts (SA)*

Special Bibliographic Notes related to special journal issues (separates) and indexing/abstracting:

- indexing/abstracting services in this list will also cover material in any "separate" that is co-published simultaneously with Haworth's special thematic journal issue or DocuSerial. Indexing/abstracting usually covers material at the article/chapter level.
- monographic co-editions are intended for either non-subscribers or libraries which intend to purchase a second copy for their circulating collections.
- monographic co-editions are reported to all jobbers/wholesalers/approval plans. The source journal is listed as the "series" to assist the prevention of duplicate purchasing in the same manner utilized for books-in-series.
- to facilitate user/access services all indexing/abstracting services are encouraged to utilize the co-indexing entry note indicated at the bottom of the first page of each article/chapter/contribution.
- this is intended to assist a library user of any reference tool (whether print, electronic, online, or CD-ROM) to locate the monographic version if the library has purchased this version but not a subscription to the source journal.
- individual articles/chapters in any Haworth publication are also available through the Haworth Document Delivery Service (HDDS).

Information Technologies: Teaching to Use–Using to Teach

CONTENTS

ABOUT THE EDITORS

Frank B. Raymond III, DSW, is Professor and Dean of the College of Social Work at the University of South Carolina. He has been a social work educator for 26 years and a dean for 18 years. His publications have been primarily in the area of technology, social work management, corrections, health care and social work education administration. Dr. Raymond has held many state and national leadership positions with the National Association of Social Workers, the National Association of Deans and Directors of Schools of Social Work and the Council on Social Work Education.

Leon H. Ginsberg, PhD, is a Carolina Distinguished Professor at the University of South Carolina College of Social Work, where he has been a faculty member since 1986. In the 1970s and 1980s, he served as Commissioner of Human Services and later as Chancellor of the Board of Regents in West Virginia. He was formerly Director and Dean of the School of Social Work at West Virginia University and, in the 1960s, was Associate Professor of Social Work at the University of Oklahoma. He is the author of several books and articles on social work and human services. Dr. Ginsberg chaired the *1997 Information Technologies Conference: Using to Teach–Teaching to Use* where these papers were presented.

Debra Gohagan, MSW, is Assistant Professor at Mankato State University in Mankato, MN. She has 20 years of practice experience with children and families in child welfare, health, and mental health settings. She is currently completing the doctoral program at the University of South Carolina College of Social Work. Her research focus is the use of technology as instructional tools for social work educators.

The articles in this volume are revised versions of papers presented at the *1997 Information Technologies Conference: Using to Teach–Teaching to Use*, held in Charleston, South Carolina, September 7-9, 1997.

Introduction

Frank B. Raymond III
Leon Ginsberg
Debra Gohagan

The decade of the nineties brought an explosion in the use of information and computer-based technologies. Higher education, in particular, is experiencing a significant impact from this rapid growth and diffusion. Colleges and universities are working to meet the challenge to prepare graduates to work and live in this rapidly changing technology-enhanced environment. There are even predictions that use of this technology will reshape and possibly replace the existing educational environment.

The impact of the rapid growth and diffusion of information technologies is affecting social workers in all types of settings. Social work educators are struggling to keep pace with the impact of the technology explosion as they prepare graduates for practice activities in a technology-enhanced environment. Even with the increased use of information technologies in social work education, there continues to be much fragmentation, duplication, and isolation in these efforts to prepare the profession for the 21st century. Educators need a venue to exchange information about the use of technology to enhance teaching and learning activities. The University of South Carolina's College of Social Work, with assistance of a Council on Social Work Education Millennium grant, sponsored the first national conference devoted specifically and completely to the use of information technologies in social work education. This conference, the *1997 Information Technologies Conference: Using to Teach–Teaching to Use*, was held in Charleston, South Carolina, September 1997.

Frank B. Raymond III, DSW, and Leon Ginsberg, PhD, are affiliated with the College of Social Work, University of South Carolina, Columbia, SC. Debra Gohagan, MSW, LISW, is Assistant Professor at Mankato State University, Mankato, MN.

[Haworth co-indexing entry note]: "Introduction." Raymond, Frank B. III, Leon Ginsberg, and Debra Gohagan. Co-published simultaneously in *Computers in Human Services* (The Haworth Press, Inc.) Vol. 15, No. 2/3, 1998, pp. 1-5; and: *Information Technologies: Teaching to Use–Using to Teach* (ed: Frank B. Raymond III, Leon Ginsberg, and Debra Gohagan) The Haworth Press, Inc., 1998, pp. 1-5. Single or multiple copies of this article are available for a fee from The Haworth Document Delivery Service [1-800-342-9678, 9:00 a.m. - 5:00 p.m. (EST). E-mail address: getinfo@haworthpressinc.com]

This conference provided social work educators the opportunity to discuss and prepare for technology-based instruction as the 21st century approaches. Participants shared technological resources, increased their knowledge of available technologies, developed skills in the use of these technologies, and established working relationships with peers from around the world. Educators presented information about models of how to teach social work subject matter through the use of technology. These models addressed the institutional, educational, and practice issues involved in expanding these technology-based applications.

Educators also presented the results of research projects that addressed questions about the effectiveness of technology-based teaching and learning activities. This research addressed the profession's concerns about the ability of technology-based instructional approaches to help students master content, think critically, interact rationally, and develop cognitive and ethical perspectives when using technology-based instruction.

This volume contains selected articles based upon the presentations at this conference. These articles present the authors' efforts to employ information technologies to meet the needs of social work education, and include examples of the use of technology to teach social work knowledge, values, and skills across the curriculum. The articles are grouped into two sections. Section 1, *Using to Teach*, contains examples of how technology is used to deliver social work education and to teach specific components of the social work curriculum. Section 2, *Teaching to Use*, includes articles that discuss efforts to integrate into the social work curriculum content on the use of technology in social work practice. These articles cover a range of perspectives, such as an international view on the role of information technology in Britain and Malaysia; training approaches for faculty development; and computer-based software that has the potential to transform the manner in which curriculum objectives are met.

USING TO TEACH

Social work educators have been using information technologies to deliver the curriculum for many years. Social work education has used interactive television (ITV) for distance education learning for almost twenty years. The University of South Carolina's College of Social Work was the first social work program to offer coursework by ITV in 1980. There are now more than 50 schools of social work that regularly provide access to social work education through distance education modalities. The use of web-based technology to provide a venue for teaching students outside of the traditional classroom environment is pushing the boundaries of distance education definitions. In spite of the profession's years of experience with distance education, questions continue to exist about the effectiveness of distance education as a teaching medium for social work education. Several authors report on research projects that measure the effectiveness of ITV/distance education and web-based approaches for delivery of course content.

Several authors report on activities in which technology is used not only as a tool for delivering information, but also as a tutor for teaching knowledge, values, and skills in research. *Forster and Rehner* describe the evaluation of a part-time graduate program delivered through distance education. Students' academic performance and student and teacher surveys suggest that distance education courses are comparable to on-campus courses in instructional quality. *Patchner, Petracchi, and Wise* also report on a research project in which students taking a foundations research methods course in a traditional classroom were compared with students taking the course via ITV. Their findings revealed no statistical significance between groups in outcomes based on final examinations, written papers, and final course grades.

Freddolino shares information and lessons learned about the process of developing and managing distance education programs in social work education. He, like the other authors in this section, describes the effectiveness and efficiency of this teaching modality, as well as its limitations.

Stocks and Freddolino describe teaching a research methods course entirely over the Internet, with no meetings on campus. Their research examined student outcome data including grades and student satisfaction, student attitudes toward technology, extent of technology use by students, and the impact of technology on classroom relationships.

Forte reports on a project that employs the use of a statistical software application in teaching an undergraduate applied statistics course. Standardized instruments were used to measure statistics anxiety and math readiness. Forte also assessed student perceptions of the use of this technology as a teaching tool. Student responses were positive to the use of this technology as an instructional tool.

Resnick describes the development of a computer-based, multi-media approach to teaching social work skill development in practice courses. This application, *Paraphrase*, is a useful tool for teaching interviewing skills, one of the most basic of skills required for practice activities.

Interest in methods for using the Internet to teach social work courses is high. *Miller-Cribbs and Chadiha* discuss the use of information technology in a foundation level, human diversity course in a master's program. Course assignments enable students to develop skill in the use of the Internet to find information about diverse groups and to evaluate relevant websites. Technology becomes a tool for finding and building knowledge as well as skills in working with diverse groups.

Galambos and Neal present instructional approaches using computer simulations and Internet linkages to teach policy and macro social work skills in a baccalaureate curriculum. This article presents information about the use of two on-line political simulation games and the use of the Internet to access information.

TEACHING TO USE

It is difficult to keep up with the demands of preparing social workers for our technology-enhanced society. In this section, educators report on institutional and societal issues that influence educators' efforts to prepare students. Articles include information about the future of information technology, an application of technology in practice, two case studies of information technology in other countries, a model for preparing educators to teach and use technology, and a discussion about incorporating specific software in the social work curriculum.

Butterfield presents information about the state of the art in information technologies in social work practice. He focuses on the potential growth areas of information technologies and provides a guide for establishing the direction of future educational innovations.

Schoech and Bolen describe the use of a technology application that is an example of the future possibilities in employing technology in practice settings. They report on a support system developed to improve workplace performance by providing on-demand access to the integrated human service agency information. The type of software application they describe can be developed to meet the needs of a variety of practice settings and is therefore appropriate for inclusion in the social work curriculum.

The issue of planning for the future growth of information technologies, as well as dealing with current trends, is affecting social work educators around the world, as demonstrated in the articles by Rafferty and Chong. *Rafferty* discusses the diffusion of communication and information technology in social work education in Britain where a national emphasis on developing and integrating technology across all areas of higher education drives this effort. CTI Centre for Human Services, whose mission is to provide resources, training, and support to social work educators interested in using technology as a teaching tool in the curriculum, coordinates these activities for social work education in Britain.

Chong discusses the growing emphasis on incorporating technology in the Malaysian governmental and societal infrastructure. Chong suggests that the integration of information technology is necessary for social work professionalization in Malaysia. Chong also suggests that given limited resources in Malaysia, including professional social workers, information technologies offer efficient means for providing staff development, distance education access, telesocial work, and networking activities.

Just as the profession needs models for distance education, it also needs models for training social work educators to use technology across the curriculum. *Stafford and Namorato* present a case study in which a university provided the resources and support to assist faculty to enhance their skills in using and teaching with technology. This university's approach included supporting technology purchases, establishing a faculty development lab, and providing an intensive training program for teaching faculty to use and develop technology-based teaching tools. The authors describe their collaborative efforts to integrate information from their respective fields in order to develop a multi-media application for teaching social welfare history.

Technology-based instructional tools have the potential to transform the delivery of social work course content. The debates about 'literacy versus competency' and 'infusion of content versus separate courses' become less relevant. *Crook and Brady* describe their efforts to use a web-based program that incorporates all course delivery activities such as assignments, grading, and course management. This type of courseware product changes the context of course design and delivery for the instructor.

Finally, *Tompkins and Southward* describe the use of geographical information systems (GIS) technology in social work education. The authors remind readers of the profession's heritage in the use of GIS. They suggest that this software application makes significant contributions to the processes by which social and economic justice concepts are taught across the social work curriculum. Using the newer technology-based GIS applications has the potential to integrate knowledge and skill-building activities across several fields of practice and curriculum areas such as research, practice, policy, and management classes.

SECTION 1:

USING TO TEACH

Part-Time MSW Distance Education:
A Program Evaluation

Michael Forster
Timothy Rehner

SUMMARY. An evaluation of a part-time master's of social work program including 18 hours of interactive video instruction examined student academic performance, instructors' ability to achieve instructional objectives, interactions among students and between students and faculty, and quality of instructional environment. The evaluation was conducted following 12 hours of interactive video, "distance" coursework. Results of grade comparisons and surveys of students, faculty and staff suggest that distance education courses are comparable to the main campus courses in instructional quality. Students and faculty voice concerns, however, about limitations on interaction and spontaneity imposed by the interactive video environment. *[Article copies available for a fee from The Haworth Document Delivery Service: 1-800-342-9678. E-mail address: getinfo@haworthpressinc.com]*

KEYWORDS. Distance education, interactive video, MSW programs, educational program evaluation

Michael Forster, PhD, is Assistant Professor of Social Work and Coordinator of the Master's Program, and Timothy Rehner, PhD, is Assistant Professor of Social Work and Coordinator of the Bachelor's Program, The University of Southern Mississippi School of Social Work.

Address correspondence to the authors at: The School of Social Work, The University of Southern Mississippi, Box 5114, Hattiesburg, MS 39406.

This article is the revised version of a paper presented at the *1997 Information Technologies Conference: Using to Teach–Teaching to Use*, held in Charleston, South Carolina, September 7-9, 1997.

[Haworth co-indexing entry note]: "Part-Time MSW Distance Education: A Program Evaluation." Forster, Michael, and Timothy Rehner. Co-published simultaneously in *Computers in Human Services* (The Haworth Press, Inc.) Vol. 15, No. 2/3, 1998, pp. 9-21; and: *Information Technologies: Teaching to Use–Using to Teach* (ed: Frank B. Raymond III, Leon Ginsberg, and Debra Gohagan) The Haworth Press, Inc., 1998, pp. 9-21. Single or multiple copies of this article are available for a fee from The Haworth Document Delivery Service [1-800-342-9678, 9:00 a.m. - 5:00 p.m. (EST). E-mail address: getinfo@haworthpressinc.com]

INTRODUCTION

Distance learning promises to revolutionize higher education (Drucker, 1997; Garrison, 1989; Schlossberg, Lynch & Chickering, 1989; Wulf, 1995). Yet distance education remains controversial among many faculty on quality and other grounds (Blanch, 1994; Blumenstyk, 1996), and poses interrelated instructional (Day, 1995) and evaluative (Kember, 1995) challenges. Instructional quality of distance courses comparable to traditional classroom experience is not a given without appropriate and effective modification of course delivery methods, and in some cases course content (Cyrs & Smith, 1990). While the interactive video environment seeks to duplicate the classroom experience through a variety of technologies, problems of assuring the attention and engagement of distant learners in particular persist (Owens, Pace & Finneran, 1995). Of particular concern to many educators, too, is preserving the relationship component of the educational experience when students are learning "at a distance" from the instructor (Freddolino, 1996).

The purpose of this study was to evaluate a part-time MSW program with a substantial distance education component. The program, based at a satellite campus and including several interactive video classes, was designed to be qualitatively equivalent to the main campus parent program. The study was initiated because administrators and faculty wanted to assess whether students in main campus and remote groups were in fact receiving comparable educational experiences. In particular, faculty and administrators want to ensure that instructional quality was not compromised by the use of interactive video classes.

BACKGROUND

The University of Southern Mississippi (USM) School of Social Work's MSW program initiated a part-time distance education program in the Fall of 1996. It was introduced in south Mississippi as a means of strengthening social work education on the Gulf Coast, a region that has experienced some of the greatest population growth in Mississippi, and as a response to requests by prospective students and social service agencies that needed professionally trained social workers. Prior to this present extension of the Hattiesburg MSW program to the Gulf Coast, some local residents pressed on several occasions to establish a local part-time MSW program through the USM Gulf Park campus, located 60 miles south of Hattiesburg in Long Beach. In August 1996, the two campuses were linked via an interactive video network. This technology made it feasible, given the limited resources (notably faculty) for the Hattiesburg campus, to offer a part-time MSW program on the Mississippi Gulf Coast.

The part-time program, approved by the Council on Social Work Education, was a three year plan that called for a new cohort of 15-20 students to be admitted every other year. Eighteen (18) semester hours (6 courses) of the 60-hour curriculum were taught "live" on the Hattiesburg Campus using interactive video technology. In most but not all cases, the faculty who taught a course via the interactive video component also taught a non-IVN section of the same course in a traditional format during the same semester. The remaining 42 hours were taught in a traditional format by faculty from the Hattiesburg campus who drove down to the Gulf Park Campus. Table 1 identifies the courses included in the three year part-time curriculum plan that were taught via IVN technology.

Equipment and Instructional Support

The "Interactive Video Network" (IVN) developed by the University of Southern Mississippi offers near-state-of-the-art capabilities. The University system is a MediaMax (VTEL) 486 CODEC, which is the heart of VTEL's advanced group conferencing systems. The IVN system operates over public and dedicated T-1 circuits. The system supports full-motion two-way video with up to 30 frames per second and at transmission rates of 384 Kbps and above.

Each room has two mounted cameras with zoom capacity and four mounted TV monitors, two front and two back, so that participants facing either way can see both their own and the remote site. Student tables are arranged classroom style, facing the faculty workstation. Individual micro-

TABLE 1. Three Year Part-Time Curriculum Plan

Year #1	Year #2		Year #3	
Fall	*Fall*		*Fall*	
SWK 601 HBSE I*	SWK 637	Research II	SWK 653	Assessment
SWK 605 Policy*				
SWK 608 Practice I	SWK 642	Field II	SWK 673	Field III
Spring				
SWK 602 HBSE II*	*Spring*		*Spring*	
SWK 609 Practice II	SWK 666	Commun*	SWK 658	Advanced
SWK 634 Diversity	SWK 674	Families		Interventions
Summer	SWK 696	Groups	SWK 673	Field III
SWK 617 Research I*				
SWK 641 Field I	*Summer*			
	SWK 635	Mangmt*		
	SWK xxx	Elective		
	SWK xxx	Elective		

* represents courses that were taught via IVN technology

phones are arranged along the student tables and turned on and off by the students before and after they speak.

Faculty workstations in IVN classrooms included an ELMO visual presenter that provides the option of viewing slides, transparencies, 3-D objects, and written work at all conference sites. A Power PC 6100 for graphic presentations and connectivity to the Internet and World Wide Web is available for both DOS and MAC system users. A VCR is available to play taped resources. A touch pad is used to operate all the foregoing equipment. Each classroom is also equipped with a telephone, fax machine, copy machine, and large white grease board.

In addition to the actual technology, the University provided some added support for faculty teaching via IVN. During all telesessions, each site had a technician on hand to operate the equipment. Technicians at either site could operate the cameras, monitors and visual presenters at the remote site. The University also ran a shuttle between both campuses, a minimum of three times per week, that was used to transport handouts, exams, and other material.

The School of Social Work also provided an on-site support person that was present in all the remote classes. This program facilitator was a graduate of the USM Hattiesburg MSW program and had been a student of the faculty that taught the IVN courses. She was available to students for face-to-face contact and acted as a bridge between students and instructors. In addition to proctoring exams, collecting and distributing assignments and facilitating activities that were a part the faculty members' classroom experience, she established rapport with students, conducted formal and informal formative evaluations and took attendance. Instructional faculty were also expected to make monthly visits to the Gulf Park site, thereby reversing "local" and "remote" sites four times during the semester.

RESEARCH QUESTIONS

The following questions structured our evaluation of the part-time MSW IVN program.

- Was the academic performance of the "remote" students as good as that of the "onsite" students?
- What were faculty's impressions regarding the achievement of instructional objectives?
- How were levels of interaction/relationship (between faculty and students and student to student) affected by the IVN format?
- How would faculty and students adapt to the "electronic classroom"?
- What would students recommend that could strengthen the effectiveness of IVN instruction?

METHODOLOGY

The data used for program evaluation were collected at the end of the 1997 summer session. The first year Gulf Park students had, at that point, completed their third semester. Students represented in each group (Gulf Park/remote and Hattiesburg/main campus) were convenience samples and included all the students that were registered for those courses. The outcome variables used in this study included students' final semester grades, semi-structured interviews with each of the three faculty members who taught the IVN courses and with the program facilitator. A 14 item student feedback survey was also used. This purposive-made survey focused on students' perceptions related to learning in an IVN context. About half the items asked students to compare their "remote" IVN experience to "on-site" class experiences on a three-point scale ranging from "better," "the same," or "not as good." Items explored students' perceptions of their interactions and accessibility to instructors as well as fellow students. Instructor's overall teaching effectiveness and the students' perceptions of their ability to learn were evaluated. Included were three (3) open-ended questions related to strengths and limitations, as well as recommendations for IVN instruction.

Characteristics of Students

Eighteen (18) students were accepted into the part-time program in the Fall of 1996. All the students were working full time in social service agencies during their first semester in which they took 9 hours of course work. This 100% employment rate among the part-time students was approximately five times that of the first-year class that began classes at the same time on the main campus. Overall, there were not any significant differences between the two groups. Both student groups were overrepresented by white women (85%). Fifteen (15%) of the students were males and about the same number were African Americans. It is interesting to note that the majority (72%) of Gulf Park students were 26-35 years old while the Hattiesburg students were much more scattered across the age continuum with the largest group under 25.

FINDINGS

Academic Performance

We found virtually no difference between the academic performance of Gulf Park and Hattiesburg students as measured by final course grades. A significant difference between the mean scores for both the Gulf Park and

Hattiesburg groups was not found. The composite grades for each class, both remote and on-site, are listed in Table 2. Overall, it appears that students in traditional courses (non-IVN) received grades that were slightly higher than did students who were in IVN classes, regardless of site.

Although grades were not substantially different between sites, faculty and the program facilitator indicated an awareness that remote students in IVN classes often had greater difficulty sustaining their attention than did students in on-site classes. In fact, 25% of Gulf Park and 53% of Hattiesburg students thought that they were at a learning disadvantage when in an IVN class. Numerous comments on student survey items further suggested that they felt their academic performance was somewhat compromised when they were in IVN as compared to on-site classes. Some typical student remarks read,

> It is difficult to concentrate on the instructor's lecture when all you can look at is the screen.

> It's very difficult to learn from the students at the remote site; interaction is difficult.

> I like a flesh-and-blood teacher to help me learn difficult material.

> I feel inhibited asking questions in IVN classes.

Achievement of Instructional Objectives

Faculty and the program facilitator reported that instructional objectives were as effectively met in IVN remote course sections as in main campus sections. Some adjustments in instructional delivery were necessary to accommodate distant learners. They did note that it was difficult to cover the same amount of class content in IVN teleclasses due to time spent in dealing

TABLE 2. Mean Course Grades by Campus

Course	IVN/GP		IVN/Hatt	
	GPAs	Ns	GPAs	Ns
601	3.44	18	3.44	26
602	3.44	18	3.44	24
605	3.77	18	3.64	14
617	3.35	18	3.50	04

GPAs	Gulf Park	Hattiesburg
IVN	3.50	3.50
On-Site	3.61	3.59

with equipment, attending to students at two rather than the traditional single site, and in building in a greater number of "engagement" activities. Faculty discovered that it was useful if not essential to reexamine both course content and instructional methods in light of IVN realities. In at least one case, SWK 605, the instructor undertook a substantial modification of the course in order to maximize instructional impact (Forster, 1997), including the introduction of numerous visuals and a variety of interactive exercises not previously used in the traditional format.

Students largely concurred with the perception of faculty and the classroom facilitator, though main campus students were somewhat more critical. Among the remote students, nearly all the respondents (96%) indicated that faculty's ability to achieve instructional objectives and teaching effectiveness were "about the same" in both IVN and on-site classes. At the main campus, fewer students (47%) perceived faculty to be as effective in the IVN context as they were in the traditional classroom. More than a third of the main campus students (35%) reported that faculty were less effective when teaching through IVN technology.

Interactions/Relationships

Faculty were surprised that interactions with students were as good as they were in IVN classes. However, faculty reported that in comparison with on-site classes, their ability to interact and engage with the distant students "casually" and "spontaneously" was severely constrained. All faculty were accustomed to frequent interaction with students in the physical classroom, and found classroom interactions through the medium of IVN equipment "difficult" and "cramped." To some degree the difficulty of interactions dissipated as the courses progressed and the instructors felt more "at-home" in the electronic environment. Following are some of the faculty comments about the restricted interactional/relationship building processes that were observed.

It's just hard to know students you only see on a screen.

The immediate feedback from students, not only through comments, but their non-verbal communications, is not there.

You can make 'eye contact' with the camera, but the sense of immediate contact is missing.

It is as though the faculty member had "forgotten" the remote class as they gave sway to their preference for on-site interaction with students.

Students were almost evenly split regarding their sense of relationship with the IVN instructors. No students felt that IVN technology improved the interaction between student and faculty. Main campus students (59%) that had the faculty member in the on-site location for at least 75% of the time thought that the faculty-student relationship was about the same as it was in the traditional classroom. At the remote site, where the faculty only spent about 25% of total class time, only 47% of the students thought that the faculty-student relationship was about the same. Some student comments on this issue were:

I favor an "in-the-flesh" instructor.

I didn't enjoy classes as much when the instructor was at the other site. I felt awkward talking with the teacher, having to push the microphone button and so on.

I kept thinking of those movie scenes where you go to visit someone in prison and you have to talk through the glass with a phone.

Taking IVN classes in Gulf Park must be horrible, since the instructor isn't there most of the time.

Faculty observed that student to student interactions, particularly at the main campus location, were about the same as they had always been in the traditional classroom. The interactions of students between the main campus and remote locations, however, were minimal and frequently "strained." The main campus class sizes may have contributed to this strain because the main campus sections were usually the largest. One faculty emphasized that classes should ideally remain evenly balanced with no more than thirty students total between both sites. The program facilitator, only present at the remote location, was particularly aware of a "polarization" between the two classes that began in the first semester and has continued to be an ongoing issue that faculty had to address.

Students' perceptions of the student to student interactions were similar in terms of how they related to one another at their respective sites. Students at the remote site (71%) considered their student to student interactions to be "better than" or "as good as" what they were in other traditional courses. The main campus students (76%) rated their own student to student interactions as "about the same" as it was in traditional classes. The majority of the remote students (82%) considered the between-site student to student interactions as "satisfactory" as compared to only 47% of the Hattiesburg students. The differing perceptions of the between site student to student interactions was probably responsible for some of the polarization that faculty noted above. Several students' comments reflected their awareness of the between-site tension and polarization.

I felt a good deal of antagonism from the other site.

It was almost as if we were in competition with one another.

I don't know where it came from, but I picked up a lot of 'attitude' from the other students.

There was tension in the classes. . . . Those guys couldn't take a joke, it got to where you didn't want to say anything to them.

I heard through the grapevine that Gulf Park students (remote) would criticize us (main campus) when their microphones were off.

Electronic Classroom

In general, faculty were satisfied with the overall classroom environment. Instructors reported that by the third telesession, the physical environment itself felt quite comfortable. In comparison to the traditional, "standard" classroom, the IVN classroom is in some ways preferred. As one instructor noted, "I'd like *all* classrooms to come equipped with an 'Elmo' projector, internet access, and built-in VCR." Faculty reported that they felt most constrained by the microphones. Faculty typically could wear a portable microphone that allowed movement around the room. Students, however, had to remain fixed to their table microphones. Further, tables themselves had to remain in fixed positions in order to accommodate microphone cords, which placed some limitations on the kinds of activities students might be instructed to do. The most frequently noted electronic classroom problem, which was reported consistently from both sites, was room temperature, a problem that was not inherently related to the classes being IVN.

Students at the two sites were nearly equally critical of the environment. No student considered the IVN environment "better than" that of the face-to-face classroom. About a third of each class rated the atmosphere as "not-as-good" as a traditional class.

Only minor problems were noted with the performance of the equipment or transmission. Classes experienced a "frozen" video image on two occasions, although in each instance the audio signal remained intact. Once, for over 15 minutes, a VCR did not function properly. Periodically, the audio signal was problematic, with static or mysterious "feedback" emerging. On two occasions technicians had to "reboot" systems during class breaks to eliminate the audio feedback. The most common and fully controllable problem involved the students' use of microphones. Students would either forget to press the microphone button before speaking (hence not being heard at the other site) or forget to turn off the microphone after speaking, creating odd noises. The most significant faculty complaint was the quality of the video image of the distant site. The monitors were small and it was difficult if not impossible to make out the identity of students without consulting a seating chart. Further, unless the students were concentrated, it was usually impossible to view the entire remote class from a single camera position.

Student Recommendations

Students suggested strengthening the program in several ways. They consistently wanted to have more on-site interaction with faculty, at both the structured and casual level. They were particularly interested in the development of strategies that would increase the amount of spontaneity that occurred in the classroom. They suggested addressing this by increasing the number of visits made by the instructor to the remote site. They favored an alternating faculty schedule that would equally divide the instructor's time between the main and remote campuses. They also thought that spontaneity would be enhanced if each student had a microphone as opposed to having to share one, which is now the case. Finally, they suggested creating additional opportunities for students from both sites to interact in person so to develop some relationships that could then carry over into the classroom.

Many reported being self-conscious about speaking in class and actually being distracted by the technology, which increased their overall self-consciousness. This sometimes occurred when they started to speak and saw themselves on the TV monitors. Students also wanted the classroom to have as few distractions as possible. They wanted faculty to be better prepared regarding the actual operating of the technology so they could respond to any equipment failures. All these distractions were problematic because they resulted in a loss of concentration and focus. A number recommended TV monitors with better resolution so it would be easier to distinguish persons on the screens. Several suggested that the number of IVN courses be kept to an absolute minimum.

DISCUSSION

Student grade performance did not measurably suffer as a result of IVN classes, and faculty did not note significant differences in the overall performances of student groups. The most relevant finding here, however, may be the students' *perception* of being at some learning disadvantage in the interactive video classes as compared to traditional classes. Interestingly, twice the number of main campus students, who had the instructor present 75% of the time, believed that the IVN format made it more difficult for them to learn than did remote students. It may be that familiarity with the classroom and the equipment was a decisive factor. Though our study did not control for the number of IVN classes students had taken, all remote students had taken four IVN classes, while most main campus students had taken only one or two. Perception of academic performance, in other words, may well increase along with familiarity with the environment. Also contributing to more favorable ratings by remote students is likely to have been these students' recognition that the MSW program would not be available without integral reliance on IVN classes. Without interactive video, no learning whatsoever would be possible. Main campus students, on the other hand, were more likely to view IVN classes as an educational nuisance to be endured.

Faculty, the program facilitator, and virtually all students at the remote site felt that instructional objectives were met at least as well in IVN classes as in traditionally taught classes. However, the main campus students who participated in IVN classes were not as convinced. We are inclined to interpret the difference between the student groups in terms of the two factors noted above. Remote students had by the time of the survey become quite familiar with the IVN format, and, further, recognized that IVN classes were essential to the instructional program. As a result, their emotional stake in recognizing equivalent IVN quality was greater than that of main campus participants in the IVN classes.

We believe our data validate the central importance of "relationship" to the controversy over the use of distance education formats in graduate social work education. The strongest feelings about IVN classes from faculty and from both student groups were expressed on this issue. While faculty might be said to have been pleasantly surprised that interactions were overall better than expected, the consensus was that the IVN format detracts from the quality of student-to-student and faculty-to-student interactions. The largest number of student suggestions related to improving face-to-face interaction and relationship building. It appears that the students' sense of relationship to the faculty member directly increased relative to the amount of time that faculty member spent in actual direct contact with the students. Alternative methods of communication, such as special phone "office hours," use of email, and dismissing the main campus class a few minutes early to talk only with the remote students, helped establish and maintain a sense of connection. Particularly noteworthy seems to be the strong group polarization noted by faculty, facilitator, and virtually all students. To some degree this polarization may represent an essentially healthy group identification, especially among the remote students, who progress through the part-time program as a single cohort. Comments suggest, however, that "polarization" is indeed an appropriate descriptor, with feelings of strong antagonism between the groups that at times hindered the learning environment. It seems clear that this phenomenon was at least facilitated by the distance format and the sharing of the instructor by two groups. Preventing or at least curtailing the development of unhealthy inter-group competition and antagonism appears to be a challenge for interactive video instruction in the program.

Our evidence further suggests that faculty, in control of a wide range of equipment, warm up to the interactive video environment fairly quickly. Students are less enthusiastic, with a significant minority at both the remote and main campus sites considering it inferior to a traditional classroom. This negative valuation, interestingly, seems to have little to do with equipment performance, in itself rated positively, but rather with the constraints on spontaneity and normal interaction imposed by the equipment. A number of students at each site commented, for example, that they disliked having to turn a microphone on and off before and after speaking each time. Others complained about the limited view of the other class afforded by the television monitors. These constraints on spontaneous engagement, in turn, seem to invite students' distraction and inattention.

Students made numerous recommendations for incremental improvements to interactive video classes, suggesting both an acknowledgment of IVN's usefulness and an awareness of important limitations. Recommendations focused on improving interactions and relationship development among students and between students and faculty, again providing evidence of the pivotal significance of the interpersonal dimension of graduate social work education.

CONCLUSION

The primary finding of this study was that the education received by both groups (main campus and remote) was comparable. The technology itself and the two locations did not compromise student performance or the achievement of instructional objectives. In short, IVN courses structured as they were in this case did not place the distant learner at a significant disadvantage.

It seems clear that remote students recognized the essential role of the technology in providing them with graduate education and, as a result, they were most satisfied with IVN classes. The main campus students, on the other hand, were less satisfied, presumably because they had to "give up" something that they might have kept (i.e., access to faculty) if not for the remote group. Clearly, all students preferred regular on-site contact with instructors, and seemed to experience a sense of "second-class status" when instructors were physically at the other site. The apparent conflict, or "polarization," between groups related primarily to the competition for the instructors' time and attention. The potential for such conflict seems inherent to this form of distance education, and is, therefore, a salient issue for educational planners to address.

REFERENCES

Blanch, G. (1994). Don't all faculty want their own tv show? Barriers to faculty participation in distance education. *DEOSNEWS: The Distance Education Online Symposium 4*(1).

Blumenstyk, G. (January 26, 1996). Faculty group calls for caution and curbs on distance education. *Chronicle of Higher Education*, p. A20.

Cyrs, T.E., & Smith, F.A. (1990). *Teleclass teaching: A resource guide* (2nd ed.). Las Cruces, NM: New Mexico State University Center for Educational Development.

Day, P.J. (1995, October). Discussion proposal: Does distance teaching equal distance learning? Paper prepared for the Baccalaureate Program Directors Meeting, Nashville, TN.

Drucker, P. (March 10, 1997). Universities won't survive. *Forbes.*

Forster, M. (1997). *Modifying a graduate social welfare policy course for interactive video instruction.* Paper delivered at the 1996 Annual Program Meeting of the Council on Social Work Education, Chicago, IL.

Freddolino, P. (1996). The importance of relationships for a quality learning environment in interactive video classrooms. *Journal of Education for Business, 71*(4).

Garrison, D.R. (1989). *Understanding distance education: A framework for the future.* London: Routledge.

Kember, D. (1995). *Open learning courses for adults: A model of student progress.* Englewood Cliffs, NJ: Educational Technology Publications.

Owens, E.N., Pace, S., & Finneran, S. (1995). *Compressed video network faculty handbook.* Hattiesburg, MS: University of Southern Mississippi Teaching-Learning Resource Center.

Schlossberg, N.K., Lynch, A.Q., & Chickering, A.W. (1989). *Improving higher education environments for adults.* San Francisco: Jossey-Bass.

Wulf, W.A. (1995). Warning: Information technology will transform the university. *Issues in Science and Technology* (Summer).

Outcomes of ITV
and Face-to-Face Instruction
in a Social Work Research Methods Course

Michael A. Patchner
Helen Petracchi
Sharon Wise

SUMMARY. This study compared students enrolled in a foundations research methods course utilizing face-to-face instruction with students taking the course via ITV. Students receiving face-to-face instruction scored better on the mid-term, but there were no statistically significant differences on the scores of the final examination, the written paper, or the final course grade. No statistically significant differences were found on a research and statistics knowledge test or on scores of a scale measuring students' attitudes toward research. Both groups were favorable to ITV. *[Article copies available for a fee from The Haworth Document Delivery Service: 1-800-342-9678. E-mail address: getinfo@haworthpressinc. com]*

KEYWORDS. Distance education, distance learning, interactive TV, teaching research, foundations curriculum, off-campus education, continuing education

---

Michael A. Patchner, PhD, is Professor and Associate Dean, Helen Petracchi, PhD, ACSW, is Assistant Professor, and Sharon Wise, MS, is Doctoral Candidate, School of Social Work, University of Pittsburgh.

Address correspondence to: Michael A. Patchner, PhD, University of Pittsburgh, School of Social Work, 2112 Cathedral of Learning, Pittsburgh, PA 15260 (E-mail: patchssw+@pitt.edu).

[Haworth co-indexing entry note]: "Outcomes of ITV and Face-to-Face Instruction in a Social Work Research Methods Course." Patchner, Michael A., Helen Petracchi, and Sharon Wise. Co-published simultaneously in *Computers in Human Services* (The Haworth Press, Inc.) Vol. 15, No. 2/3, 1998, pp. 23-38; and: *Information Technologies: Teaching to Use–Using to Teach* (ed: Frank B. Raymond III, Leon Ginsberg, and Debra Gohagan) The Haworth Press, Inc., 1998, pp. 23-38. Single or multiple copies of this article are available for a fee from The Haworth Document Delivery Service [1-800-342-9678, 9:00 a.m. - 5:00 p.m. (EST). E-mail address: getinfo@haworthpressinc.com]

New technologies permit delivery of credit courses and continuing education offerings to students at distant locations. Such technologies provide individuals, lacking access to traditional educational settings, opportunities to engage in professional education and development. According to a study conducted by the Council on Social Work Education's Commission on Accreditation, 17% of those responding to a survey offered all or part of their baccalaureate or master's programs via distance education (Lockhart & Wilson, 1997). Recent standards issued by the Council on Social Work Education recognize the increasing role technology has the potential to play in social work education, assuring that attention will be given to quality content and delivery.

Interactive Television (ITV), sometimes referred to as interactive video or video conferencing, is a recent technological development with applications for social work education. ITV is a fully interactive video and audio system where courses can be taught from one location to students located at a distant site. With ITV, on-campus students can see and hear the instructor in person while the instructor can simultaneously see distant students via a large screen television or another monitor and can hear them via audio equipment. The two-way audio and video provide for nearly instantaneous communication.

This study evaluates the effectiveness of distant technology utilizing interactive television in teaching a research methods course. More specifically, this study compared the performance of students enrolled in a beginning graduate social work research course which utilized face-to-face instruction with students who simultaneously took the course at a distant location via interactive television. Additionally, students' attitudes toward distance education as well as their experiences in this course were evaluated.

REVIEW OF THE LITERATURE

Distance education includes any instruction that occurs when students are located a geographic distance from the instructor and teaching site. As a result of the technological explosion of the 1980s and 1990s, a variety of technological media (including video, audio, computer and multi-media) are currently available to social work educators enabling us to provide expanded educational opportunities for adult learners. The course under discussion, for example, permitted a large urban school of social work to utilize interactive television (ITV) with distant students wanting to enroll in a foundation research course while remaining in their home community.

Distance education has been utilized within social work education for well over a decade (Jennings, Siegel, & Conklin, 1995; Weinbach, Gandy, & Tartaglia, 1984). Nevertheless, distance education offerings in social work are considered to be in their infancy (Lockhart & Wilson, 1997). Distance education is seen as having the greatest utility and being especially valuable for off-campus programs serving part-time students and for offering continuing education (Blakely, 1994; Blakely & Schoenherr, 1995; Conklin & Osterndorf, 1995). According to Lockhart and Wilson, the state-of-the-art technology for distance education in social work, which this study utilized, "appears to be two-way audio and video systems with compressed signals that minimize the time separation between sender and receiver" (1997, p. 5).

A review of the social work distance education literature reveals a paucity of literature directed at the delivery of social work foundation courses delivered to adult learners utilizing ITV. The extent to which schools of social work have incorporated ITV into existing foundation curriculum is also limited, with only three studies available in the literature. Heitkamp (1995) evaluated ITV in North Dakota where the technology was used to provide baccalaureate and graduate social work courses to rural communities located between 90 and 370 miles from the main campus. In this evaluation, distant rural learners performed as well as the on-campus students with their satisfaction with the course mirroring that expressed by the on-campus students. Similarly, Jennings, Siegel and Baskind (1992) found no significant differences between distant students registered in a foundation social policy course offered via ITV in student attendance, classroom performance or overall satisfaction with the course. However, when Thyer, Polk, and Gaudin (1997) compared live instruction with two-way interactive television in a required MSW course, "Social Work with Abusing and Neglecting Families," they found live instruction rated significantly higher than instruction utilizing two-way interactive television.

Absent from this social work distance education literature are discussions of the utilization of ITV in a foundation research course where students are also involved actively in learning the research process through evaluating their medium. Hence, this course was considered a dynamic first step in providing experiences for students to learn the research process while simultaneously applying it. This article, then, attempts to fill a gap in the social work educational literature by describing an assessment of student learning in a school of social work that utilized ITV to deliver a foundation research course; a course in which students were evaluating their learning concurrent with the learning experience itself.

METHODOLOGY

Two groups of students were enrolled in a beginning graduate-level social work research course. One group of students (n = 13) received face-to-face instruction while the other group of students (n = 8) simultaneously received the course at a distant site via interactive television. ITV allowed the instructor to teach the course in one classroom while simultaneously broadcasting the course to another classroom at a distant site. The students receiving face-to-face instruction took this course on the main campus of the University while students who utilized ITV took the course at a regional campus approximately two hours driving time from the main campus. The instructor of the course reversed student roles once during the course, visiting the distant site and delivering a lecture in-person which was simultaneously delivered via ITV to students on the main campus (otherwise considered the face-to-face students). With the exception of this one lecture, students on the main campus received face-to-face instruction and students at the distant site received instruction via ITV.

This course utilized an ITV classroom on both campuses. Both classrooms had television cameras, microphones on the tables where students sat, a technical booth with a technician operating the equipment, and several large screen TVs. The ITV format allowed students to interact between sites and to engage in discussions with virtually no time delay between students' statements, questions, or responses. Aside from utilizing a temporary classroom at the distant site for the first three classes, the technical difficulties experienced in delivering this course were kept to a minimum.

Foundations of Social Work Research was a beginning research methods course required for students in the MSW program. The students met once a week on Friday afternoons throughout the 15-week term (January-April) for three hours, including a short break. The course consisted of lectures with some brief in-class assignments primarily focused on developing the research skills necessary to conduct the class project, a project designed to evaluate the effectiveness of ITV for teaching research methods. The course was a survey of research methods and addressed foundation knowledge and skills needed for understanding research and beginning competence for designing and conducting basic studies. Included in this course were the following topics: concepts and definitions of common terms in research, ethics, formulating research problems, sampling, single subject and group research designs, needs assessments and program evaluation, measurement and sources of data, questionnaire construction, reliability and validity, and data analysis. All students were required to take objective mid-term and final examinations based on the content in the lectures and readings. In addition, students submitted final papers written in the format of a journal article. The final paper was based on the class project which was an evaluation of the effectiveness of ITV versus face-to-face instruction in delivering a research methods course. Thus, students evaluated the course, while simultaneously acting as subjects in their evaluation.

Evaluation of the course incorporated a pre-test, post-test comparison group design. Pre-test and post-test measures included a multiple choice examination measuring students' research knowledge, a semantic differential scale assessing students' attitudes toward research, and a similar semantic differential scale assessing students' attitudes toward ITV. A multiple choice examination, comprised of 50 items assessing basic knowledge of research and statistics, was a test used by the School of Social Work to determine whether students were knowledgeable enough to exempt from Foundations of Social Work Research and progress directly to an advanced research course. The semantic differential scales included 13 bipolar adjectives rated on a 7-point continuum and added together to yield a total score. The two lead statements for the respective semantic differential scales were *"The Foundations of Social Work Research course is:"* and *"Utilizing Interactive TV to take this course is:"*. These lead sentences were followed by 13 pair of bipolar adjectives (e.g., exciting-dull, difficult-hard, etc.) rated on a 7-point continuum. Each semantic differential scale had a possible range from 13 to 91. The multiple choice examination and the two semantic differential scales were administered to the students on the first day of class and during the twelfth class of the 15-week term.

Students' performance on the mid-term examination, the final examination, and the final research paper were evaluated as well. The mid-term examination, given on the seventh week of the term, consisted of 50 questions of which 22 were true-false items, 21 were multiple choice, and 7 were short answer. The final examination, administered on the last day of the term, included 71 items of which 27 were true-false, 27 were multiple choice, and the remaining 17 questions required short answers. The mid-term and final examination grades were calculated as the percent of the total which were correct. The students' research papers were blind-graded by the instructor and assigned a letter grade. These letter grades were converted to a percentage grade with A+ = 98%, A = 95%, A− = 92%, B+ = 88%, B = 85%, B− = 82%, etc. To calculate the final grade for the course for each student, the scores on the mid-term examination, the final examination, and the final paper were averaged together with equal weights applied to each.

The students in the class participated in designing a questionnaire which included a section assessing demographic characteristics of the two groups of students. Background information regarding students' age, gender, marital status, employment status, student status, paid and volunteer experience, among other variables were included in the questionnaire. On each of these variables, comparisons were made between those receiving the course face-to-face and those receiving the class via ITV.

During the final week of the foundation research course, an additional survey was mailed to students at the distant site and distributed in class to on-campus students. The survey instrument was adapted from one used by the University of North Dakota to evaluate student experiences on their compressed video network (Haga and Heitkamp, 1995). The purpose of this survey was to provide an evaluation of the student's experiences in this course, independent of their course assignments. This assessment was important because it was not associated with the course in any way. Both on-campus and distant students were provided with a stamped envelope addressed to the independent faculty evaluator; an instructor at the school who had nothing to do with course delivery. Students were asked to return their completed surveys at their convenience and were assured that survey results would not be shared with the instructor or the graduate student assistant until after final grades for the course had been submitted to the University registrar.

FINDINGS

All eight of the students receiving ITV instruction were part-time students and were taking this course through the School of Social Work's continuing education program. Thus, none of these students were enrolled in the MSW program, but four indicated they had definitely planned to apply to the MSW program. The remaining four indicated they probably would apply to the MSW program at some point in the future. In contrast, 78.6% of the students receiving face-to-face instruction were enrolled in the MSW program with the remaining 21.4% (3 students) being employees of the university, taking the course through their employee benefits, but anticipating they would be applying to the MSW program at some point in the future. Of all the face-to-face students, 64.3% were part-time with the remaining 35.7% being full-time students.

Table 1 illustrates that the students at both locations were remarkably similar in their demographic composition (i.e., no statistically significant differences were found). All of the students were female with the exception of one male who was enrolled in the face-to-face instruction section of the course. The average age of the ITV students was 36 years while the average age of students receiving face-to-face instruction was 35.1 years. Of the students receiving ITV instruction, 87.5% were employed full-time with 12.5% being employed part-time; none were unemployed. On the other hand, of the students receiving face-to-face instruction, 64.3% were employed full-time, while 21.4% were part-time employees, and 14.3% were unemployed. Students in the ITV class had an average of 9.3 years of paid experience in the human services and 6.8 years of volunteer experience while students receiving face-to-face instruction had 6.1 years of paid human services experience and 5.7 years of volunteer experience. Students receiving ITV instruction reported having had an average of 1.9 undergraduate or graduate courses in research or statistics with 62.5% indicating they had some previous re-

TABLE 1. Students' Demographic Characteristics: Comparison of Students Having Instruction via ITV versus Those with Face-to-Face Instruction

	Type of Instruction	
Characteristic	**ITV (n = 8)**	**Face-to-Face (n = 14)**
Age (Ave. Years)	36.0	35.1
Gender		
Female	100%	92.9%
Male	0%	7.1%
Marital Status		
Never Married	14.3%	42.9%
Married	71.4%	42.9%
Divorced/Separated	14.3%	14.2%
Enrolled in the MSW Program		
Enrolled	0%	78.6%
Not Enrolled	100%	21.4%
Student Status		
Full-Time	0%	35.7%
Part-Time	100%	64.3%
Current Employment Status		
Full-Time	87.5%	64.3%
Part-Time	12.5%	21.4%
Not Currently Emp.	0%	14.3%
Paid Experience in Human Services		
Average Years	9.3	6.1
Volunteer Experience in Human Services		
Average Years	6.8	5.7
Courses in Research or Statistics		
Average Courses	1.9	2.4
Previous Research Experience		
Had Experience	62.5%	57.1%
Had No Res. Exper.	37.5%	42.9%
Experience with Using ITV		
Had Experience	12.5%	7.1%
No Prior Experience	87.5%	92.9%
One-way Commuting Time		
Average No. of Minutes	31.9	24.8
Weekly Study Time		
Ave. No. of Minutes	156.9	132.9

search experience. Similarly, students receiving face-to-face instruction re-ported having had an average of 2.4 research or statistics courses with 57.1% indicating they had some previous research experience. ITV students also indicated they averaged a 31.9 minute commute each way to and from class and spent an average of 156.9 minutes studying each week, while students receiving face-to-face instruction averaged a 24.8 minute commute and 132.9 minutes of study time each week.

Attitudes toward the research class did not differ significantly between the two groups of students. However, both students receiving face-to-face in-struction and instruction via ITV improved their attitudes toward research at the time of the post-test, albeit not significantly. As illustrated in Table 2, students in both groups were positive about the research course at the time of the pre-test, with this positive attitude persisting until the end of the course. Indicative of a positive attitude toward the course is the low rate of absentee-ism among the students. All students had good attendance records with no statistically significant differences between on-campus and distant students in this regard. On average, the group receiving ITV instruction were absent from .4 classes while the group receiving face-to-face instruction missed 1.4 classes. In the event of an absence, a videotape of each class was produced and made available to students at both sites for them to view at their conve-nience. Again, despite the majority of this course being offered during the winter months and students knowing they had access to a videotape of the class if they were absent, attendance was remarkably good. Similarly, stu-dents' attitudes toward using ITV were relatively positive at the beginning of the course, as measured by the semantic differential scale during the pre-test, and continued to be positive at the end of the term, as measured during the

TABLE 2. Comparison of Students' Attitudes: Students Having Instruction via ITV versus Those with Face-to-Face Instruction (N = 22)

	Type of Instruction	
Attitude	**ITV** **mean[a] (n = 8)**	**Face-to-Face** **mean[a] (n = 14)**
Attitude Toward the Research Class		
Pretest	58.9	55.0
Post-Test	65.6	63.8
Attitude Toward Using ITV		
Pretest	65.4	63.2
Post-Test	66.3	63.8

[a]13-Item Semantic Differential Scale

post-test (see Table 2). ITV students were slightly more positive about ITV technology than their on-campus counterparts, both at the pre-test and at the post-test. However, these differences toward technology were not statistically significant.

Despite having had an average of one-half a course less of undergraduate or graduate instruction in research and statistics (1.9 courses for students having instruction via ITV vs. 2.4 courses for students having face-to-face instruction), students at the distant site scored slightly higher on the pre-test of the research exemption examination (albeit not statistically significant) than their on-campus, face-to-face counterparts. Students receiving instruction via ITV averaged 67.0% on the pre-test while students receiving face-to-face instruction averaged 63.9% (see Table 3). The scores of both groups improved significantly from pre-test to post-test with the class receiving ITV instruction averaging 75.3% on the post-test of the research exemption examination ($t = -3.4$, $df = 7$, $p = .01$) while on-campus face-to-face students averaged 75.7% ($t = -8.1$, $df = 13$, $p = .0001$). With approximately one-half of the questions on the research exemption examination related to a basic understanding of statistics, the research exemption examination included a fair amount of content on statistics as well as content on research. The Foundation of Social Work Research course, however, focused primarily on methods for conducting social work research and included only limited content on the application of statistics for social work research. Nonetheless, both groups of students improved significantly in their research knowledge and had nearly identical post-test scores on the research exemption examination.

TABLE 3. Comparison of Students' Performance: Students Having Instruction via ITV versus Those with Face-to-Face Instruction (N = 22)

Performance Measures	Type of Instruction	
	ITV mean (n = 8)	Face-to-Face mean (n = 14)
Research Exemption Exam		
Pretest	67.0	63.9
Post-Test	75.3	75.7
Course Requirements		
Mid-Term Exam[a]	83.9%	90.9%
Final Exam	79.0%	84.1%
Paper	90.1%	91.7%
Course Average	84.4%	89.2%

[a]P < .05

Students in the course were evaluated according to three criteria–performance on the mid-term examination, performance on the final examination, and the grading of the written paper. The grades on each of these were averaged together to obtain a final grade for the course. Table 3 illustrates the average grades received by the students on each of these measures. On the mid-term examination, the final examination, the paper, and the course average, the students receiving ITV instruction averaged the following grades: 83.9%, 79.0%, 90.1%, and 84.4%, respectively. In comparison, the students receiving face-to-face instruction scored: 90.9%, 84.1%, 90.1%, and 88.4%, respectively. With the exception of the mid-term examination (t = -2.3, df = 20, p < .05) there were no statistically significant differences between the two groups of students on these measures. In general, those students receiving face-to-face instruction had only one graduate-level course prior to taking Foundations of Social Work Research. Students receiving face-to-face instruction had been taking courses as part of their MSW program or as employees of the University taking courses in preparation for applying to the MSW program. As a consequence, students receiving instruction via ITV did not have as much recent experience with preparing for and taking examinations. This may explain the statistically significant differences found in the performance of the two groups of students on the mid-term examination.

Of the 22 students enrolled in the course (14 on-campus and 8 at the distant site), 16 students (approximately 63%) returned their surveys to the independent faculty evaluator. By site, 64% (n = 9) of on-campus students and 88% (n = 7) of the distant ITV students responded to the survey as requested.

Initially, students were asked the grade they expected to receive in the course. This question was considered important because it was hypothesized that students who expected lower grades would be more negatively biased in their survey responses than students who expected to receive higher grades. Interestingly, on average, the distant ITV students accurately expected lower grades in the course than their on-campus counterparts (with about half expecting "B" grades; only one on-campus student expected to receive a "B" in the course).

Students were also asked to respond to three distinct categories of questions. First, students were asked about the technical aspects of their learning experiences. Second, students were asked to assess the teacher's interactive skills, specific to this technology. Finally, students were asked about resource availability in order to compare the experiences of students on-campus receiving face-to-face instruction with the experiences of the distant students receiving the course via ITV. Unfortunately, there were not large enough and consistent enough responses to perform the appropriate Chi-square test to analyze students' responses to these sets of questions. However, cross-tabulations of responses by location were possible.

Questions Regarding Technical Aspects of the Course: These questions asked students to assess their ease in viewing the monitor and in the sound quality of audio transmissions, including experiences with transmitting human images, videotapes or other instructional aids. Generally, both groups of students were pleased with the various video transmissions viewed on their monitors. However, a concern was indicated by one on-campus student receiving face-to-face instruction about the clarity and understandability of sound transmissions. This is not an entirely unexpected result given that clarity of sound in ITV is where technicians expend most of their efforts (Spirek, 1995).

Questions Regarding the Instructor's Interactive Skills: Questions regarding the teacher's interactive skills queried students about their assessment of the course instructor's ability to convey verbal and non-verbal communication. Again, students who had received instruction face-to-face as well as the distant ITV students indicated they were pleased with the instructor's ability to make himself clearly and easily understood, both verbally and non-verbally. Both on-campus as well as distant students were also asked to assess the instructor's quality of interaction with distant students during course lectures. Interestingly, one on-campus student felt that the amount and quality of interaction between the classroom instructor and distant students was inadequate during lecture. Yet, all students were in general agreement that the instructor was adequate in making himself available to students outside the classroom sessions.

Questions Regarding Resource Availability: Questions regarding resource availability should be paramount to schools of social work contemplating the delivery of courses to distant students. We must be mindful to ensure comparability of the learning experience for our distant students with our on-campus students. Unfortunately, we generally have less control off-campus over the availability of books, required readings, etc. In this assessment, distant ITV student experiences with resource availability did not appear to differ from the experiences had by their on-campus peers. All students generally agreed that textbooks and classroom materials (including the return of papers and tests) were available in a timely fashion. However, one distant ITV student felt the library and research facilities at the distant site were inadequate and inaccessible.

Finally, students were asked whether the course met their expectations and whether or not they would enroll in another course delivered in this format. Approximately 89% of the students receiving face-to-face instruction and 72% of the distant ITV students who responded to this survey felt their expectations for this course were either met or exceeded (almost half of the distant ITV students felt their expectations were exceeded). While there were no statistically significant differences between on-campus students and the distant ITV students in their responses to this question, one on-campus student was joined by two distant students in indicating the course did not meet their expectations. Yet, 100% of students who responded to this survey indicated they would enroll in another course if it were offered in the interactive television format.

LIMITATIONS

The convenience sample and small number of students in each class prevent generalizing the findings beyond this study. Moreover, the small number of students in each class prevents differences between the two classes from being significant when statistical tests are computed. There may also be unknown differences between the two groups of students which may have affected the results of this evaluation in unknown ways (for example, one group of students live in a more rural environment while the other group of students live in a more urban area). Perhaps the most important limitation, however, is the fact that the face-to-face instruction was not the traditional face-to-face instruction which administrators, faculty, and students normally expect. The face-to-face instruction in this study was impacted by the following factors: students receiving face-to-face instruction were in an ITV classroom surrounded by very technical equipment, there was a technician present at all classes, the instructor used many outlines and charts which were projected onto television monitors, and each student had to press a button to activate a microphone whenever a question was asked or a comment was made. Despite these limitations, this study contributes to the existing knowledge regarding distance learning in social work education and demonstrates that further research is needed to understand the efficacy of distance technology for student learning.

CONCLUSION AND DISCUSSION

This study demonstrated that students at a distant site receiving instruction via ITV performed as well as students receiving face-to-face instruction in a foundation social work research methods course. Students in both groups would have preferred face-to-face instruction, but felt that ITV was a very acceptable mode of instruction for those having no other means of access to such education.

The explosion of telecommunication technologies allows social work educators to increase educational access to potential students who might previously have been neglected. Potential students lacking resources or easy access to a school's on-campus programs may find a course offered through distance technology more accommodating of their own schedules and more appealing. An interactive course that attracts distant students in need of the beginning foundation courses also serves as a recruitment tool for the school by making course offerings available to a larger pool of students. Moreover, interactive television also allows the instructor to utilize guest experts who might otherwise be unable to travel to the distant location to offer a lecture.

Students at both sites in this study expressed a desire for more interaction with the other group of students. This is a major challenge in distance education (Barker, 1992; Beare, 1989; McNeil, 1991). Offering a social work education course via ITV, while simultaneously having face-to-face instruction with another class, requires creativity and planning to promote both formal and informal interaction among the students. The ITV system for this research class was not available except during class time, thus not allowing for 'down time' communication between the two groups of students. Future classes may want to explore the option of allowing interaction between sites during these periods.

In this study the instructor made one trip to the distant class. The experience was quite positive in that the instructor and the students were able to interact in a manner different from their interactions over ITV. The interaction during this visit was less formal and more personal. Students received more individualized attention. Moreover, during this visit, when the lecture was presented face-to-face to the students at the distant site, the students were more spontaneous, more readily engaged the instructor, asked more questions, and made more comments than normal. The opposite was true for the other class (normally the on-campus class) who received this one lecture via ITV. This experience helped the students gain a better understanding of and a new perspective on one another. This supports Hult's (1980) finding that an instructor visiting a distant site has a positive affect on student attitudes.

According to the National Center for Education Statistics, ITV is currently the most widely used technology for the delivery of distance education courses (American Council on Education, 1997). This study is the first step in a research agenda designed to evaluate the effectiveness of the ITV instruction in social work foundation education. The next step will be to evaluate course delivery by comparing face-to-face and distant students with students enrolled in this course as it is delivered in the traditional on-campus classroom. Under these conditions, all three groups of students will complete the same course requirements (mid-term, final exam, and written paper) as well as the pre-test, post-test measures (i.e., baseline examination of research knowledge, the assessment of attitudes toward research as well as an assessment of their attitudes toward and experiences with ITV). Comparing three groups of students (students receiving instruction via ITV, students receiving face-to-face instruction in the ITV classroom on-campus, and traditional on-campus classroom students) is anticipated to provide a more orthogonal research design, thus allowing us to make more definitive statements regarding the potential of ITV technology for social work foundation education.

Utilizing ITV has allowed this School of Social Work to extend a graduate-level research methods course to students who otherwise would not have had the opportunity to take this course in their community. As social work education approaches the new century, more and more accredited programs will offer opportunities to students at a distance. As Ohler (1995) has stated, "in the Industrial Age, we go to School. In the Communication Age, schools can come to us."

AUTHOR NOTE

Michael A. Patchner, PhD, is Professor and Associate Dean at the School of Social Work, University of Pittsburgh. Dr. Patchner has been teaching research methods for nearly 20 years. He has extensive experience in teaching research and other courses to non-traditional students in off-campus locations. He has numerous publications including research articles evaluating part-time social work education, and is the co-author of two research methods texts, *Planning for Research* and *Implementing the Research Plan*. He has been teaching research via ITV since 1996.

Helen Petracchi, PhD, ACSW, is Assistant Professor at the University of Pittsburgh, School of Social Work. Dr. Petracchi has been actively involved in distance education for more than 12 years delivering workshops, continuing education offerings, and credit courses. Dr. Petracchi has regularly presented papers on distance education at the CSWE Annual Program Meeting since 1989 and has published articles on distance learning in the *Journal of Continuing Social Work Education* and the *Journal of Baccalaureate Social Work*.

Sharon Wise, MS, is currently a doctoral candidate at the University of Pittsburgh, School of Social Work. Prior to her graduate work at the University of Pittsburgh, she served as an adjunct instructor at West Virginia State College where she developed and implemented a distance education program for the department of social work. She is currently a fellow at the John F. Kennedy Center for Developmental Disabilities, Health Sciences Division at the University of Colorado at Denver. She has made national and international presentations on using technology for the delivery of social work education.

REFERENCES

American Council on Education (1997). *Research Briefs: Most Colleges Offer Distance Education Courses*. Washington, D.C.: Author.

Barker, B. (1992). *The Distance Education Handbook. An Administrator's Guide for Rural and Remote Schools*. Washington, D.C.: Office of Educational Research and Improvement.

Beare, P. (1989). The comparative effectiveness of videotape, audiotape, and telelecture in delivering continuing teacher education. *The American Journal of Distance Education, 3* (2), 57-66.

Blakely, T.J. (1994). Strategies for distance learning. *Journal of Continuing Social Work Education, 6* (1), 4-7.

Blakely, T.J. & Schoenherr, P. (1995). Telecommunication technologies in social work distance education. *Journal of Continuing Social Work Education, 6* (3), 8-12.

Conklin, J.J. & Osterndorf, W. (1995). Distance learning in continuing social work education: Promise of the year 2000. *Journal of Continuing Social Work Education, 6* (3), 13-17.

Grimes, P.W., Krehbiel, T.I., Nielsen, J.E., and Niss, J.F. (1989). The effectiveness of Economics USA on learning and attitudes. *Journal of Economic Education, 20* (2), 139-152.

Haga, M. & Heitkamp, T. (1995). *Evaluation results of an innovative social work distance education program.* A paper presented at the Annual Program Meeting of the Council on Social Work Education, San Diego, California.

Haynes, K. & Dillon, C. (1992). Distance education: Learning outcomes, interaction, and attitudes. *Journal of Education for Library and Information Science, 33* (1), 35-45.

Heitkamp, T. (1995). *Social work education at a distance: An innovative approach.* A paper presented at the Annual Program Meeting of the Council on Social Work Education, San Diego, California.

Hobbs, V. (1990). Distance learning in North Dakota: A cross-technology study of the schools, administrators, coordinators, instructors, and students. Two-way interactive television, audiographic tele-learning, and instruction by satellite. ERIC Document Reproduction Service ED 328225.

Hult, R.E. (1980). The effectiveness of university television instruction and factors influencing student attitudes. *College Student Journal, 14* (1), 5-7.

Jennings, J., Siegel, E. & Baskind, F.R. (1992). *Teaching techniques for instructional interactive television.* Warrenton, Virginia: Learning Technology Institute.

Jennings, J., Siegel, E. & Conklin, J.J. (1995). Social work education and distance education: Applications for continuing education. *Journal of Continuing Social Work Education, 6* (3), 3-7.

Lockhart, L. & Wilson, S. (1997). Distance Education: A Summary of Survey Results. *Social Work Education Reporter, 45* (2), 5.

McNeil, D.R. (1991). Computer conferencing project. Final report. Washington, D.C.: Academy for Educational Development, Inc.

Ohler, J. (1995). Forward. *The Online Chronicle of Distance Education & Communication. May 1995.* Online: Internet.

Spirek, M. (1995). *The impact of Math Boosters on its viewing audiences: An external multimethod assessment of the 1994-1995 season.* Paper presented at the 11th Annual Conference on Distance Teaching and Learning, Madison, Wisconsin.

Thyer, B.A., Polk, G. & Gaudin, J.G. (1997). Distance Learning in Social Work Education: A Preliminary Evaluation. *Journal of Social Work Education, 33* (2), 363-367.

Weinbach, R.W., Gandy, J.T., & Tartaglia, L.J. (1984). Addressing the needs of the part-time student through interactive closed-circuit television: An evaluation. *Arete, 9* (2), 12-20.

Building on Experience:
Lessons from a Distance Education
M.S.W. Program

Paul P. Freddolino

SUMMARY. Using data from interviews with students completing the first half of an entire M.S.W. degree program delivered through distance education and a comparable group of students on the main campus, this paper focuses on many of the key issues asked about electronically mediated graduate education in social work: positive and negative aspects of the program; costs and benefits of participation; and overall perspectives on students' experiences. *[Article copies available for a fee from The Haworth Document Delivery Service: 1-800-342-9678. E-mail address: getinfo@haworthpressinc.com]*

INTRODUCTION

The role of universities is changing. They no longer provide a body of knowledge in one field which their alumni/ae utilize through lengthy unidimensional careers. Now, universities host many people returning in search of education and training in new and different fields, or for advanced training in their present fields.

How we provide graduate social work education is changing too, as are the

Paul P. Freddolino, PhD, is Professor and Coordinator of Distance Education, School of Social Work, Michigan State University, 254 Baker Hall, East Lansing, MI 48824. E-mail:freddoli@pilot.msu.edu

An earlier version of this paper was presented at the 1997 Annual Program Meeting of the Council on Social Work Education, held in Chicago, Illinois, March, 1997.

[Haworth co-indexing entry note]: "Building on Experience: Lessons from a Distance Education M.S.W. Program." Freddolino, Paul P. Co-published simultaneously in *Computers in Human Services* (The Haworth Press, Inc.) Vol. 15, No. 2/3, 1998, pp. 39-50; and: *Information Technologies: Teaching to Use–Using to Teach* (ed: Frank B. Raymond III, Leon Ginsberg, and Debra Gohagan) The Haworth Press, Inc., 1998, pp. 39-50. Single or multiple copies of this article are available for a fee from The Haworth Document Delivery Service [1-800-342-9678, 9:00 a.m. - 5:00 p.m. (EST). E-mail address: getinfo@haworthpressinc. com]

characteristics of our students. As evidenced by the 1995 Council on Social Work Education (CSWE) teleconference on "The Use of Distance Education in Social Work" (CSWE, 1995), previous expansion through off-campus programs is now being supplemented by courses offered through electronic communications media such as satellite and compressed video to reach new student populations (Blakely & Schoenherr, 1995; McFall, Freddolino, Flynn, Downs, & Herrick, 1994).

The expansion of programming via "distance education"–whereby students are linked by means of some type of electronic communications medium– eventually led to the development and approval of "Guidelines for Distance Education Proposals in Social Work" (Commission on Accreditation, 1995). Based on extensive comments from social work educators, the guidelines are meant to apply to any program "proposing to offer a year or more of their course work" using distance education.

For schools of social work contemplating developing a distance education degree program, the guidelines provide a valuable starting point for thinking about the multitude of interrelated dimensions which must be addressed in any program design. What they do not provide, and what the social work literature is only now beginning to address, is any real pragmatic sense of how these issues play out in the hard, cold reality of actually delivering such a distance education program with real social work students and real social work faculty (Freddolino, 1996, March; Petracchi & Morgenbesser, 1995).

This paper seeks to expand the practical knowledge base in this area by reporting some of the results of an extensive ongoing evaluation of a CSWE-approved distance education M.S.W. degree program at Michigan State University. During the Spring, 1996 semester, students in the program completed the first year field and methods sequences, and they thus reached the half-way point in the four-year program. This is a preliminary report, but it addresses many of the key issues being asked about electronically mediated graduate education in social work. These issues include such topics as reasons for selecting a distance learning program; positive and negative aspects of the distance learning technology; costs and benefits of participation in the program; and an overall perspective on the students' experiences.

BACKGROUND

In response to considerable demand from potential students in northern rural areas of the state, the faculty of the School of Social Work at Michigan State University approved a new Distance Education Initiative (DEI) in 1993. For the initial undertaking the faculty have implemented two part-time graduate degree programs using electronically mediated instruction. One program is based in Marquette in the Upper Peninsula, 400 miles from the main campus, and the other is centered in Gaylord in the northern part of the lower peninsula, approximately 200 miles from campus.

At each site, 50-75 students completed the first of two courses designed to be taken prior to formal application for admission to the Master of Social Work degree program. This two-course re-introduction to academic life was intended to permit potential applicants to experience again the "complications" inherent in adding course work to their already full lives, and thus to self-select out of the process *before* applying to the program if the obstacles seemed insurmountable. This was an important consideration for the students, and it was also very important for the program because once students were admitted and completed several courses, the program would not be able to replace any students who dropped out.

Eventually, 50-55 students were admitted at each site when the application process was completed, and about 50 actually matriculated at each site. Based on our experience with prior outreach programs conducted by the School using commuting faculty, it is expected that 35-40 students will complete the program at each site in May, 1998. All requirements for the M.S.W. degree will be able to be completed *on site*, an opportunity made possible only through the use of relatively new instructional technology–interactive instructional television (IITV)–to complement a human presence.

The social work programs at MSU use one of the emerging practices for electronic distance education, a technology known as compressed video. The video signal is "compressed" in that only the portion of the video image that changes from one frame to the next is actually transmitted. This permits the use of a narrow and thus less expensive bandwidth for signal transmission. These lower-cost compressed video systems are used for many of the interactive instructional television course offerings at colleges and universities across the country, including many in social work (Siegel, Conklin, Jennings & Flynn, 1996).

In the DEI programs, instruction generally originates on Michigan State's main campus, where it is simultaneously transmitted to both distant sites. (At least once in each course, however, instruction originates at each of the other sites when faculty visit with the students on site.) There is generally a group of students in the classroom with the primary instructor, as well as groups of students in the classrooms at the distant sites, with an adjunct faculty member at each site. Faculty and students at each of the sites are able to see each other and speak with each other interactively, through the use of cameras, microphones, and television monitors.

In addition to the in-class adjunct faculty member at each site, the DEI programs have established the equivalent of a satellite site in Marquette and Gaylord, with staff composed of part-time advisors, field instruction coordinators and liaison staff, and administrative support staff; in addition, technical services staff are hired through a contract with the host facility. The basic thrust of this effort has been to establish a set of human relationships to complement and frame the technology (Freddolino, 1996).

METHOD

Sample. All students in the DEI programs in Gaylord and Marquette have been interviewed using a structured instrument. In addition, many of the East Lansing students who completed their first year social work methods courses in the interactive linked classes with the DEI students have also been interviewed.

Demographic information about the students in Marquette and Gaylord who completed the initial courses reveal two groups quite similar in terms of ethnicity, gender, undergraduate grade point average (GPA), percentage of students working in human service agencies while in the course, and length of past human service work experience. Typically, students in both sites are white females with undergraduate GPAs in the 3.10-3.15 range, working in a human service agency during the program, and with about 7.5 years of experience in the human service field.

The data do show some differences, however. Whereas 32.9% of the Marquette students had earned a BSW degree, only 9.6% of the Gaylord students had. This difference reflects the presence of a BSW program right in Marquette (at Northern Michigan University), and the absence of any similar program within about 100 miles of Gaylord. While all students commuted some distance to get to class, the Marquette site seemed to be equally distant from the students' work and home, whereas the Gaylord site was on average less than half the distance from students' homes than from their work. In summary, the two groups of students at the distant program sites seemed more alike than different from each other.

By contrast, students on the East Lansing campus tend to be younger, slightly more ethnically diversified, with higher undergraduate GPAs and less experience in the human service field. A smaller segment of the East Lansing students are working in a human service agency while completing the M.S.W. program.

Instrument. In order to gather information on the wide range of topics required for the evaluation of the DEI program, a structured, open-ended telephone interview instrument was prepared in collaboration with the students in Gaylord and Marquette who were going to be completing the interviews. A first draft was prepared by the author, and then subsequent drafts were prepared as the instrument was fine-tuned together with the student-interviewers.

Topics covered include students' academic and professional backgrounds;

their motivation for entering the DEI program; their own knowledge and use of various technology components–VCRs, computers, and so forth; how well the interactive technology is thought to be working and how appropriate it is for the different courses; library and other resources which generally enhance social work programs; socialization to the school of social work, the university, and the profession; exams, assignments, and grading; the nature and quality of advising; field instruction supervision, liaison, and related issues; and overall program support.

Procedure. The majority of the interviews were conducted during the summer of 1996 by students in Gaylord and Marquette who signed up for independent study credit in research methods. The remainder were collected by graduate student research assistants in East Lansing during the fall of 1996. Each respondent was contacted by phone, and an appointment was made for the telephone interview. Each interview was audio tape-recorded, and the student interviewer completed a verbatim transcription of each interview.

Analysis process. To date, the analysis has involved four graduate students and the author in a fairly traditional approach using the identification of multiple themes in the responses to each question. During this phase of the analysis we have erred on the side of generating more themes rather than fewer themes to illustrate the range of responses. All coding activities involved at least two people dealing with the data independently, followed by comparison and discussion of coding until mutually agreeable codes were developed.

Subsequent analysis will produce a smaller set of more complex themes for each question, together with the exploration of themes within individual respondents–profiles or "types" of students, if you will. These analyses will be reported in subsequent papers.

RESULTS

The primary goal of this component of the overall DEI evaluation is to provide some "broad brush" contextual detail concerning the thoughts, values, perceptions, preferences, and suggestions of the two groups of DEI students and their East Lansing counterparts. The intent is to develop a picture of the students and the program together, in order to understand more about what the experience has been like and how it can be improved.

Reasons for Selecting the MSU Program (Q1a)

In reviewing the data it becomes clear very quickly that this question means very different things to the students on campus and the DEI students in

Marquette and Gaylord. For the East Lansing students the question was interpreted as "why did you choose MSU as opposed to another program?" and the answers involved such factors as "the reputation of the school" (35.1%) and the respondents' "familiarity with the program" (18.9%).

In Marquette and Gaylord, the question was interpreted to mean "why did you choose MSU as opposed to not entering an M.S.W. program?" About 45% identified "career opportunity" or "job advancement" as reasons, and 31% noted their desire for the M.S.W. credential. About 14% liked the "flexibility of the part-time structure," although 14% also acknowledged the "lack of other programs" as a reality. It is interesting to note that about half of the respondents at all three sites noted the close and convenient location of THEIR site as a reason for selecting the program.

Certainly the time may come when students might actually have a choice between a distance education program and the traditional on-campus mode. This scenario may come to pass as more course work becomes available through the Internet as well as through interactive video. In such an environment some students may choose the distance education version because it offers more time flexibility and shorter commuting times, while other students choose the on-campus program because they value the higher levels of socialization provided by a college campus.

Positive Aspects of the Interactive TV System (Q8)

There appears to be no doubt in the minds of the DEI students in Gaylord (62.2%) and Marquette (65.9%) that the most important positive aspect of the interactive TV system is that it "allows one to get an M.S.W. education off-campus." As one of the students from Marquette expressed it, "This sure beats commuting 400 miles each way!!!" In East Lansing, the two related themes of "getting different perspectives/responses" (43.2%) and being able to "interact with other locations" (35.1%) were mentioned most frequently. Both Gaylord (32.4%) and Marquette (56.1%) also valued this "ability to interact with other locations."

Among themes identified fewer times, there were some very interesting sentiments expressed. Five students in each of the DEI locations identified "immediate access to the professor at MSU" as one of their positives. Five students in East Lansing liked being "exposed to the perspectives of older, more experienced students" in the two DEI sites, and one person in each DEI site also mentioned this. Finally, three students in East Lansing said there were "no positives" in the interactive TV system, while no one in Marquette or Gaylord stated this.

Limitations or Problems with the Interactive TV System (Q9a)

A difference in perspective between on-campus and distance learning students appears again in the responses to this item. About one quarter of the students in both Marquette and Gaylord indicated that "not having the professor on site" was a limitation. By contrast, the largest number of students in East Lansing (37.8%) noted "time delays due to technology" as a limitation. Between 24 percent and 32 percent of the students in each site commented that "glitches in technology" were a shared burden at times throughout the system.

The comments from the East Lansing students point to a very real limitation that faculty have noted throughout their experience in this setting. It is taken as a given that some amount of time will be lost from both (1) coping with audio and/or video glitches that make repetition of some content necessary; and (2) "checking in" with each of the sites linked by the technology to see if there are questions or comments. Each of the faculty has attempted to deal with this aspect in a variety of ways, including the use of more written material as handouts, using presentation software to prepare computer-generated graphics and outlines, and reworking lectures to get points across more succinctly.

Student comments about technology glitches point to an interesting aspect of the technology in use in this program. Specifically, despite the focus on the interactive *video* used in the classroom, the dimension of the technology that is much more significant in causing problems was the *audio*! As in other situations in everyday life, we can generally cope more easily with distortions in a video image as long as we can hear what's going on.

Several other comments from students centered on the effect of the technology on the process in class, and these were fairly evenly divided among the three sites. For example, 10.4 percent noted that the system "deters class participation" and that it is "hard to get discussion going on TV." The sense that "people get uncomfortable on camera" was mentioned by 16.5 percent of the students. Finally, a "lack of human contact" was cited by 13.0 percent.

Assessment of the People Who Ran the Equipment (Q9b)

In describing the MSU approach to distance learning we have stressed the importance of relationships as the building block of the program, and these relationships include the task-oriented relationships with the technical staff people in all three sites (Freddolino, 1996). Overall, the staff generally received ratings of good (23.5%), very good (19.1%), and excellent (18.3%). The staff on campus received slightly better scores on average, but this is not surprising because (1) there are generally more people involved with each class, and (2) some of these folks are full time professionals. Students did note in their comments that "some people were better than others," and that "personnel have varied dramatically in their abilities," especially at one of the distant sites. Finally, it is of interest to note that 11.3 percent of the students commented that basically "the problems have been with the technology, not the personnel."

Most Important Benefits Obtained from Participation to Date (Q49)

For the students in East Lansing, the benefit mentioned most often–by 48.6 percent of the respondents–had nothing to do with the distance learning situation. For these students the benefit came from increased knowledge from field instruction and the application of theory. The students in Marquette and Gaylord, in comparison, mentioned increased knowledge of social work ethics, roles, and theory most frequently (25.0%), followed by professional and personal growth (21.6%). These differences reflect the higher levels of practice experience already accomplished by the students in Marquette and Gaylord. Skill building and networking were also mentioned frequently.

Most Important/Difficult Costs and Sacrifices (Q50)

The similarities across the three sites in the expression of costs and sacrifices was truly surprising, and the students' comments suggest that we have been successful–if that is the word–in achieving a high level of comparability!! Regardless of their location, students were most likely to talk about two dominant themes: time and money.

Comments related to time pointed to many dimensions of this phenomenon. In addition to a general description of the importance of this sacrifice, 32.2 percent of the students mentioned the impact of the program on "time away from family." Students at the Gaylord site mentioned the "need to learn to manage time" more than the other sites, while students in Marquette mentioned time lost to commuting more frequently. Almost a quarter of the students on campus mentioned the "lack of a social life," reflecting the fact that this group might have been more likely to even HAVE a social life prior to starting the program! The comments about money were general and across the board, noted by 44.3 percent of the respondents.

In one of the distance sites almost a quarter of the students indicated some form of "stress" in response to this question, whereas hardly anyone at the other two sites used this concept. Respondents at all three sites mentioned the "impact on the paid employment situation," as well as the sense that their participation was "hard on the family."

Taken together, the responses appear to indicate that the students at the two distance sites have been fairly well socialized into the rigors and burdens of participation in an intensive M.S.W. program. Their responses suggest that their experiences are very similar to those of the students completing the program on campus. The frequent mention of stress related to time and time management suggests that greater attention should be paid to these issues during recruiting, and extra support and information should be provided to students in the early stages of participation in the program.

If You Had It to Do Over, Would You Begin This M.S.W. Program? (Q61)

Near the end of the interview we asked one of those existential types of questions intended to capture the essence of an issue. The full wording of the question was: *"If you had it to do over again, and if you knew then what you know now, would you begin this M.S.W. program? Please comment."*

The overall responses are captured in Table 1 below. For large majorities in all three sites, the answer was in the affirmative. In tallying the comments provided by the students, we found some interesting variations among the three sites. For example, more than twice as many students in East Lansing mentioned increased knowledge and/or experience as one of the positives. They were also more frequent in noting the positive quality of the program.

At the same time, somewhat to our surprise, 81 percent of all negative comments related to the cost of the program came from the students in East Lansing; we would have expected more of these complaints from the off-campus students. The students in Marquette and Gaylord, on the other hand, were more frequent in noting the amount of time the program took, a reflection of having added participation in the M.S.W. program to lives already fairly full. For some of the students in Marquette, the answer was quite simple. Twenty-two percent of these respondents very simply stated that "it was the only program available."

There are many more questions in the interview which are in the midst of the analysis process at the present time, and these data will be reported in a variety of other papers and reports. Based on a very quick scan of the tran-

TABLE 1. Responses to the Question: "If you had it to do over again, and if you knew then what you know now, would you begin this M.S.W. program?

Answer	East Lansing	Marquette	Gaylord
Yes	33	34	30
No	3	7	2
Unclear, undecided	1	–	5

scriptions from the 115 interviews, we can present some very preliminary additional results.

In general, it appears that students are generally satisfied with most aspects of the courses and the program as a whole, but certain issues (e.g., access to e-mail, level of the material for students with extensive practice experience, etc.) were noted as problematic. Comparisons between the two distance sites and among these two sites and the linked classes on campus reveal no statistically significant differences in perceptions of the learning environment, and few differences in grades. Differences that do appear in the data relate to environmental factors–room temperature, comfort of seats, and so forth (less satisfaction in the distance sites); and choice of electives (again lower at the distance sites).

CONCLUSION

The strong impression created by these extensive interviews with students in all three sites is that the MSU School of Social Work's Distance Education Initiative is a viable alternative to the "traditional" program, but that it certainly is not anyone's *preferred* option. It certainly has costs as well as benefits for all participants.

For the distance site students, the obvious benefit is the opportunity to complete an accredited MSW program while maintaining jobs, family life, and community ties. They complain about the time involved, the commuting, the impact on family, the discomforts in the classroom–but overwhelmingly, if they had it to do over again, a large majority would begin the program.

The perspective of students in East Lansing is different. For them, the cost is time lost to the technology that they do not even need! A benefit reported is the opportunity to interact with other students from different parts of the state, students who are known to have more extensive experience in the field. Many of the other complaints and benefits of the students in all three sites are basically identical, and they are what you would expect from most graduate social work students: it takes time, it costs money, and it certainly is not a whole lot of fun!

The data have pointed out to the faculty that one aspect of the "message" that we have been trying to convey has not yet been communicated very clearly or convincingly. In the early stages of the program we were very apologetic about the need to teach to students in Marquette and Gaylord "through" the electronic medium of interactive television. We were even more apologetic to the students on campus, for whom we could provide very little justification for their participation in the distance education classroom. But as we gained more experience with the ITV system, and as we became more familiar with the applications of this technology in practice, especially in rural areas of Michigan, we have moved from describing the interactive TV system as something we simply teach "through" out of necessity, to something that we actually teach "about." We are now much more likely to offer to students concrete demonstrations of how interactive television is already part of the practice environment in such fields as mental health and health care (Freddolino, Nordling, & Olsen, 1998). The absence of any mention of this concept in the data strongly suggests that we have a long way to go in demonstrating this value.

AUTHOR NOTE

Paul P. Freddolino, PhD, is Professor of Social Work at Michigan State University, where he is also Coordinator of Distance Education in the School of Social Work. Most of his research has been in the area of program evaluation, including numerous studies in mental health, health care, education, and social services. Recent studies have included evaluations of an interactive video system linking numerous high schools; a study of a breast cancer support group operating through videoconferencing technology which links four communities; and interviews with employees of a regional medical center who use videoconferencing, focusing on their perceived training needs.

REFERENCES

Blakely, T. J. & Schoenherr, P. (1995). Telecommunication technologies in social work distance education. *Journal of Continuing Social Work Education, 6* (3), 8-12.

Commission on Accreditation, CSWE (1995). *Guidelines for social work distance education programming.* Alexandria, VA: Author.

Council on Social Work Education–CSWE (1995). *The use of distance education in social work teleconference.* Alexandria, VA: Author.

Darkenwald, G. G. (1989). Enhancing the adult classroom environment. In E. R. Hayes (Ed.), *Effective teaching styles* (pp. 67-75). New Directions for Continuing Education, no. 43. San Francisco: Jossey-Bass.

Freddolino, P. P. (1996). The importance of relationships in creating a quality learning environment in an interactive TV classroom. *Journal of Education for Business, 71,* 205-208.

Freddolino, P. P. (1996, March). *Creating quality learning environments in distant interactive TV classrooms: Efforts and results.* Paper presented at the Annual Program Meeting of the Council on Social Work Education, Washington, DC.

Freddolino, P. P., Nordling, C., & Olsen, L. (1998, March). *Demonstrating the value of interactive television (ITV) for students taking ITV courses on Campus.* Paper presented at the Annual Program Meeting of the Council on Social Work Education, Orlando, FL.

McFall, J., Freddolino, P. P., Flynn, M., Downs, M., & Herrick, J. (1994, April).

Maintaining quality in distance education: MSW programs delivered via interactive audio-visual systems. Paper presented at the Biennial Midwest Social Work Education Conference, St. Paul, MN.

Petracchi, H. E. & Morgenbesser, M. (1995). The use of video and one-way broadcast technology to deliver continuing social work education: A comparative assessment of student learning. *Journal of Continuing Social Work Education, 6* (3), 18-22.

Siegel, E., Conklin, J., Jennings, J., & Flynn, S. A. N. (1996). *The directory of accredited schools of social work that utilize distance learning.* (Available from the Department of Social Work, Southern Connecticut State University, 501 Crescent Street, New Haven, CT 06515.)

Evaluation of a World Wide Web-Based Graduate Social Work Research Methods Course

J. Timothy Stocks
Paul P. Freddolino

SUMMARY. This paper reports on the evaluation of a world-wide web-based social work research methods course in experimental design. The course was taught entirely on the Internet, with no meetings on campus. The same instructor taught another section of the same course during the same semester on campus. Descriptive process data and comparative student outcome data (grades and satisfaction) are presented. Recommendations are made for others considering such courses. *[Article copies available for a fee from The Haworth Document Delivery Service: 1-800-342-9678. E-mail address: getinfo@haworthpressinc.com]*

KEYWORDS. Computer assisted instruction, computer attitudes, educational program evaluation, social work education

Over the past few years, off campus social work courses and programs have been offered through electronic media in the form of interactive televi-

---

J. Timothy Stocks, PhD, is Assistant Professor, and Paul P. Freddolino, PhD, is Professor, School of Social Work, Michigan State University.

Address correspondence to the authors at: School of Social Work, 252 Baker Hall, Michigan State University, East Lansing, MI 48824-1118 (E-mail: stocks@pilot. msu.edu or paul.freddolino@ ssc.msu.edu).

[Haworth co-indexing entry note]: "Evaluation of a World Wide Web-Based Graduate Social Work Research Methods Course." Stocks, J. Timothy, and Paul P. Freddolino. Co-published simultaneously in *Computers in Human Services* (The Haworth Press, Inc.) Vol. 15, No. 2/3, 1998, pp. 51-69; and: *Information Technologies: Teaching to Use–Using to Teach* (ed: Frank B. Raymond III, Leon Ginsberg, and Debra Gohagan) The Haworth Press, Inc., 1998, pp. 51-69. Single or multiple copies of this article are available for a fee from The Haworth Document Delivery Service [1-800-342-9678, 9:00 a.m. - 5:00 p.m. (EST). E-mail address: getinfo@haworthpressinc.com]

sion (Blakely & Schoenherr, 1995; McFall et al., 1994). This modality has been used to deliver individual social work courses as well as degree programs to students in widely dispersed geographic areas (Black, 1997; Coe & Elliott, 1997; Forster, 1997; Freddolino, 1997; Stocks, 1997). A concurrent phenomenon has been the growth of various forms of educational computer applications. Among the newer and more interesting developments is computer-mediated communication (CMC).

CMC is a generic term for a variety of communications systems using computers and networks, which includes e-mail and hypertext environments such as the worldwide web. It has been used for a wide array of educational purposes including undergraduate and graduate courses, seminars, role plays, peer counseling, and self-help groups (Hiltz, 1986, 1990; Miller, 1991; Wells, 1992; Schutte, 1997). In a time when the costs of electronic communication are decreasing and the costs of transportation, buildings, light, and heating are increasing, the utilization of electronic communication technologies in education, and particularly on line CMC, is likely to increase (Clinksdale, 1986; Wittock, 1986; Romiszowski & Mason, 1996).

One aspect of CMC is the on line discussion group. It has been proposed that these groups tend to enhance class interaction since participants may receive feedback from any other participant. This feedback may be of any length since the asynchronous nature of e-mail conferencing does not require a fixed time limit for a communication (Feenberg, 1989; Harasim, 1989; Moore, 1991). Some research also supports the notion that computer mediated communications tend to be more democratic and group discussion oriented than those in classrooms or other electronic communication media (Harasim, 1989; Levin, Kim, & Riel, 1990; Siegel et al., 1986).

However, a reported difficulty with educational CMC is the open-ended demand on instructor time (Paulsen, 1992). Since communication is asynchronous, the instructor faces requests, questions, and comments from students at all times, not just within class periods. Thus, the on line class is a particularly time consuming proposition.

This paper describes a graduate social work research course taught via CMC over the Internet.

METHODS

Course Design

The course was the first in a two-course sequence designed to provide students in the Master of Social Work program with a basic grounding in research skills. It was titled "Social Work Research I: Experimental and

Quasi-Experimental Designs." Research I is typically offered in the Winter/ Spring semester.

Two sections of the course were offered–one entirely over the Internet and another in a classroom on campus. The same instructor (the first author) taught both sections. Lecture content and assignments were the same for both sections.

Students in the Internet section accessed text lectures at a course website. The lectures were posted at the website each week, giving students a week to read the lecture. At the end of this period, lecture and textbook content for the week were discussed on a listserv™ discussion group limited to class members. Class participation was evaluated based upon the frequency, relevance, and quality of postings to the list.

Lectures remained available on the website after the week's discussion so that students could refer back to them.

Study questions covering assigned textbook readings and lecture material were also posted at the website each week. Students answered the questions using forms input on the website. The instructor returned students' answers with corrections via e-mail.

Students also had to write a critical evaluation of a journal article evaluating threats to internal validity.[1] These papers were submitted in word processor file form as attachment files on an e-mail message.

A term paper describing the results of a single subject evaluation was submitted by mail. Many students did not have access to and/or competency using graphics applications. Therefore, it was judged that requiring e-mail submission of the term paper was too involved a process to be justified at the time.

There was also a final examination. This examination was not given over the Internet. Students either had to come to the campus to take the examination or arrange for a proctor. This was done to comply with host University regulations concerning security of examinations.

Students in the On Campus section had the same assignments (including study questions) as those in the Internet section. These students did not have access to the Internet course website nor did they have access to the Internet class discussion list (although they did have a listserv™ discussion list of their own).

"Lecture" material for the Internet section consisted of written lectures and graphical examples (i.e., charts and figures) illustrating lecture content posted on the worldwide web. Study questions covering assigned textbook readings and lecture material were also posted at the website each week. Students answered the questions using a form on the website that e-mailed their answers to the instructor. The instructor returned students' answers with corrections via e-mail.

Lectures in the On Campus class were presented using a Powerpoint™ format. Powerpoint™ slides consisted of outlines using section headings from the posted web lectures and all the graphical examples from the website. Lecture notes were copies of the text material presented on the website. Students received a handout at each class session showing all slides for the day's lecture. This handout was designed to allow students space to take notes.

Evaluation Design

Measures

Since the distributions of dependent variable scores were skewed in most instances, a mean would tend to give a biased estimation of the central tendency of the distribution. The standard deviation (based in the symmetric normal distribution) would likewise give an inaccurate picture of the variability of scores. The results have been reported using unbiased indicators, namely, the median as the measure of central tendency and the 25th and 75th percentiles as indicators of variability.

Computer Attitude Scale. The Computer Attitude Scale is a 30-item rapid assessment instrument developed by Loyd and Gressard (1984). This scale is designed to measure the respondent's comfort with computers. Higher scores are held to indicate greater magnitude of comfort.

This instrument was administered at the beginning of the course and at the course's conclusion. Alpha Coefficients for the two administrations were .968 and .960, respectively, implying little random measurement error. The retest reliability coefficient was .861. The lower retest coefficient suggests that this instrument was sensitive to changes between administrations.

Technology Use Inventory. The Technology Use Inventory is a 24 item rapid assessment instrument designed to evaluate an individual's perception of personal proficiency with technology. It is the proficiency subscale of the Educational Technology Skills Inventory (Iowa Educational Technology Training Institute, 1996). Higher scores are held to indicate a greater sense of proficiency than lower scores. Inventory items are evaluated on a four-step scale (unfamiliar with item; no experience; some experience; proficient). The inventory items may be found in Figure 1.

This instrument also was administered at the beginning of the course and at its conclusion. Alpha Coefficients for the two administrations were .921 and .925, respectively. The retest reliability coefficient was .738. Again, the high Alpha Coefficients suggest little random error, and the lower retest coefficient suggests sensitivity to between administration changes.

Classroom Relationship Inventory. A 35 item Classroom Relationship Inventory was administered at the conclusion of the course.[2] The items were

FIGURE 1. Technology Use Inventory

1. Create a document in a word processor.
2. Create a spreadsheet.
3. Use computer-administered assessment software.
4. Create a newsletter using desktop publishing.
5. Create a computer presentation using presentation software.
6. Use e-mail (electronic mail).
7. Participate in an Internet discussion group (e.g., Listserv, Majordomo).
8. Participate in a Usenet news group.
9. Use live Internet chat (e.g., IRC).
10. Access an online database (e.g., library catalog).
11. Use an online service (e.g., CompuServe, AOL).
12. Browse the Internet.
13. Browse the World Wide Web.
14. Access information on a CD-ROM disk.
15. Install a program on a computer hard drive.
16. Configure software to communicate with other computers/networks.
17. Install an internal computer adapter/card (e.g., sound card, modem card).
18. Troubleshoot malfunctioning computer hardware.
19. Troubleshoot a malfunctioning printer.
20. Troubleshoot malfunctioning computer software.
21. Use a camcorder to record a videotape.
22. Use an audio cassette recorder to make a recording.
23. Use a CD player to play back a recording.
24. Use a speakerphone.

selected and adapted from the Adult Classroom Environment Scale (Darken-wald, 1987). These items deal with aspects of the interactive environment within the class. A summative score is not derived from this inventory. Instead, individual items are evaluated. They are evaluated on a seven-step scale from "strongly disagree" to "strongly agree." The inventory items may be found in Figure 2.

Background Information. Information was collected on background variables–age, gender, concentration/major, current credit load, hours spent employed, work experience in human services, and miles traveled to class. Additionally, information was collected on technology related variables–use of computers at work, use of computers in previous classes, access to a home computer, access to a home computer with a modem, and having an e-mail account in the previous year.

Use of E-Mail. The frequency of private e-mail messages to the instructor was recorded for each study participant. Also the frequency of e-mail messages to a class listserv ™ discussion group was recorded.

Course Grade. Each student's grade was recorded. Grading was on a 100-point scale.

FIGURE 2. Relationship Inventory

1. The class is flexible enough to meet students' individual needs.
2. Most students participate in class discussions.
3. Each student is expected to learn the same thing.
4. Students often share personal experiences in class.
5. Students are allowed to select assignments that are of personal interest to them.
6. Students rarely interact with one another during class.
7. Students are able to achieve personal learning goals.
8. The teacher tries to help students to succeed.
9. The teacher tries to find out what individual students want to learn.
10. The teacher talks down to students.
11. Students are given the opportunity to learn at their own pace.
12. The teacher encourages students to do their best.
13. Students help to decide the topics to be covered in class.
14. Students are often bored in class.
15. The teacher makes all decisions in class.
16. Students in the class feel free to disagree with each other.
17. The teacher follows the lesson plan even if students are not interested.
18. The students pay attention to what the teacher is saying.
19. Students in the class enjoy working together.
20. The teacher respects students as individuals.
21. The teacher dominates classroom discussion.
22. The class is relevant to student life experiences.
23. Students are free to question course requirements.
24. The teacher likes the students in the class.
25. The teacher requires that things be done his or her way.
26. Students in the class work well together.
27. The class is enjoyable.
28. The teacher cares whether or not the students learn.
29. Students look forward to the class.
30. Students in the class learn from one another.
31. The form of the class encourages development of friendships.
32. The teacher cares about students' feelings.
33. Students often ask the teacher questions.
34. Students participate in setting course objectives.
35. A few students dominate class discussions.

Group Interview. An evaluator (the second author) other than the instructor conducted a group interview using a modified focus group approach. A notice was placed on the Internet section's listserv ™ discussion group, and six students agreed to participate. Since many students chose the Internet section so as to be free of the requirement to be on campus at certain times, it was not surprising that only six students chose to attend the focus group meeting. Interview topics included:

1. how students spent course-related time;
2. the role of the listserv ™ discussion group in regard to asking questions;

3. the nature (direct e-mail, discussion group e-mail, telephone, face-to-face) and extent of contact among students in the Internet section and with students in the On Campus section; and
4. strengths and limitations of the course.

The interview lasted for 80 minutes and was audiotaped for later analysis.

Survey. Students in the Internet section received a brief self-administered survey with their final examination. Survey content included queries about expectations for the course and how these were met; the nature and extent of contact with other class members; the role of "community"; contact with the instructor; suggestions for the future; and whether or not the respondent would take another Internet course. Eight out of 24 students (33%) returned the survey, a response rate lower than hoped for. One explanation for this low response rate would be that the final examination and other required forms had to be completed at the same time as the survey (which was voluntary).

Research Participants

Participants were graduate students enrolled at a major state university. All but two of the students were enrolled in the MSW program. The other two were graduate students from other departments at the university. Of the sixty students who signed up for the course, 36 enrolled in the On Campus section and 24 enrolled in the Internet section. Although there was not random assignment[3] to sections, the student samples were similar on most pre-test variables (see Tables 1 and 2).

However, there were meaningful differences between the Internet and On Campus groups on two variables–Computer Attitude Scale (CAS) and Technology Use Inventory (TUI) scores. Students in the Internet section tended to score higher on both instruments, indicating somewhat more comfort with computers and more experience with technology than their On Campus contemporaries. Still, as can be seen in Table 2, there was considerable score overlap between the sections.

RESULTS

There were no significant differences between pre- and post-intervention scores for the Computer Attitude Scale (see Figure 3).

However, there were significant differences for Technology Use Inventory scores using the Wilcoxon Signed Ranks Test at the .05 criterion. Individuals in both the Internet and On Campus sections tended to self-report increases in technological proficiency (see Figure 4).

TABLE 1. Background Characteristics

Variable	Percentiles	Section	
		On Campus	Internet
Miles to Class[NS]	25th	5	6.25
	50th	23	11
	75th	135	86
		n = 36	n = 24
Years in Human Services[NS]	25th	1	1
	50th	3	3
	75th	7.625	6
		n = 34[b]	n = 24
Hours a Week Worked[NS]	25th	5.25	16
	50th	16	20
	75th	21	37.5
		n = 34[b]	n = 23[a]
Credits Current Semester[NS]	25th	12	9.25
	50th	13	12.5
	75th	13	13
		n = 36	n = 24
Age[NS]	25th	23	24
	50th	25	27
	75th	39	34.25
		n = 36	n = 24
CAS Score*	25th	34.00	39.25
	50th	49.00	54.00
	75th	53.00	57.00
		n = 35[a]	n = 19[c]
TUI Score*	25th	29.00	35.00
	50th	34.43	39.00
	75th	40.00	48.00
		n = 35[a]	n = 19[c]

* $p < .05$; Mann-Whitney/Wilcoxon Test
[NS] = Not Significant
[a] one score missing
[b] two scores missing
[c] five scores missing

TABLE 2. Background Characteristics

	Section	
Variable	**On Campus**	**Internet**
Computer Use at Job/Placement[NS]	55.6% n = 36	69.6% n = 23[a]
Computer Use in Previous Course[NS]	86.1% n = 36	100% n = 23
Concentration[NS] Clinical Administration Other	91.7% 5.6% 2.8% n = 36	87.5% 8.3% 4.2% n = 23
Computer at Home[NS]	72.2% n = 36	75.0% n = 23
Computer at Home with Modem[NS]	52.8% n = 36	75.0% n = 23
Prior E-Mail Account[NS]	88.9% n = 36	87.5% n = 23

[NS] = Not Significant; χ^2 Test
[a] one score missing

Of the 35 items in the Classroom Relationship Inventory, five showed significant differences:

10. The teacher talks down to students.
11. Students are given the opportunity to learn at their own pace.
14. Students are often bored in class.
21. The teacher dominates classroom discussion.
31. The form of the class encourages development of friendships.

Students in the Internet section were less likely to agree with items 10, 14, 21, and 31 than their peers in the On Campus section (see Figure 5). They were more likely to agree with item 11 than were the On Campus students.

Differences in variability of response were apparent for items 21 ("The teacher dominates classroom discussion.") and 31 ("The form of the class encourages development of friendships."). The interquartile range for the Internet section responses was approximately 3 to 4 times as great as that in the On Campus section.

Mann-Whitney/Wilcoxon tests showed significant ($p < .05$) differences

FIGURE 3. Computer Attitude Scale (25th, 50th, and 75th Percentiles)

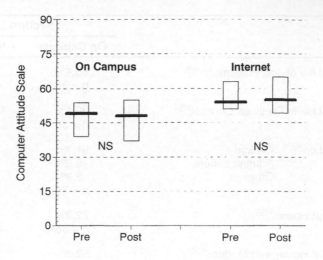

FIGURE 4. Technology Use Inventory (25th, 50th, and 75th Percentiles)

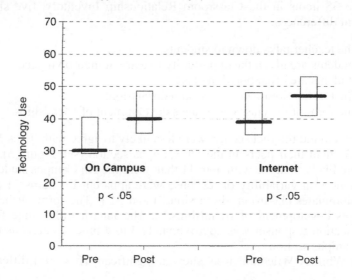

FIGURE 5. Relationship Measures (25th, 50th, and 75th Percentiles)

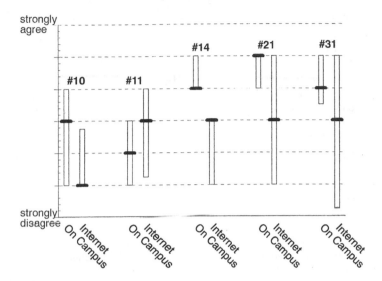

between On Campus and Internet sections with respect to frequency of use of e-mail. Students in the On Campus section tended not to use e-mail to communicate with the instructor (median = 0; interquartile range = 1) while Internet students would contact the instructor more frequently (median = 6.5; interquartile range = 4.5). Similarly, On Campus students were less frequent users of the class list (median = 2; interquartile range = 4) than Internet students (median = 8.5; interquartile range = 11).

There were no significant differences between sections on grade points (see Figure 6). Overall, students in the Internet section seemed to score slightly higher than those in the On Campus section.

Six variables were evaluated within sections as to their association with grade: frequency of off list e-mail, frequency of on list e-mail, Computer Attitude Scale score, Technology Use Inventory score, access to a computer with a modem at home, and whether they had an e-mail account prior to entering the course (see Table 3).

For the On Campus section, only the presence of a prior e-mail account was significantly associated with grade. Individuals who already had an account tended to have higher grades with prior e-mail account status accounting for 16.6% of the variance in grade.

Within the Internet section, three variables were significantly associated with grade: frequency of off list e-mail, Computer Attitude Scale score, and access to a computer with a modem at home. Computer Attitude Scale score had the strongest association with grade (24.6% of variance explained), fol-

FIGURE 6. Grades (25th, 50th, and 75th Percentiles)

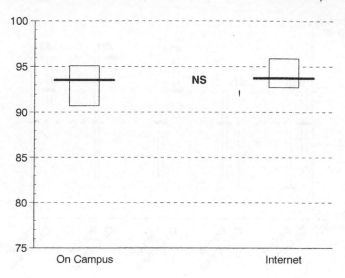

TABLE 3. Correlations with Grades

Variable	Section	
	On Campus	Internet
Off List E-Mail	− .193NS	+ .425*
On List E-Mail	+ .137NS	+ .377NS
Computer Attitude Scale	+ .133NS	+ .496*(1)
Technology Use Inventory	− .059NS	+ .169NS(1)
Home Computer with Modem	+ .127NS	+ .469*
Prior E-Mail Account	+ .407*	+ .041NS

* p < .05
NS = Not Significant
(1) five scores missing

lowed by access to a computer with a modem (22.0% of variance explained), and frequency of off list e-mail (18.1% of variance explained).

There was overall concordance between interview and survey responses of the Internet students. Positive aspects mentioned more than once included the following:

- Students perceived greater flexibility in time scheduling. They could "attend" lecture whenever they chose.
- Many students thought it was easier to ask questions–both of the instructor and other students–via e-mail instead of in person.
- As distinct from an on campus class, students could read lecture notes several times to improve understanding.
- Students saw themselves as being more able to set the pace at which they worked.
- The listserv ™ discussion group was seen as central to keeping students in contact with the instructor and each other. There was a consensus among respondents that the course could not have worked without the list.

The instructor also found the Internet discussion list to be an extremely important component of the course. An unanticipated benefit of the list was that on list student discussions seemed more thoughtful than classroom discussions.

Negative aspects mentioned more than once included these areas:

- The technology did not always work well (e.g., difficulties accessing the system, e-mailing papers, breakdown of chatrooms). The instructor also mentioned this as a major difficulty.
- Some students as well as the instructor found the volume of messages on the listserv ™ discussion group difficult to handle. Also, messages on the list were often seen as not being personally useful.
- Students missed face-to-face contact and relationship with the instructor and classmates. Some of the students met together face-to-face to study for their final examination. It is interesting to note that this was, to some extent, organized via on-list and off-list e-mail.
- Feedback from the instructor to work submitted and to questions asked on the class list took longer than expected.

Technical difficulties were a barrier for both students and instructor. One incident involved the submission of a paper via e-mail. Students had been instructed on how to attach word processor files to an e-mail message and submit them. The papers were submitted, but many students gave their files the same name. Thus, subsequent submissions replaced previous ones. It took approximately three weeks to finally get these papers properly submitted.

On one occasion, the instructor was attempting to upload the lecture for a week and was unable to do so. The lecture files on the server had already used up the allocated space. As a result, the lecture went online late.

Even something as simple as returning papers took longer on the Internet. Once papers had been graded, the word processor files were attached to an e-mail and sent back to the student. Returning papers took about eight times longer than in a traditional on campus class.[4]

These difficulties accounted for many of the delays in instructor feedback experienced by students. Rather than answer e-mail, the instructor was occupied with solving technical problems.

DISCUSSION

Student performance was comparable in the two sections. Overall grades were similar. Since communication tended to be via e-mail in the Internet section, it is not too surprising that students in the Internet section made more use of e-mail than did their On Campus classmates. However, despite this difference in "practice" during the semester, both groups reported similar increases in proficiency with technology. Student comfort with computers as measured by the CAS remained about the same from beginning to end of the course for both sections.

Three relatively strong predictors of higher grades for the Internet section were greater comfort with computers, availability of a computer with modem at home, and high frequency of private e-mail to the instructor. It seems reasonable that students who were more comfortable with computers would find it easier to perform in an environment where communication was mediated by computer. The availability of a computer and modem at home would also make classwork easier. Finally, private e-mail may be analogous to a visit to the instructor during office hours. These students would have the benefit of additional clarification and development not available to students who did not make such contact.

However, while the effect sizes for these variables were fairly large, it should be born in mind that the range of grades in both the Internet and On Campus sections was fairly narrow. Students tended to perform well even when their comfort with computers was low, they lacked access to the course from home, and they did not directly contact the instructor with questions.

Students in the On Campus and Internet sections tended to resemble each other on the background variables as well. Only two pre-intervention variables showed a statistically significant difference between sections–Computer Attitude Scale (CAS) score and Technology Use Inventory (CAS) score. Students in the Internet section tended to score in ways that indicated greater comfort with computers and greater proficiency with technology than their On Campus counterparts.

However, these "significant" differences were slight. The interquartile range for the CAS scores within the two sections was a little under twenty while the difference between section medians was five. The within section interquartile range for the TUI was around twelve while the difference was around five. For both variables the degree of overlap in scores was greater than the degree of difference. Overall, the two sections seemed more similar than different.

Still, CAS score was positively correlated with grade in the Internet section (but not the On Campus section). Also, students in the Internet section tended to have higher CAS scores than those in the On Campus section. This raises the possibility that selection bias may have had some role in the differences between sections.

Results from the Classroom Relationship Inventory were consistent with interview results. More Internet section students reported feeling able to learn at their own pace than On Campus section students. This was paralleled by reports from Internet class interviewees that they saw greater flexibility in time scheduling and being more able to set their own work pace. These findings were similar to those in Schutte's (1997) study of an Internet undergraduate social statistics class. As compared with an On campus section, Shutte's Internet students perceived a higher degree of flexibility than the On campus students although the differences were not significant at the $\alpha = 05$ level.

Internet section interviewees thought it was easier to ask questions via e-mail than in person. Similarly, Internet section students were less likely to feel that the instructor dominated class discussion than were students in the On Campus section. Likewise, Internet section students were less likely to characterize the instructor as talking down to students. These tend to support earlier findings (Harasim, 1989; Levin, Kim, & Riel, 1990; Siegel et al., 1986) that computer mediated communications may be more democratic and group oriented than those in classrooms or other electronic communication media.

On the other hand, students in the Internet section tended to find their class format less conducive to the development of friendships than students in the On Campus section. This was echoed in the interviews where respondents reported missing in person contact with the instructor and each other.

Both students and instructor sometimes found the volume of e-mail difficult to handle. This parallels Paulsen's (1992) report of greatly increased time demands on instructors. Since there was no fixed class time, students could make comments, ask questions, or request clarification at any time. This meant that the instructor was, in a sense, always on call. Technical problems also led to greater difficulties for instructor and students.

CONCLUSION

Overall, the educational experience for students in the Internet section was comparable to that of the students in the On Campus section. Performance as measured by grade was the same for the two sections. Students in the Internet section tended to find the flexibility inherent in the design of the course a positive feature. They found the lack of face-to-face interaction a negative one.

Teaching this Internet course was extremely time-consuming. It is definitely not "labor saving." However, it is an effective way of taking social work education to individuals who find it difficult to attend a university or commute to a studio for an interactive television class. For social work educators engaged in outreach work, the Internet course is a valuable resource.

RECOMMENDATIONS

- The online course is an appropriate way of meeting the needs of students who find it difficult to attend an On campus class. We would recommend it for courses where *immediate* instructor feedback is not a necessary component of the course.
- Because of the amount of labor entailed in preparing a course to be taught over the Internet, instructors should be *released* from teaching one course in the semester prior to teaching the online course. This would provide the instructor with the time to adequately prepare the course as well as reasonable compensation for the additional effort involved in such preparation.
- Technical support is extremely important. When this course was set up, there was little technical support available to the instructor. Subsequently, more professional support became available to instructors. These included not only programmers, but individuals trained in graphic design. Currently, it is much easier to set up an Internet course at this institution than it was as recently as a year ago.
- Internet instructors would be well-advised to make use of the capacities of the computer to *automate* certain repetitive operations Inherent in teaching. As we enter the second iteration of this course, we are using more self-testing with automated feedback using Javascript ™ applets.
- Students should find it easy to obtain and provide *feedback*. Our website format has been redesigned to make it easier for students to send messages to the listserv ™ discussion list or to the instructor. Specifically, a "question" link has been provided periodically throughout the "lecture." The link contains a message telling students that questions posed to the class list count as class participation, while questions sent privately to the instructor do not.
- Students should be provided with frequent *prompts* for discussion on the class list. A new feature throughout the course is the "thought problem" link. Within the lecture, a potentially controversial question is posed to the student. The question is followed by a link to the listserv ™ discussion list with a reminder that contributing to the discussion will raise one's class participation grade.

- It is possible that students might be able to *personalize* the instructor and each other more if they met face-to-face before the class met or early in the semester. Such meetings have been set up in another Internet class taught within our school as well as in the second iteration of this class with ambiguous results. Less than one-third of the students elected to attend such a session. It is also important to realize that the very reasons why a student chooses an Internet class may militate against attending a face-to-face meeting. Students with difficult schedules or who are living at some distance from the campus may not be able to attend.
- It would be useful to know the role played by pre-existing student *beliefs* on student outcomes. For example, what role is played by beliefs about the importance of face-to-face student-student and student-instructor contact? Similarly, *expectations* about the nature of student-student and student-instructor contact in an Internet course may be important.

NOTES

1. Originally, there were two papers–one on internal validity and one on external validity. The second assignment had to be dropped due to technical difficulties surrounding transmission of papers via e-mail.

2. A modified form of this inventory was administered at the beginning of the course. Items were the same, but students were asked to evaluate items on a seven-step scale from "highly undesirable" to "highly desirable." No significant differences were found between the Internet and On Campus sections for any of the items.

3. The sample for this study was a convenience sample. This, combined with the non-random assignment of students to sections, makes the probability values in the statistical tests questionable. In this paper, the tests are simply used as an arbitrary way of dividing effects into stronger and weaker categories.

4. Returning a paper via e-mail requires that an e-mail message be addressed, a subject line be typed for the message, and the file containing the corrected paper be attached to the message. After this has been accomplished, one must wait for the server to clear the message before the next one may be set up. It took the instructor an average of one minute and six seconds to send each corrected paper.

For a class of 33 students, it took four minutes and ten seconds to hand back papers. This is a little less than eight seconds per paper.

REFERENCES

Black, J. (1997). *From a distance: The partnership between field education and distance education technology.* Paper presented at the 43rd Annual Program Meeting, Council on Social Work Education, Chicago, IL.

Blakely, T. J. & Schoenherr, P. (1995). Telecommunication technologies in social work distance education. *Journal of Continuing Social Work Education, 6*(3), 8-12.

Clinksdale, B. G. (1986). Teleconferencing: A new dimension for the business education class. *Journal of Education for Business, 62*(3), 127-130.

Coe, J. & Elliott, D. (1997). *An evaluation of teaching direct practice in distance education programs for rural settings.* Paper presented at the 43rd Annual Program Meeting, Council on Social Work Education, Chicago, IL.

Darkenwald, G. G. (1987). Assessing the social environment of adult classes. *Studies in the Education of Adults, 19*(2), 127-136.

Feenberg, A. (1989). The written world: On the theory and practice of computer conferencing. In R. Mason & A. R. Kaye (Eds.), *Mindweave: Communication, computers, and distance education* (pp. 22-39). NY: Pergamon.

Forster, M. (1997). *Modifying a graduate social welfare course for interactive video instruction.* Paper presented at the 43rd Annual Program Meeting, Council on Social Work Education, Chicago, IL.

Freddolino, P. (1997). *Building on experience: Lessons from a distance education MSW program.* Paper presented at the 43rd Annual Program Meeting, Council on Social Work Education, Chicago, IL.

Harasim, L. M. (1989). Online education: A new domain. In R. Mason & A. R. Kaye (Eds.), *Mindweave: Communication, computers, and distance education* (pp. 50-62). NY: Pergamon.

Hiltz, S. R. (1986). The "virtual classroom": Using computer-mediated communication for university teaching. *Journal of Communication, 36*(2), 95-104.

Hiltz, S. R. (1990). Evaluating the virtual classroom. In L. M. Harasim (Ed.), *Online education: Perspectives on a new environment* (pp. 133-183). NY: Praeger.

Iowa Educational Technology Training Institute. (1996). *Educational Technology Skills Inventory.* IA: Iowa Educational Technology Training Institute, University of Northern Iowa.

Levin, J. A., Kim, H., & Riel, M. M. (1990). Analyzing instructional interactions on electronic message networks. In L. M. Harasim (Ed.), *Online education: Perspectives on a new environment* (pp. 185-214). NY: Praeger.

Loyd, B. H. & Gressard, C. P. (1984). Reliability and factorial validity of computer attitude scales. *Educational and Psychological Measurement, 44,* 501-505.

McFall, J., Freddolino, P., Flynn, M., Downs, M., & Herrick, J. (1994). *Maintaining quality in distance education: MSW programs delivered via interactive audiovisual systems.* Biennial Midwest Social Work Education Conference, St. Paul, MN.

Miller, A. J. (1991). *Applications of computer conferencing to teacher education and human resource development.* Proceedings of the International Conference on Computer Conferencing. Columbus, OH: Ohio State University.

Moore, M. G. (1991). *Computer conferencing in the context of theory and practice of distance education.* Proceedings of the International Conference on Computer Conferencing, 1-9. Columbus, OH: Ohio State University.

Paulsen, M. F. (1992). The NKI electronic college: Five years of computer conferencing in distance education. In M. F. Paulsen (Ed.), *From bulletin boards to electronic universities: Distance education, computer-mediated communication, and online education.* University Park, PA: The American Center for the Study of Distance Education.

Romiszowski, A. J. & Mason, R. (1996). Computer-mediated communication. In D. H. Jonassen (Ed.), *Handbook of research for educational communications and technology* (pp. 438-456). NY: Simon & Schuster Macmillan.

Schutte, J. G. (1997). Virtual teaching in higher education: The new intellectual superhighway or just another traffic jam. <http://www.csun.edu/sociology/virexp. htm>.

Siegel, J., Dubrovsky, V., Kiesler, S., & McGuire, T. W. (1986). Group processes in computer-mediated communication. *Organizational Behavior and Human Decision Processes, 37,* 157-187.

Stocks, J. T. (1997). *Using computer generated visuals to enhance interactive television classes.* Paper presented at the 43rd Annual Program Meeting, Council on Social Work Education, Chicago, IL.

Wells, R. (1992). *Computer-mediated communication for distance education: An international review of design, teaching, and institutional issues.* (ACSDE Monograph No. 6). University Park, PA: The American Center for the Study of Distance Education.

Wittock, M. (1986). *The handbook of research on teaching.* NY: Macmillan.

Less Pain, More Gain:
Computer Applications
for Teaching Applied Social Statistics

James A. Forte

SUMMARY. Applied social statistics is typically one of the most dreaded courses in a social work program. Technological advances in computer applications offer tools to lessen the pain and increase the gains associated with teaching and learning statistics. This paper reports on a modest research project resulting in a computer-based approach to teaching Applied Social Statistics. This approach makes full use of MicroCase, a statistical software package. Results of evaluative efforts which appraised the computer technology-enhanced statistics course are presented. Course format, classroom procedures, workbook and homework assignments, evaluation tools, and teaching strategies are also suggested. *[Article copies available for a fee from The Haworth Document Delivery Service: 1-800-342-9678. E-mail address: getinfo@haworthpressinc.com]*

KEYWORDS. Applied statistics, computer technology, teaching

Computers have had a profound impact on everyday life and social work. Of special importance to social work faculty is the availability of computer technology which is relatively easy to use and which will perform all the

James A. Forte, MSW, PhD, is Associate Professor of Social Work, Christopher Newport University, Social Work Program, 50 Shoe Lane, Newport News, VA 23606 (E-mail: jforte@cnu.edu).

[Haworth co-indexing entry note]: "Less Pain, More Gain: Computer Applications for Teaching Applied Social Statistics." Forte, James A. Co-published simultaneously in *Computers in Human Services* (The Haworth Press, Inc.) Vol. 15, No. 2/3, 1998, pp. 71-87; and: *Information Technologies: Teaching to Use–Using to Teach* (ed: Frank B. Raymond III, Leon Ginsberg, and Debra Gohagan) The Haworth Press, Inc., 1998, pp. 71-87. Single or multiple copies of this article are available for a fee from The Haworth Document Delivery Service [1-800-342-9678, 9:00 a.m. - 5:00 p.m. (EST). E-mail address: getinfo@ haworthpressinc.com]

tedious, dull and anxiety-producing arithmetical tasks previously necessary in Applied Social Statistics courses.

Despite gains in computer assisted instruction, many students enter statistics courses with meager quantitative proficiency. Taylor (1990, p. 31) reported on a national assessment of high school math achievement and noted that students "perform dismally in the ability to apply their knowledge and skills to problem-solving work." Only 6.4% of these students could solve multi-step or algebra problems. Math weakness and aversion continues through college (Schacht and Stewart, 1990). Glisson and Fischer (1987) state that social work students have the lowest quantitative GRE scores of any student group. Royce and Rompf (1992) found that social work students have more math anxiety and finish fewer math courses than other university students. Moreover, 41% of those enrolled in a statistics course reported previously failing math. Witkin, Edleson, and Lindsey (1980) replicated an earlier study (Weed and Greenwald, 1973) of the statistical competence of social work graduates. Only two of a sample of 128 social work practitioners–including 79 with undergraduate degrees–could identify eight common statistical symbols. Kreuger (1987, in Taylor, 1990) identifies key causal factors. These include: minimal math preparation; late introduction to data analysis; an anti-quantitative bias; little appreciation for the power of analytical models; and minimal mental imagery useful in thinking about quantitative concepts. In appreciation of students' views of social statistics, one textbook writer titled his monograph, *Sadistic Statistics* (Horowitz, 1981).

Many faculty share an aversion to statistics. Bogal and Singer (1981) reported that three-fourths of their sample viewed their students as highly apprehensive and negatively predisposed toward research courses. In two surveys of faculty attitudes, research was rated by undergraduate social work educators as the lowest priority curriculum area (Forte & Mathews, 1994; Griffin & Eure, 1985). Social work faculty admit to low interest and involvement in research projects and prefer teaching (Faver, Fox, Hunter, & Shannon, 1986). Rubin (1992), in an extensive review of undergraduate research education, reports on the related widespread practice of delegating statistics courses to non-social work faculty. Undergraduate social work educators, especially in small programs, feel pressured by CSWE to include research content essential to practice evaluation but feel unable to satisfy this directive.

Progress has been made in identifying educational principles which may aid social work majors to begin "numerate" careers (Paulos, 1988). First, students must be helped to overcome their anxiety toward math. The creation of an atmosphere that supports confidence building efforts for nervous students should be the primary teaching objective (Blalock, 1987). Unchecked statistical anxiety interferes with learning (Taylor, 1990), leads to over-reliance on memorization (Blalock, 1987), increases the likelihood of academic failure (Schacht, 1991), frustrates the teacher (Schacht & Stewart, 1990), and contributes to avoidance of quantitative analysis (Rounds & Hendel, 1980). Second, computer competence should be an integral part of all social work education including statistical training (Ezell, Nurius, & Balassone, 1991; Glisson & Fischer, 1987; Smith, 1983). Computer related content and practice prepares the student for future learning possibilities, for career and personal computer accomplishments, and for professional communication with computer specialists (Munson, 1988 in Ezell, Nurius, & Balassone, 1991). More and more research and consequent social science data analysis is being done with the help of computers (Bainbridge, 1989). User-friendly computer based applications offer an opportunity to implement both educational principles. This paper describes a teaching approach refined by the author incorporating computer usage and the MicroCase statistical application.

CHOICE OF COMPUTER APPLICATION

In the Fall of 1991, faculty in one department at Christopher Newport University (CNU) agreed to work together on a pilot program. The project aimed to integrate the MicroCase statistical software package and its companion display package, ShowCase, into a variety of courses in the Sociology and Social Work curriculum (Hartmann, 1991). MicroCase Analysis System, a product of the MicroCase Corporation, is a statistical analysis program for IBM or IBM compatible microcomputers (Cognitive Development, 1990). The MicroCase package offers a student-friendly approach to teaching students data management and basic statistical analysis techniques.

MicroCase was selected because of its usefulness in a variety of areas important to beginning students (Monette, Sullivan, & Dejong, 1990). These included its inclusion of current General Social Survey (GSS) data sets with many cases and variables, its speed, and its capacity for handling large data files entered by the student. It has also been positively reviewed in the social science literature (Chin, 1990; Kearl & Gordon, 1992; Seufat, 1989; Silver, 1991). Silver (1991) recommended the main menus as appealing visually and accessible to students. Cursor movement allows for easy selection of tasks and function keys provide useful help screens such as abbreviated codebooks. MicroCase can be easily used at home, allowing students self-paced interaction with the statistical program. In addition, MicroCase provides a wide variety of statistical procedures allowing for univariate, bivariate, and multivariate data analysis. The ShowCase companion software allows for the use of the GSS data set, a cross-cultural data set, a criminology data set, and other social science data sets in classroom visual presentations.

FEATURES OF A COMPUTER-ORIENTED STATISTICS COURSE

The Baccalaureate Social Work Curriculum Policy Statement emphasizes training for practice evaluation and teaching quantitative data analysis (Council on Social Work Education, 1992). Currently, however, there is little social work literature about the teaching of social work statistics and few empirical studies evaluate the effectiveness of particular teaching approaches. Social work educators preparing to teach statistics sail into uncharted territory (Rosenthal & Wilson, 1992). Social work statistics education is a new, complicated, and understudied area for most teachers. However, recent progress in the production of computer-assisted statistical software offers an opportunity for productive technological transfer. Developmental research was used to systematically incorporate MicroCase statistical software into a social work program (Forte, 1995; Reid, 1979; Rothman, 1992; Thomas, 1979, 1992).

Identification of the Central Problem

There seems to be a consensus that students' anxiety about math and statistics is the major obstacle to effective learning (Tobias, 1978). Blalock (1987) insists that the instructor must overcome students' fears and resistances about math before any other educational objective can be achieved. Schacht (1991) adds that statistics anxiety adversely affects student performance. Royse and Rompf (1992) note that students who replace their anxiety with comfort and confidence are likely to become professionals committed to practice evaluation and knowledge generation. In an exploratory investigation, Schacht and Stewart (1990) learned that student anxiety is amenable to change through creative and supportive teaching strategies. Only in one atypical social work study, did researchers find that social work students both valued statistical training and gained in statistical competence (Basom, Iacono-Harris, & Kraybill, 1982).

Course Objectives and Arrangements

In the CNU social work program, applied social statistics is taught by social work or sociology faculty. Clearly contracted relationships with non-social work faculty and ongoing communication about the major-specific needs of social work students avoids problems. Our classroom arrangements mixes social work students with students from other disciplines. Course objectives are those recommended for undergraduate social statistics courses (Glisson & Fischer, 1987; Lazar, 1990; Taylor, 1990). The course was also conceptualized as a place in the curriculum for students to increase their computer literacy (Ezell, Nurius, & Ballasone, 1991; Glisson & Fischer, 1987). The statistics course is part of the research sequence and students are advised to take it following an introductory course on research methods and tools. As recommended also (Glisson & Fischer, 1987; Lazar, 1990), the applied statistics course is described as a start on an educational continuum. Students can keep the MicroCase package–textbook, workbook, and student version of the statistical software–and carry out advanced statistical projects for other courses and graduate school using their undergraduate research faculty as consultants.

Components of Computer-Assisted Statistics Course

The CNU approach makes major use of MicroCase's computer-assisted teaching products and strategies. Use of such software can be taught in a few hours or less. Students spend more time analyzing the meanings and implica tions of data while reducing time learning statistical formulas and calculating statistics. With computer assisted statistical instruction, students can work with or without the aid of the instructor depending on their own comfort level. Opportunities are thus provided for very important hands-on learning (Royse & Rompf, 1992) and for socialization to the use of computing as part of the college culture (Dubrovsky, Kiesler, Sproull, & Zubrow, 1986).

Computer assisted statistical instruction also enables instructors to teach statistical concepts, principles, and procedures in an active and engaging manner. The teaching role changes from one emphasizing the communication of complex statistical formulas to one emphasizing illustration, support, and exploration. Instructors can more easily make the case for the value of statistics. For example, teaching computer-based statistical skills offers learning that for more and more students will be directly transferable to work settings. Teachers who use the assistance of computer software need less math expertise. With certain statistics software (Hudson, 1985), teachers can even dramatically reduce time spent in grading statistics homework assignments.

Since piloting the use of MicroCase, two related resources have become available: an applied social statistics text with a parallel computer lab workbook (Fox, 1992a; Fox, 1992b); and MircoCase Explorit: The American Survey, a CD-ROM with 20 years of the National Opinion Research Center's General Social Survey's allowing for cross-year and trend analysis (MicroCase Corporation, 1997). These would nicely add to a MicroCase-based course.

The CNU approach uses an on-campus computer laboratory, a necessary compliment to classroom education (Nurius & Mutschler, 1984; Smith, 1983). MicroCase is available through a network on any of 25 terminals. Students receive a manual offering guidelines and discussing issues related to computer usage. The class first participates in a 30 minute orientation session. Following the orientation, lab usage is optional. For students who attend, lab work follows a set routine. In class, the workbook assignment is discussed. Statistical concepts and procedures in the assignment are explained and the MicroCase commands and tips on running the procedures are reviewed. Actual lab sessions are held frequently–but students can work at home or leave early, as they prefer. The students can also use lab time to complete the workbook assignment or work on practice statistics problems. As recommended by Smith (1983), technical support staff and the instructor are available at each lab session. At the next class, students report on their computer experience and interpret the MicroCase printout of the computed statistics.

Computer-oriented assignments are of two kinds: workbook assignments and homework assignments. Workbook assignments are drawn from the MicroCase workbook and each focuses on a particular statistical procedure. Specific directions are available in the workbook. These assignments take from 20 to 40 minutes to complete and the final product is either a computer printout or handwritten notes in the workbook taken from the data and statistics displayed in graphic and visual form on the terminal. Workbook assignments typically include two parts: first, the collaborative small-team examination of research questions and variables recommended by Fox; second, the examination of variables chosen by the student to address a personally interesting research question. A student interested in women's issues, for example, might choose gender as one major variable and study gender issues across assignments. This overall approach to computer assignments supports cooperative learning and rewards individual initiative and extra effort (Hudson, 1985).

During the semester, students work at home or in the lab independently to complete three homework assignments: a descriptive statistics assignment; an inferential statistics assignment; and a bivariate analysis assignment. Students complete these on their own time. All steps and procedures necessary to complete the homework have been covered in the related MicroCase workbook assignments and in class lectures. The homework assignment serves as the test of each student's progress in computer usage, statistical understanding, and statistical expression.

The use of the MicroCase statistical software is complimented by more traditional teaching strategies. These include: efforts to create a relaxed and supportive classroom atmosphere (Lazar, 1990); classroom examination of excerpts from research reports (Holcomb, 1992); the use of humor to reduce tension (Maier, 1980; Schacht and Stewart, 1990; Schacht, 1991); discussion of real-life statistical illustrations, often found in newspapers; practice in solving statistical puzzles and identifying published statistical lies (Huff, 1954); and illustrations from the instructor's own data analysis and presentation experiences.

EFFECTIVENESS
OF MICROCASE-BASED STATISTICAL EDUCATION

The MicroCase evaluation project focused on the assessment of the contribution of MicroCase to changes in the level of student anxiety, to improvements in statistical competence, and on overall satisfaction with the incorporation of MicroCase (Forte, Healey, and Campbell, 1994). A self-report evaluation instrument was developed to measure these and a few other variables.

Measures

Since a valid and reliable measure of statistics anxiety could not be located, statistical anxiety was operationalized as a ten-item adaptation of the Mathematical Anxiety Rating Scale (MARS). Math and statistics anxiety are considered similar phenomena (Schacht and Stewart, 1990). The MARS is a 94 statement Likert-like paper and pencil instrument composed of descriptions of situations that might arouse different levels of mathematics anxiety. The MARS is considered to have good test-retest reliability (Suinn, Edie, Nicoletti, & Spinelli, 1972), high internal consistency (Richardson & Suinn, 1972), as well as good construct validity when correlated with the math section of the Differential Aptitude Test (Suinn, Edie, Nicoletti, & Spinelli, 1972). The MARS-R has also been successfully validated with a group of social work students (Royse & Rompf, 1992). Items with relevance to the teaching of social statistics were selected from the set of all items and were maintained as originally designed with the only change being the inclusion of the phrase "or statistics class" after the word math. Possible responses range from "1" for not at all to "5" for very much. Total scores on the adapted MARS range from 10 indicating no fear of statistics to 50 indicating great fear of statistics in all areas.

To determine the general level of mathematical competence and readiness for applied social statistics, all students completed Healey's Math Self-Test (Healey, 1991). Problems involved performing mathematical tasks like multiplication and division, interpreting basic math symbols, rounding off, and completing computations on a series of numbers. The Math Self-Test was scored and the final score represented the number of problems correct. The range of possible scores was 0 for no correct answers and 28 for all correct answers. Perceived competence at the completion of the course was also measured as an item asking about the student's expected final grade: A, B, C, D, or F. Grades on statistics homework assignments and on the statistics exams might also serve as useful measures of improvements in statistical competence.

The instrument for evaluating student satisfaction with MicroCase was developed by the author and modeled after Flynn and McDonald (1991). Two dimensions were assessed. The first, satisfaction with the software's contribution to learning, asked students to rate the extent to which software use aided: (1) understanding the text, the lectures, and the use of the computer; (2) completing computer lab assignments; and (3) increasing knowledge of social statistics. The second, satisfaction with specific features of computer assisted instruction, asked students to rate attributes of the statistical software and computer lab service. Relevant software attributes include the visual layout, the student control of learning pace, the social science data set available through the software, the data printouts, the time available for lab work, and the quality of lab consultation. Seabury and Maple (1993) recently offered a slightly different format for appraising student reactions to computer assisted instruction. Their format might be used in future evaluations.

Additional information about the student's efforts to use MicroCase was operationalized as survey questions–first, the number of minutes per week spent at the computer terminal, and second, the number of completed computer assignments. Official class evaluations were used to obtain basic demographic information and qualitative information about student responses to specific aspects of the course. Additional background information about the student's previous math experience and grades, previous computer experience, grade point average, and major was obtained through short items on the self-report instrument.

Method of Data Collection. The evaluation project was a one group-pretest/posttest design. Due to practical limitations, students could not be randomly assigned to the MicroCase project and a control condition. Ninety-eight students enrolled in three statistics classes in Fall 1991 and Spring 1992 participated in the study. Students were undergraduate social science or social work majors. One instructor was an experienced statistics instructor who, in fact, "wrote the book" and the other, the social work research instructor (and author of this paper), had only one year of previous formal classroom teaching experience.

During the first week of class, students completed the pretest instrument which included the statistics anxiety scale, the Math Self-Test, and the questions about previous math and computer courses. The self-report instrument was completed within 30 to 45 minutes in the classroom following a brief introduction by the classroom teacher. During the last week of class, students completed the posttest instrument which included the statistics anxiety scale, the satisfaction with MicroCase scales, and open-ended questions about use of the computer application. Students were told that the researchers would not examine the posttest instruments until after grades were posted.

Hypotheses. Goals for the pilot study of the use of the MicroCase computer-based application were modest. If students reported a decrease in anxiety with statistical material and an increase in competence in using social statistics, MicroCase would be deemed a valuable addition to the educational program. Three hypotheses were tested. First, it was expected that statistical anxiety as measured by the shortened MARS would be significantly lower at the end of the semester. Second, there would be a statistically significant, positive relationship between involvement with MicroCase (perceived involvement, perceived amount of time on the computer, and self-reported completion of computer assignments) and expected final grade. Third, students would favorably react to the integration of MicroCase into the course. Specifically, students would report on a five-point scale a score of 1 "strongly agree" or 2 "agree" on each item of the "Assessment of MicroCase" section. Due to the lack of research on teaching with MicroCase, predictions about student's ratings of specific features of MicroCase were not made.

Results. Of the 98 students who began the study, seven either dropped the class or did not complete the posttest instrument. The remaining had a roughly equal mix of men (45%) and women (55%). Of the 79 participants who reported their race, 65 identified that they were white, 11 were black, 2 were Hispanic, and 1 said other. The students were predominantly young–42 reported an age of 19 to 22, 23 were 23 to 30 years of age, and only 17 reported that they were over 30. Although young, most of the students were close to completion of their college education. Almost 90% of the students were in their junior or senior year. No student was voluntarily enrolled in the social statistics class. All 83 students were required to take the course as either a distribution or a major requirement.

Students varied in their math, social statistics, and computer backgrounds. Students reported previous college math work ranging from 1 to 4 courses with an average of about 2 courses. Most students (n = 63) had at least one previous computer course while 8 had 2 computer courses and one person had three such classes. Less than half the student group, 40 students, reported useful nonacademic experience with computers. Basic math competency measured by the Healey Math Self-Test ranged from 4 to 28 with a mean math score of 19.9.

Of the 87 students who completed both the pretest and posttest measure, 28 were enrolled in the Fall class and 59 were enrolled in one of the Spring classes. Although the study participants were not randomly selected, a T-test procedure was used to gauge the direction and the size of changes in statistical anxiety. As indicated in Table 1, for all the students, there was a change in the expected direction, that is, the mean rating of statistical anxiety declined from 32.55 to 27.91, a difference of 4.64.

For students enrolled in the Fall class with the novice statistics teacher, the decline was smaller. The pretest mean of 31.07 fell to 27.39 for a statistically insignificant difference of 3.68. The greatest change in the level of student

TABLE 1. Comparison of Student Mean Statistical Anxiety Score Before and After Use of MicroCase

Class	Before MicroCase	After MicroCase	Difference	T-Value
All Students (n = 87)	32.55	27.91	− 4.64	3.16*
Fall Students (n = 28)	31.07	27.39	− 3.68	1.32
Spring Students (n = 59)	33.18	28.15	− 5.03	2.90

*p < .01

anxiety occurred for students taught in the Spring semester by the experienced faculty. A mean anxiety score of 33.18 at the beginning of the semester declined by 5.03 to 28.15 following student involvement with MicroCase. For the whole student group and for the students in the Spring semester classes, statistics anxiety lessened significantly.

Additional bivariate data analysis provides some support for the observation that better students seemed to make greater use of MicroCase in reducing their anxiety. Using the Pearson correlation procedure, for example, it was found that the higher the score on the basic math competency test, the lower the reported anxiety after the use of MicroCase (r = − .265, p < .05). Additionally, the better the expected final grade, the lower the anxiety at the end of the semester (r = − .428, p < .01).

If MicroCase is an important part of the learning process, it is reasonable to expect that greater involvement with MicroCase will relate to better grades. Univariate statistical analysis shows that students varied in how involved they became with the computer and MicroCase. Relative involvement with the lab was measured as students' perception of their effort with Micro-Case relative to other students. Of all the students, 62% (n = 43) claimed that they were as involved as the average student while 25% (n = 17) reported that their involvement was greater than that of the average students and nine students, 13% of the item's respondents, were less involved. Students also estimated the time devoted to MicroCase usage. The mean weekly time was 48 minutes with a range from 10 minutes to 4 hours spent at the computer. Finally, students reported how many required workbook assignments they completed. In the Fall class, students reported a mean number of 8 assignments completed of a possible 9 while in the Spring sessions, students averaged 3 completed assignments of a possible 5 for the semester.

Pearson's correlation procedure was used to measure the association between the three measures of involvement with MicroCase and expected final grade. Table 2 summarizes the results of this analysis.

As indicated in Table 2, there were statistically significant relationships between expected grade and two measures of involvement. The nature of the relationships was as expected. Study results show that the greater the number of lab assignments completed, the higher the expected final grade (r = .335) and the greater the perceived relative involvement, the higher the expected final grade (r = .254). The item, minutes per week using MicroCase, however, was not related significantly nor in the expected direction to expected final grade. It may be that the better students quickly and adeptly used MicroCase to run a procedure and provide a printout. In contrast, the struggling students who expected lower grades may have needed more time on the computer.

Many specific features of MicroCase were related significantly and in the expected direction to the final grade. In rank order, the final grade was correlated with student agreement that MicroCase individualized learning (r = .377, p < .01), that the time allocated to MicroCase use was right (r = .354, p < .01), that the MicroCase use of the General Social Survey data set was relevant (r = .341, p < .01), that MicroCase helped with understanding the text (r = .299, p < .01), that the student could control his or her own progress (r = .283, p < .01), that MicroCase gave useful feedback about the computer usage (r = .254, p < .05), that the class review of printouts was helpful (r = .254, p < .05), that MicroCase increased knowledge of statistics (r = .243, p < .05), and that MicroCase increased lecture comprehension (r = .239, p < .05). In sum, with few exceptions, positive ratings of MicroCase features were related to the expectation of a good final grade.

As expected, students reported positive assessments of the contribution of MicroCase to three aspects of their learning experience. A mean of 1 suggests strong agreement about MicroCase's value while a 2 indicates agreement. As shown in Table 3, students agreed that MicroCase contributed to their completion of assignments (2.0 mean rating), to their knowledge of social statistics (2.1 mean rating), and to their understanding of computer usage (2.3 mean rating). These were respectively the top three ranked items.

TABLE 2. Correlations Between Expected Final Grade and Measures of Degree of Involvement with MicroCase

Expected Grade	Measure of Involvement	Pearson Coefficient
Grade	Number of Lab Assignments	.335**
Grade	Relative Involvement	.254*
Grade	Time Using MicroCase	−.037

* p < .05, ** p < .01

TABLE 3. Rank Order by Means of Items Assessing MicroCase's Contribution to Student Learning

Rank	Item	Mean
1	Helped with lab/homework assignments	2.0
2	Increased knowledge of social statistics	2.1
3	Helped understanding of computer use	2.3
4	Helped comprehension of lectures	2.7
5	Increased understanding of text	2.7

Possible rating ranged from "1," strong agreement to "5," strong disagreement

The value of MicroCase for understanding classroom lectures, rank 4, and for understanding the course text, rank 5, was less clear. For both, means were close to neutral (2.7 mean rating). Students neither agreed nor disagreed that MicroCase helped them with learning in these two areas.

Students reported fairly positive satisfaction with each of the specific features of the MicroCase statistical analysis software. They judged the General Social Survey data set used by MicroCase as relevant and they liked their degree of control over their learning pace (2.1 mean rating for each). Students found the visual layout attractive (2.2 mean rating), the time assigned for computer usage sufficient (2.2 mean rating) and movement through Micro-Case tasks easy (2.2 mean rating). Additionally, students believed that Micro-Case helped them individualize their learning (2.3 mean rating) and they valued classroom review of statistical printouts (2.3). About the overall use of MicroCase, students (2.4 mean rating) agreed that this was a satisfying experience. These fairly positive ratings are supported by the qualitative remarks of the students. Students liked the colors of the display, found Micro-Case usage simpler than expected, thought MicroCase was a tremendous improvement over the previous software, and enjoyed working with the software.

DISCUSSION

Students gained in their comfort with statistics by the end of the semester. Students who were most involved with MicroCase expected the highest final grades and students reported satisfaction with both the contribution of Micro-Case to their learning and with specific features of MicroCase. The statistically significant but educationally minor changes in the level of anxiety may be explained in several ways. First, one of the instructors was teaching this course for the first time and his own uncertainty and anxiety might have affected negatively the students' comfort. Greater declines in anxiety reported by the students in the senior instructor's class lend support to this explanation. Moreover, this course was taught in an evening section, from 7:00 to 9:40 p.m., a notoriously difficult time to maintain student enthusiasm. Second, some students may bring so much anxiety to a required statistics class that even a minor decline over one semester is an accomplishment. Thus, faculty might expect that a very satisfying one semester computer experience with statistics will not undo a long history of math phobia. It is noteworthy, for instance, that though declines in anxiety were small, the evaluations of MicroCase were generally favorable. Moreover, it is possible that the full power and value of the software system may not have been assessed in this pilot study. Nevertheless, this preliminary investigation indicates that students liked MicroCase, viewed it as a helpful supplement to their learning of statistics, and believed its use contributed to good grades.

Social work programs desiring to use teaching products like MicroCase might consider several issues. First, preparation for such a teaching assignment will help. Interested faculty can participate in national and regional conferences like the 1997 University of South Carolina's "Information Technologies for Social Work Education" conference that included training in the use of new information technologies and in statistical instruction. The annual Baccalaureate Program Directors (BPD) conference with its regular sessions on teaching research, the summer program of the Inter-University Consortium for Political and Social Research (ICPSR), and the twice annual Quantitative Instruction on American Society (QIAS) workshops are other examples of skill development opportunities. Or, faculty might purchase a statistical software project for their own computer use, and then carry out a small research project that requires univariate, bivariate, and inferential statistics. Lessons mastered from this kind of exercise can be later transferred to the classroom. Second, initial service as a social work statistics instructor may seem less intimidating if support is obtained. For example, the novice teacher in a small program might first team teach a statistics class with a senior sociology or psychology professor. Or, as in the author's case, the novice might teach as an apprentice to an experienced statistician. Through regular consultation, the expert can aid the novice in dealing with teaching tricky quantitative material. Or, the novice teacher might closely use teaching materials developed at other teaching institutes. Initial use might be cookbook fashion, but mastery and innovative use will occur as confidence with the basics is attained. Finally, even for the experienced statistics instructor, students can be allies in the implementation of teaching innovations and the maintenance of high quality. Regular feedback from students will both ease the introduction of new approaches and maintain student engagement through the recognition of their perceptions and concerns.

Additional improvements in the MicroCase-oriented approach are possible in several areas. First, although the Fox text and workbook effectively contribute to student learning, teaching materials that more fully integrate social work practice, research, and statistics are preferable (Lawson & Berleman, 1982) and should be sought. Second, at the undergraduate level, statistics education should lead to skillful practice evaluation and knowledge generation (Rubin, 1992). More needs to be done so that computer-based statistics learning is supported by field instructors (who currently lack such interest and expertise) and reinforced by field placement opportunities for the use of data analysis skills (Poulin, 1989). Statistical software packages such as MicroCase offer ways to insinuate statistical concepts into many other parts of the undergraduate curriculum. These possibilities are yet to be pursued. Third, this summary of one applied social statistics approach suggests a static use of prefabricated teaching technologies. Further exploration regarding the creative and spontaneous adaptation of this approach to emergent class processes and problems would be useful. Analysis of qualitative data from consumers of the approach might enrich our understanding of such interactive learning processes. Fourth, the 1997 University of South Carolina conference and recent publications indicate that faculty are experimenting with alternative strategies for enriching computer-based statistical education. These include: on-line, distance learning approaches to Applied Social Statistics; the use of multi-media presentations to enhance lectures and class activities; the integration of alternative statistical software such as "SPSS for Windows" into courses (Karp, 1995); and the inclusion of computer-assisted qualitative data analysis as a contrast to quantitative analysis. These strategies offer much potential for development by innovative faculty.

CONCLUSIONS

A computer-assisted instructional approach to statistics education offers promise as an innovative way to teach the subject. Such an approach should include a significant experiential learning component offered in a relaxed, anxiety-dampening atmosphere. Teaching social statistics is enhanced with user-friendly computer software packages and structured teaching materials such as workbooks and social work specific text content. Social work statistical education must be sensitive to the variability in student needs and capacities specific to numeracy. The CNU social work and sociology faculty believe that we have made some progress in using MicroCase to develop an approach responsive to these pedagogical issues. This paper offers lessons based on our experiences. Combined with the reports of other educators using the latest computer and information technologies, social work faculty can now select from many new and exciting tools to deepen their effectiveness.

REFERENCES

Bainbridge, W.S. (1989). *Survey research: A computer assisted introduction.* Belmont, CA: Wadsworth Publishing Company.

Basom, R.E. Jr., Iacono-Harris, D.A. & Kraybill, D.B. (1982). Statistically speaking: Social work students are significant. *Journal of Education for Social Work*, 18, 2, 20-26.

Blalock, H.M. Jr. (1987). Some general goals in teaching statistics. *Teaching Sociology*, 15, April, 164-172.

Bogal, R.B. & Singer, M.J. (1981). Research course work in the baccalaureate social work curriculum: A study. *Journal of Education for Social Work*, 17, 2, 45-50.

Council on Social Work Education (1992). *Curriculum policy statement for baccalaureate degree programs in social work education.* Alexandria, VA: Council on Social Work Education.

Dubrovsky,V., Kielser, S., Sproull, L., & Zubrow, D. (1986). Socialization to computing in college: A look beyond the classroom. In R.S. Feldman (Ed.), *The social psychology of education* (pp. 313-340). Cambridge, England: Cambridge University Press.

Ezell, M., Nurius, P.S., Balassone, M.L. (1991). Preparing computer literate social workers: An integrative approach. *Journal of Teaching in Social Work*, 5, 1, 81-99.

Faver, C.A., Fox, M.F., Hunter, M.S. & Shannon, C. (1986). Research and practice: Orientations of social work educators. *Social Work*, 31, July-August, 282-286.

Flynn, J.P. & MacDonald, F. (1991). Waterslides and landmines in computer-based education. *Journal of Teaching in Social Work*, 5, 1, 101-115.

Forte, J.A. (1995). Teaching Statistics without Sadistics. *Journal of Social Work Education*, 31, 2, 204-218.

Forte, J.A., Healey, J. & Campbell, M.H. (1994). Does MicroCase statistical software package increase the competence and comfort of undergraduate social work and social science majors? *Journal of Teaching in Social Work*, 10, 1/2.

Forte, J.A. & Mathews, C. (1994). Potential employers' views of the ideal undergraduate curriculum. *Journal of Social Work Education*, 30, 2, 228-240.

Fox, W. (1992a). *Social statistics using MicroCase.* Chicago: Nelson-Hall, Inc.

Fox, W. (1992b). *Doing statistics using MicroCase: A workbook for social statistics using MicroCase.* Chicago: Nelson-Hall, Inc.

Glisson, C. & Fischer, J. (1987). Statistical training for social workers. *Journal of Social Work Education*, 3, Fall, 50-58.

Griffin, J.E. & Eure, G.K. (1985). Defining the professional foundation in social work education. *Journal of Social Work Education*, 3, 73-91.

Hartmann, D.J. (1991). Microcomputers and curricular objectives in applied undergraduate training. *Teaching Sociology*, 19, January, 54-61.

Healey, J. (1991). *Statistics: A tool for social research.* 2nd Ed. Belmont, CA: Wadsworth Publishing Company.

Holcomb, Z.C. (1992). *Interpreting basic statistics: A guide and workbook based on excerpts from journal articles.* Los Angeles: Pyrczak Publishing.

Horowitz, G. (1981). *Sadistic statistics.* Wayne, NJ: Avery Publishing Group.

Hudson, W.W. (1985). Computer managed instruction: An application in teaching introductory statistics. *Computers in Human Services*, 1, 1, 117-123.

Huff, D. (1954). *How to lie with statistics.* New York: W.W. Norton.

Karp, D.R. (1995). Using SPSS for windows to enhance, not overwhelm, course content. *Teaching Sociology*, 23, July, 234-240.

Kearl, M. & Gordon, C. (1992). *Social psychology: Shaping identity, thought, and cognition.* Boston: Allyn and Bacon.

Kraybill, D.B., Iacono-Harris, D.A., & Basom, R.E. Jr. (1982). Teaching social work research: A consumer's approach. *Journal of Education for Social Work*, 18, 4, 55-61.

Kreuger, L.W. (1987). *Humanizing statistics for social work education.* Paper presented at the Annual Program Meeting of the Council on Social Work Education, St. Louis, MO.

Lawson, T.R. & Berleman, W.C. (1982). Research in the undergraduate curriculum: A survey. *Journal of Education for Social Work*, 18, 1, 86-93.

Lazar, A. (1990). Statistics courses in social work education. *Journal of Teaching in Social Work*, 4, 1, 1990.

Maier, H.W. (1980). Play in the university classroom. *Social Work with Groups*, 3, 1, 7-16.

MicroCase Corporation (1990). *MicroCase Analysis System.* West Lafayette, IN.

MicroCase Corporation (1997). *MicroCase Explorit: The American survey.* Bellevue, WA.

Monette, D.R., Sullivan, T.J. & DeJong, C.R. (1990). *Applied Social Research: Tools for the Human Services.* 2nd Edition. Fort Worth, Texas: Holt, Rinehart and Winston, Inc.

Munson, C. (1988). Microcomputers in social work education. *Computers in Human Services*, 3, 143-157.

Nurius, P.S. & Mutschler, E. (1984). Use of computer-assisted information processing in social work practice. *Journal of Education for Social Work*, 20, 1, 83-94.

Paulos, J.A. (1988). *Innumeracy: Mathematical illiteracy and its consequences.* New York: Hill and Wang.

Poulin, J. (1989). Goals for undergraduate social work research: A survey of BSW program directors. *Journal of Social Work Education*, 25, 3, 284-289.

Reid, W.J. (1979). The model development dissertation. *Journal of Social Service Research*, 3, 2, 215-225.

Richardson, F.C. & Suinn, R.M. (1972). The mathematics anxiety rating scale: Psychometric data. *Journal of Counseling Psychology*, 19, 6, 551-554.

Rounds, B. Jr. & Hendel, D.D. (1980). Measurement and dimensionality of Mathematics anxiety. *Journal of Counseling Psychology*, 27, 2, 138-149.

Rosenthal, B.S. & Wilson, W.C. (1992). Student factors affecting performance in an MSW research and statistics course. *Journal of Social Work Education*, 28, 1, 77-84.

Rothman, J. (1992). Creating tools for intervention: The convergence of research methodologies. In A.J. Grasso & I. Epstein (Eds), *Research utilization in the social services* (pp. 51-70). New York: The Haworth Press, Inc.

Royse, D. & Rompf, E.L. (1992). Math anxiety: A comparison of social work and non-social work students. *Journal of Social Work Education*, 28, 3, 270-277.

Rubin, A. (1992). Education for research utilization in BSW programs. In A.J. Grasso & I. Epstein (Eds), *Research utilization in the social services* (pp. 369-392). New York: The Haworth Press, Inc.

Schacht, S. (1991). What does Opus know about statistics? The cartoon technique for reducing student anxiety. In L.R. Gaydosh (Ed.), *Syllabi and instructional material for social statistics* (pp. 55-57). Washington, D.C.: American Sociological Association Teaching Resources Center.

Schacht, S. & Stewart, B.J. (1990). What's funny about statistics? A technique for reducing student anxiety. *Teaching Sociology*, 18, January, 52-56.

Schacht, S.P. (1991). What does Opus know about statistics? The cartoon technique for reducing student anxiety. In L.R. Gaydosh (Ed.), *Syllabi and instructional material for social statistics* (pp. 55-57). Washington, D.C.: American Sociological Association Teaching Resources Center.

Seufert, R.L. (1989). MicroCase: Survey analysis software. *Teaching Sociology*, 17, 1, 143-145.

Seabury, B.A. & Maple, F.F. Jr. (1993). Using computers to teach practice skills. *Social Work*, 38, 4, 430-439.

Silver, M.L. (1991). MicroCase Analysis System. *Teaching Sociology*, 19, October, 545-547.

Smith, M.J. (1983). Use of the computer in a course on data analysis in social welfare research. *Journal of Education for Social Work*, 19, 1, 74-78.

Stull, J. (1990). Other materials for use in social psychology courses: Computer software. In J. Chin (Ed.), *Social psychology: A collection of syllabi and instructional material* (pp. 241-244). Washington, D.C.: American Sociology Association Teaching Resources Center.

Suinn, R.M., Edie, C.A., Nicoletti, J. & Spinelli, P.R. (1972). The MARS, a measure of mathematics anxiety: Psychometric data. *Journal of Clinical Psychology*, 28, 373-375.

Taylor, F.A. (1990). The numerate social worker. *Journal of Social Work Education*, 1, Winter, 25-35.

Thomas, E.J. (1978). Generating innovation in social work: The paradigm of developmental research. *Journal of Social Service Research*, 2, 1, 95-115.

Thomas, E.J. (1992). The design and developmental model of practice research. In A.J. Grasso & I. Epstein (Eds), *Research utilization in the social services* (pp. 71-92). New York: The Haworth Press, Inc.

Tobias, S. (1978). *Overcoming math anxiety.* New York: Norton.

Weed, P. & Greenwald, S.R. (1973). The mystics of statistics. *Social Work*, 18, 2, 113-115.

Witkin, S.L., Edleson, J.L., & Lindsey, D. (1980). Social workers and statistics: Preparation, attitudes and knowledge. *Journal of Social Service Research*, 3, Spring, 313-322.

Paraphrase II:
A Listening Skills Training Program
for Human Service Students

Hy Resnick

SUMMARY. *Paraphrase*–A multimedia listening skills training program is presented and discussed. Major elements of the program include a definition of paraphrasing, some of its advantages and disadvantages, techniques of paraphrasing, and an example of how such a multimedia program might be used to deal with a problem of interpersonal conflict in an organization. Graphics, text, video images and audio were used in the design of the program. *[Article copies available for a fee from The Haworth Document Delivery Service: 1-800-342-9678. E-mail address: getinfo@haworthpressinc.com]*

KEYWORDS. Listening, electronic tools, skill training, human service

Training and experience as a group worker early in his social work practice, the teaching methods used by professors in doctoral education, and his own experiences as a beginning professor at the University of Washington School of Social Work led the author to dissatisfaction with traditional didactic-instructional methods.

In an ongoing search for more effective teaching and to create a classroom environment that was more interactive and involving, Dr. Resnick designed

---

Hy Resnick, PhD, is Professor of Social Work, University of Washington School of Social Work, Seattle, WA 98105 (E-mail: resnickh@u.washington.edu).

[Haworth co-indexing entry note]: "*Paraphrase II*: A Listening Skills Training Program for Human Service Students." Resnick, Hy. Co-published simultaneously in *Computers in Human Services* (The Haworth Press, Inc.) Vol. 15, No. 2/3, 1998, pp. 89-96; and: *Information Technologies: Teaching to Use–Using to Teach* (ed: Frank B. Raymond III, Leon Ginsberg, and Debra Gohagan) The Haworth Press, Inc., 1998, pp. 89-96. Single or multiple copies of this article are available for a fee from The Haworth Document Delivery Service [1-800-342-9678, 9:00 a.m. - 5:00 p.m. (EST). E-mail address: getinfo@haworthpressinc.com]

and tested a variety of in-class exercises to more fully engage students in the learning process. During the course of many such experiences and with the development of new multimedia technologies, he became intrigued with the possibilities of computer assisted learning (CAL).

After observing a visiting professor demonstrate the range of multimedia tools that could be used interactively to excite and challenge an undergraduate psychology class, Dr. Resnick realized how far behind social work education was with respect to other human service disciplines and undertook a literature search in the CAL field. This search revealed the many advantages of using CAL, including the recognition that the computer is infinitely patient, consistent, nonjudgmental, and always supportive of students learning at their own pace and in their own place. Further, CAL requires that students participate actively in the learning process and ensures that they receive feedback about their progress.

When this new technology became generally available to the academic community, Dr. Resnick began experimenting with introducing it to his students. After attaining a minimal level of proficiency with the computer, he was able to develop a computer-driven listening skills training program called *Paraphrase I*.[1] Although this first version was a simple (if not simplistic) prototype using mostly text and comprehension checks, it was a beginning for both Resnick and the school.

In developing *Paraphrase II*, Dr. Resnick used a tutorial design which allows students to interact with a computer at a time and place convenient for them. The learning model employed might best be described by the acronym PIIA, where

- P = PRESENTATION (an overview of the major components of the paraphrasing skill.
- I = ILLUSTRATIONS of correct and incorrect uses of paraphrasing, using realistic portrayals of workers paraphrasing client comments and clients' realistic responses to the paraphrases. For example, when a worker (in an incorrect and judgmental paraphrase) reaches beyond what the mother of a troubled child is saying, the client reacts angrily in the video skit. Alternatively, when the client feels understood (by a correct paraphrase), s/he responds positively with a "yeah" and a nod of the head.
- I = INTERACTIVE. After seeing and hearing definitions and examples of paraphrasing, students are given a comprehensive check which requires that they type out a paraphrase of a client's comments and send the printout to the instructor for evaluation and feedback.
- A = APPLICATION. The program includes an application module which demonstrates how the paraphrasing skill can be used in a conflict–resolution situation in an organization.

The content of the first version of *Paraphrase* was developed by Dr. Resnick,[2] and the programming was done by three different graduate students who had free time on their hands and wanted to practice the authoring languages they had learned in a computer science class. Although their part-time and volunteer status proved to be unsatisfactory, the team effort was sufficient to eventually enable a rough prototype of *Paraphrase II* on CD-ROM, by way of a small grant provided by the School of Social Work and the University.

The grant paid for video production equipment and facilities, a part-time project manager who also served as the programmer (and who was skilled in the authoring language (Authorware), a video producer and director, a graphic artist, and a pair of professional actors–all of whom worked together with Resnick to develop *Paraphrase II* (the CD-ROM version of *Paraphrase I*). This "upgrade" makes use of slides, cartoons, moving video images (skits illustrating learning points), sound (music and talk), and text, as well as professionally designed interfaces and navigation systems.

The following demonstration of *Paraphrase II* identifies its content, media formats, and the essential learning components used to heighten the learning experience of the students and specify the advantages of computer-driven instructional modules. The advantages of this electronic program over printed work, and the lessons learned, via student feedback, are discussed.

CONTENT OF PARAPHRASE II

Five content categories are addressed by the program:

1. a definition of paraphrasing;
2. the basic concepts of the paraphrasing skill;[3]
3. advantages and disadvantages of this skill;
4. incorrect (i.e., ineffective) ways of using this skill; and
5. practical applications of this skill in social work situations with clients, patients, and colleagues.

MEDIA UTILIZED IN PARAPHRASE II

A variety of media–text, video and audio clips, slides and graphics–are used in *Paraphrase II*. For example, video clips illustrating the four methods of paraphrasing are employed to clarify the text explanations. Music introduces and opens the program in a dramatic and user-friendly way. Graphics humorously portray incorrect and correct use of the paraphrasing skill (see Figures 1 and 2).

FIGURE 1

Speakers can benefit from any verbal restatement of their comments.
However, certain paraphrasing efforts are more useful than others. For
example...

When an archer aims
and shoots at an
unseen target on the
other side of a wall,
and is merely told the
shot missed — that is
unhelpful.

Speaker

Paraphraser

FIGURE 2

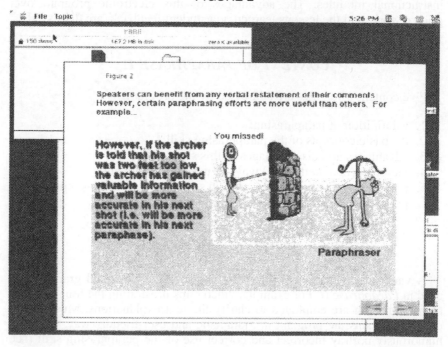

Figure 2

Speakers can benefit from any verbal restatement of their comments.
However, certain paraphrasing efforts are more useful than others. For
example...

You missed!

However, if the archer
is told that his shot
was two feet too low,
the archer has gained
valuable information
and will be more
accurate in his next
shot (i.e. will be more
accurate in his next
paraphase).

Paraphraser

ESSENTIAL FEATURES OF THE PROGRAM

Paraphrase II utilizes seven major learning components to achieve its goal of challenging and engaging students in such a way that it increases the probability of this skill being learned and used.

1. Content. This will include definitions and purposes of paraphrasing, and the specification and brief discussion of the major dimensions of this skill. The content will focus on improving students' skills in listening to the cognitive and affective messages in a communication. This will include definitions and purposes of paraphrasing and a brief discussion of the major dimensions of this skill.
2. Comprehension Checks. To assess learning, "tests" are given at intervals appropriate to the learning task.
3. Skill Practice Sessions. Practice exercises are included in the program to provide students with an opportunity to practice their newly acquired skill in a simulated situation as directed by the program.
4. E-mail. This "tool" facilitates communication with faculty if students have questions, suggestions, or answers to quizzes.
5. Interface.[4] The program is designed to be user-friendly. In a clear attractive way (see Figure 3), it informs students how to continue or exit, take comprehension checks, repeat screens, view other models of learning to listen programs, print responses to instructor's questions, get onto the e-mail program, quit, etc.
6. Video and Graphics. These media were used when the design team decided that was the best way to illustrate a learning point. Funding, of course, also played a role in the decision to use video and graphics.
7. Audio. Audio voice-over of the introduction reinforces the message programmed in the text, and makes it more interesting than simply reading.

ADVANTAGES OF PROPOSED PROGRAM OVER PRINTED WORK

Because of the variety of senses stimulated in the students who use the multimedia version of the *Paraphrase* program, and because of the opportunity for interactivity designed into the program, it is hypothesized that students will learn more quickly, with more motivation, and retain such learning longer, as well as use it more readily in real life situations, than if they were exposed to the same information in a book or article. In the latter medium–text–students relate to the content in a more passive way with fewer senses engaged.

Dramatic (not glitzy) electronic media, designed for interactiveness, are much better able to capture students' energy and imagination than books, although this is not an excuse to eliminate books from our world. Books may

FIGURE 3

offer options that electronic technology cannot. We have a decade or two to discover which media does what best.

LESSONS LEARNED

Students who have used the program report that their interest and learning are highest when:

- The video segments of the program provide a realistic look at a correct paraphrasing interaction.
- There are a variety of media utilized, such as graphics, video, slides, and text, with text being the least attractive of the media.
- The program is integrated into other instructional activities in the curriculum. The program is not intended to be used as a stand-alone device; rather, it is designed to support (usually precede) other instructional activities available in and out of the classroom. Discussion of new research, application obstacles, contexts where the skill should not be used, etc., is essential to proper application of the paraphrasing skills practiced in the program.
- Users of the program are provided with opportunities to share their experiences in small discussion groups. CAL need not isolate students in front of a computer. Interaction with a small group of students can help them internalize the learning and implications of paraphrasing, and deepen their understanding of the paraphrasing skill.

- The program realistically indicates shortcomings of the method as well as its advantages.
- The program provides students with opportunities to test their learning via comprehension checks, and teachers provide feedback and support based on the results of these checks.

CONCLUSION

Electronic Technology has proven to have some utility in higher education and public school classrooms. Social work education so far has made little use of this innovative medium to improve its educational effectiveness. *Paraphrase II* is the first of this genre to be developed and used in social work education. Preliminary testing indicates that this program did its job of teaching social work students the rudiments of one of the profession's most important skills: listening (see Figure 4). Further testing is needed to determine in what ways this tool should be employed in a professional education institution (e.g., as a stand-alone program or as a supplement to classroom instruction); the extent to which its use is warranted, given its high upfront costs; and whether different designs (i.e., more interactivity, more use of video, more

FIGURE 4

dramatic graphics, different navigational aids, etc.), might yield more impact-ful results.

Whether or not this particular skill training program is ultimately used to teach listening skills in social work education institutions, there is reason to believe that CAL programs such as *Paraphrase II* will enter the social work classroom in the 21st century and prove their value.

AUTHOR NOTE

Dr. Hy Resnick is Professor of Social Work at the University of Washington School of Social Work, Seattle, WA. His major specializations are: organization development, planned change in organizations, group processes, electronic technology in human service practice and education, and supporting the work of the newly independent republics in Europe and Asia.

NOTES

1. The paraphrasing skill is taught in traditional ways–lecture, class discussion, and role play–in the School's beginning practice courses.

2. Those active in multimedia development are of two types–content experts and programmers–who occasionally experience communication problems because of the difference in training, interests, and personal styles. A good working relationship be-tween these representatives of two quite different cultures is essential for a good product.

3. For a comprehensive overview of the listening skill, see Matthew Westra (1995), *Active Communication* (pp. 2-6, 99-11, 125-130), New York: Brooks Cole Publishing Co.

4. See K. Mullet & D. Cano (1996), *Designing Visual Interfaces: Communication Oriented Techniques*, Englewood Cliffs, NJ: Prentiss Hall ECS Professional.

Integrating the Internet in a Human Diversity Course

Julie E. Miller-Cribbs
Letha A. Chadiha

SUMMARY. Increasingly, social work educators have become aware of the impact of information technology. Electronic mail, for instance, is utilized widely in schools of social work by students, faculty, and staff. In addition, students are increasingly accessing electronic resources such as the Internet or online library resources for use in their class assignments. There are many applications of such technology in the field of social work, including practice, advocacy, networking, communication, participation in policy formation, and teaching. This paper will describe how the integration of information technology can be used in a course on human diversity. *[Article copies available for a fee from The Haworth Document Delivery Service: 1-800-342-9678. E-mail address: getinfo@ haworthpressinc.com]*

KEYWORDS. Internet, human diversity, social work education, information technology

INTRODUCTION

Addressing human diversity in social work practice has become a more salient issue with increasing numbers of non-White clients whom social

Julie E. Miller-Cribbs, MSW, is a doctoral student, and Letha A. Chadiha, PhD, is Associate Professor, George Warren Brown School of Social Work, Washington University, St. Louis, MO 63130-4899 (E-mail: jemiller@artsci.wustl.edu or lethac@ wucan.wustl.edu).

[Haworth co-indexing entry note]: "Integrating the Internet in a Human Diversity Course." Miller-Cribbs, Julie E., and Letha A. Chadiha. Co-published simultaneously in *Computers in Human Services* (The Haworth Press, Inc.) Vol. 15, No. 2/3, 1998, pp. 97-109; and: *Information Technologies: Teaching to Use–Using to Teach* (ed: Frank B. Raymond III, Leon Ginsberg, and Debra Gohagan) The Haworth Press, Inc., 1998, pp. 97-109. Single or multiple copies of this article are available for a fee from The Haworth Document Delivery Service [1-800-342-9678, 9:00 a.m. - 5:00 p.m. (EST). E-mail address: getinfo@ haworthpressinc.com]

workers serve. The concept of human diversity refers to different experiences–racial, ethnic, cultural, social, political, and economic–that people have. Along with these different experiences, social workers recognize diversity in people on the basis of differences in gender, sexual orientation, and physical disability (Beckett & Johnson, 1995). The Council on Social Work Education recommends that students in a course on human diversity are versed in knowledge and skills about these different experiences. More specifically, according to Fletcher and Devore (1997), the Council's curriculum guidelines call for courses that cover "race and racism, oppression and powerlessness, experiences of ethnic groups, and the impact of culture on social workers and their clients" (p. iv).

Increasingly, social work educators have become aware of the impact of information technology. Electronic mail, for instance, is used widely in schools of social work by students, faculty and staff. Students across disciplines are increasingly accessing electronic resources such as the Internet or on-line library resources for use in their class assignments (Halpern & Associates, 1994). There are many applications of such technology in the field of social work–including practice, advocacy, networking, communication, participation in policy formation, and teaching. However, a review of twelve exemplary human diversity course syllabi published by the Council of Social Work Education (Devore & Fletcher, 1997) has revealed that only one contains an Internet application. This paper will describe how the integration of information technology can be used in a social work course on human diversity, a foundation level course.

INTEGRATING INFORMATION TECHNOLOGY
IN A COURSE ON HUMAN DIVERSITY

This human diversity course provides students with knowledge and skills for social work practice with economically disadvantaged and oppressed people. Such people typically include ethnic minorities of color, women, people with disabilities, gay and lesbian people, and poor people. The critical concepts focused on in this course include ethnicity, culture, race, gender, social class, prejudice, stratification, power, inequality, discrimination, racism, homophobia, sexism, anti-Semitism, and oppression. Students explore the adaptive capabilities and strengths of disadvantaged and oppressed people and learn how such strengths can be used effectively in social work practice. Finally, students are expected to conduct self-evaluation by exploring how their own personal values, beliefs, and behaviors may limit their ability to conduct effective social work with people of diverse backgrounds. Students who complete this course have a better understanding not only of themselves but also of the diverse groups they will work with in practice.

Rather than taking a pedagogical approach, this human diversity course has relied on a more experiential learning format. Thus, the introduction of information technology into the course was a natural extension of the style of course already in place. This paper suggests two assignments which provide creative ways of administering and delivering social work education in human diversity. Readers may find more information about these assignments and other aspects of the human diversity course in Devore and Fletcher (1997).

Weekly journals. The first assignment is a weekly journal which reports on students' explorations of the critical concepts for the week using a variety of sources. Students are required to 'surf the Internet' on the weekly concepts of interest. They are able to choose one or more of the weekly concepts and initiate an Internet search. They are asked to describe the information they find on the Internet and discuss how it relates to the weekly topic. In the past, journal entries included students' reactions to class readings, class discussions, exercises, video presentations, guest lectures, situations in field practicum, encounters in personal life, or professional concerns. The assignment still includes the use of these experiences but now also includes the use of material found on the Internet.

Students are instructed to *focus* on topics that interest or excite them, *criticize* positions that they do not agree with, and *present* alternatives to positions discussed in class or found on the Internet. They repeat course content only insofar as it is relevant to their thoughts and feelings. Students are encouraged to think of ways in which the readings, discussions, and Internet findings illuminate an issue. Finally, they are asked to consider and discuss practice implications in each entry.

The main goals of the weekly journals include self-reflection and exploration. Therefore, students must understand that there is no 'right way' to conduct these weekly journals. The journals allow the students to reflect upon their experience in terms of learning about themselves and from others. The instructor must make the expectations for the weekly journal assignments clear as these assignments tend to be more informal in style but should not be weak in content. When grading the weekly journals, the instructor must be sure to give adequate feedback, write questions that require students to consider their feelings, or to challenge certain assumptions about a concept, theory, or a group.

Internet assignment. The second assignment, the Internet assignment, was created specifically to take advantage of information technology capabilities and took the place of a mid-term exam. For this assignment, each student is required to find a web site relevant to human diversity, particularly one that is dedicated to improving issues related to diversity. Students are asked to locate a web site and conduct a thorough investigation of the resources available to them at that site. They are encouraged to read online publications, email individual contacts, post questions on the available newsgroups, and to investigate other links to their web site. In a written assignment the students describe the role the agency web site has in improving issues related to human diversity (i.e., improving ethnic relations, combating racism, or increasing the awareness of certain groups through advocacy, information, or direct services). They then comment on the electronic resources available to them via their web site and critique their usefulness. Finally, they comment on the relevance of electronic resources for improving issues of human diversity and carefully consider the advantages and disadvantages of the use of electronic resources in the field of social work.

The main goal of the Internet assignment is for the student to think about how the Internet can be best used on several levels. On the micro level, students must learn how to obtain information through email contacts, newsgroups, or Internet searches. They must also consider how electronic resources might be used to serve individual clients. On the macro level, students consider the potential for electronic resources to be used for advocacy, collaboration, community empowerment, communication, and social change. Students explore the potential of electronic resources as social work tools and discuss optimum ways of using these tools. The potential uses of information technology are vast and this assignment serves the purpose of introducing students to those possibilities.

In addition, the students are instructed to turn in a copy of the web site they investigated for the assignment to the instructor. At the end of the semester the students' web sites are compiled and distributed to the class. This collection of web sites is a kind of human diversity Internet guide and students may be interested in some of their classmates' findings. Another option is to publish the web sites found by students on a WWW document. For example, one of the authors has published the web sites from previous courses and encourages each new class to use the web page for their own searches. This compilation also keeps the instructor informed of interesting web sites related to human diversity.

FINDINGS FROM DATA

Sixty students from four classes involving three instructors completed an evaluation of the Internet assignment (see Appendix). Students agreed overwhelmingly that the Internet assignment allowed them to access multicultural information, exposed them to different views and values, and provided more current information. They also agreed that they had the necessary computer skills to complete the assignment. Students were relatively more likely to agree than disagree that the Internet assignment helped them to hone computer skills, helped them to gain a global, cross-cultural perspective on diversity, and enhanced knowledge about diversity (see Table 1).

Unfortunately, students did not provide us with qualitative information regarding why they responded the way they did. Thus, we have to speculate the reasons students responded less favorably to certain questions. For example, a small percentage of students did not indicate that the Internet assignments improved their computer skills. Possibly, some students entered the course with a lower level of computer-related skills and therefore they were less adept at navigating the Internet. These students may have been more frustrated by the assignment, may not have participated in the computer classes offered by our school at the beginning of the semester, or may not have taken advantage of meetings with the instructors. On the other hand, some students may have entered the course with adequate to excellent computer skills and therefore did not feel that the assignments necessarily added to their existing computer skills.

Further, the authors speculate that the fact that some students did not feel that the Internet assignments allowed for international comparisons is likely due to the limitations of the course rather than the assignments. Currently, the course focuses predominately on domestic diversity issues and less on international issues. This limitation has been recognized, however, and is in the process of being remedied.

Nonetheless, results support course objectives, particularly the one noting that students completing this course will have a better understanding not only of themselves but also of the diverse groups they will work with in practice.

TABLE 1. Percentage Distribution of Students' Responses

Evaluation Questions	Strongly Disagree	Disagree	No Opinion	Agree	Strongly Agree
Access to info re: cultures	0.0	3.3	3.3	51.7	41.7
Exposure to different views	0.0	5.0	5.0	53.3	56.7
Provide current info	1.7	3.3	8.3	31.7	55.1
Sharpen computer skills	1.7	13.3	13.3	31.7	40.0
Access global perspectives	0.0	13.3	20.0	38.3	28.3
Enhance knowledge	0.0	10.0	8.3	63.3	18.3
Had computer skills	0.0	5.0	3.3	38.3	53.3
Given assistance	1.7	6.8	20.3	20.3	50.8*

N = 60   *N = 59

DISCUSSION

There are many advantages to including information technology in a course on human diversity as well as in any social work course. The following discusses the potential advantages and disadvantages.

Students have access to international/global perspectives thus allowing them to make cross-cultural comparisons. The Internet is a global twenty-four hour source of information. Often courses on human diversity are limited to discussion of diversity issues in the United States. However, the Internet can expand students' use of course materials as well as go beyond them. Through the Internet, students are able to access information regarding diversity issues worldwide. For example, ERCOMER–the European Research Centre on Migration and Ethnic Relations (http:///www.ercomer.org/)–is a university-based research institute which studies ethnic relations worldwide. From their web page, students can access newsletters, find information on newsgroups, receive online publications, receive information regarding conferences, or obtain statistics. In addition, there is a link to Race and Ethnic Relations: Conflict Resolution and the Internet, where there is an opportunity for world-wide discussion and analysis of racial and ethnic conflict. The global aspect of the Internet allows students to make cross-cultural comparisons. For example, students might compare immigration policy in Germany and the United States, or observe how different countries treat gays and lesbians. By making such comparative analyses students may envision new solutions or ideas for intervention. In some cases, students may collaborate directly with agencies using email or newsgroups.

In addition, many universities in the U.S. have various centers or organizations related to diversity and these organizations have gone on-line. Therefore, students can access information about diversity issues on other college campuses, networking and collaborating for ideas and solutions to pressing ethnic and racial issues.

Students are able to 'participate in the process' directly–involving themselves with policy formation by connecting with agencies, policy makers and local, state, and federal government officials. Many agencies and law makers involved in policy-making have web sites students can access–ask questions, sign petitions, register opinions, or write letters. Many provide policy highlights, proposals, and direct links to legislators. While obviously useful for a policy course, human diversity students can tailor their use towards policy directly related to diversity issues such as gays and lesbians in the military, sexual harassment, or affirmative action. Such work pushes human diversity beyond the micro level and gives students an opportunity to search for solutions to problems such as racism or discrimination on a more macro level. Such an exercise can be extremely satisfying to students who struggle with these issues predominately at the micro level–thus broadening their perspectives. In addition, students are able to directly involve themselves through email, petitions, or newsgroups. This may be a welcome change for students frustrated with searching for solutions on the micro level.

An excellent example of how students can use the Internet for advocacy on behalf of policy is the web site of the Feminist Majority Foundation (http://www.feminist.org/). On this site, one of the options for students is to click on a box entitled "Take Action." Located at this site is information that tells students how they may become involved with women's issues. The information is well organized and allows the students to respond directly. For example, the "Take Action" site lists over twenty actions which a student could perform. Thus, a student could click on any of these actions and become involved. For example, if the student chose the action "Urge the Department of Health and Human Services to Allow Poor Women to Escape Domestic Violence" they would find a summary and explanation of the action, a description of which states have already adopted the Family Violence Provision, a pre-written letter to Secretary Shalala, and a direct fax link to Secretary Shalala. Another action, "Urge Congress to Cut the Military Budget and Provide More Money for Domestic Programs," provides direct email and fax links to members of Congress. Students can even choose which members of Congress to contact and whether to use email or facsimile.

Students can access current information and data. The Internet can expedite the access to information. Many web pages are updated daily or weekly. Students can obtain data such as current news, statistics, legislation, and figures and tables. For example, students may access the U.S. Census Bureau where they can find recent statistical data as well as frequently requested tables, state rankings, and state or county profiles (http://census.gov/).

Newsgroups on the Internet serve as a kind of a bulletin board where students can keep in touch with local, state or federal issues and post notes requesting information on a specific topic. There are numerous newsgroups on a variety of topics available for students to access. On-line journals are also available to students. For instance, a student interested in environmental racism might access the on-line journal *Race, Poverty and Environment*, a journal dedicated to social and environmental justice (gopher://gopher.igc. apc.org:70/0./orgs/urbanhab/.RPE/Subscribe). Of course, not all information on the Internet is accurate, and students must be cautioned to manage all information carefully, questioning its validity and bias–just as they would in printed sources.

Students will be exposed to different viewpoints and information from a variety of groups and individuals and will be able to interact with them–thus expanding their horizons on topics that either complement course materials or go beyond them. On an individual level, students who spend time surfing human diversity topics will inevitably expose themselves to a variety of viewpoints and information. They may or may not agree with what they find, it may reinforce what they feel, or it could change what they believe. In essence, it has the potential to shake up students by challenging their assumptions. In addition, because anonymity does not exist in the classroom, some students may avoid exploring certain issues in class. Yet the Internet provides the user with some protection of identity and thus may encourage some students to converse with individuals on the Internet.

Students can learn and sharpen their computer skills while focusing on topics related to human diversity. Requiring students in any course to use computers is not a bad idea. Social workers must not ignore the advances in information technology but instead must embrace it and then continually search for ways in which technology can further the ideals of social work. Students cannot accomplish this task without the requisite skills. Instructors can offer sessions to students where some basic computer skills are taught, have a teaching assistant run some optional labs, or require that students attend seminars at schools where these are available. Finally, because human diversity is a foundation course, typically taken by students in the first semester, students gain computer skills early in their career. In the authors' experience, students not familiar with the Internet are amazed at the resources available to them after they have been introduced to its capabilities. Many of the students commented that the assignments got them to use the Internet and that they were glad that they did.

DISADVANTAGES

Information can be inaccurate because a mechanism that would evaluate accuracy in Internet sources does not exist. Furchgott (1997) raises questions about First Amendment rights and their application to the Internet and stresses the importance of considering the accuracy of Internet information before disseminating it to other users. A critical issue for students to consider is the medium they use for distributing criticisms about another person's products as ideas or viewpoints. Extrapolating from Furchgott's (1997) article in the *New York Times*, students may wish to post their criticisms in Usenet groups rather than build a Web site specifically to criticize. Further, Miller (1997) warns that many books and journals on-line are actually excerpts. This may be especially important for students who cannot for whatever reason validate the accuracy of information. Teachers of human diversity must teach students to cross-validate Internet facts and information with written sources, whenever these are available.

Citing sources from Internet is unclear because agreement on how to cite electronic sources is still evolving. A standard for the citation of electronic materials is not yet available. The American Psychological Association Manual of

Style, the 'gold standard' for documenting citations in most social work articles, has proposed some preliminary standards for referencing online documents (http://www.psycho.uni-osnabrueck.de/www.pages/APAWEB.HTML). The APA discusses potential authorship issues that frequently occur when online materials are used. Another good reference for citing electronic resources can be found in Li and Crane (1996).

Students can have a difficult time navigating through the amount of information available on the Internet. Miller (1997) notes that "it is not uncommon for a user to have 10,000 hits in response to a query on the Internet" (p. A44). Thus, students need instructions on how to properly use search engines to locate information. This can occur several ways through instructors, librarians, or teaching assistants. Furthermore, the authors have also found that the use of keywords on a course syllabus will help students hone their Internet searches.

On-line tutorials are available to students. The Marger (1996) textbook used in the human diversity course described in this paper designates a web page for students to access. This web site (http://www.thomson.com/rcenters/sociology/lessons/html), provides students with a glossary of technological terms and an online tutorial that explains how to 'surf' and access newsgroups and information. It also provides students with links to information on a variety of topics. Another example is Karger and Stoesz's (1998) supplement to their American Social Welfare Policy test. This guide offers information that provides students with a guide to the Internet as well as offers several useful web sites of interest to social work.

Not only can the information obtained from Internet search be voluminous, it can also be inflammatory. Various hate groups and some individuals may be very offensive to students. The flip-side of this offensiveness is that students may learn from it by opening themselves to discuss inflammatory issues with others on and off the Internet. This kind of experience fits well the goals of the human diversity course.

Such assignments may be difficult in schools without adequate resources–computers or support. Small schools, particularly those with low budgets, may simply lack the technological sophistication and consequently the ability to access Internet resources. Agencies, particularly small ones, may not afford the luxury of a telephone to accommodate a modem for Internet resources due to budget constraints. To overcome resource inadequacy, schools with adequate resources may offer workshops and continuing education courses to teach students from other schools as well as agency staff lacking Internet resources.

Using the Internet lacks direct interaction with a person. When using electronic resources instead of face-to-face interaction, the interaction is with a machine–the computer. However, as discussed previously, the computer can provide anonymity to students hesitant to discuss or inquire about sensitive issues. Obviously, social workers must have excellent communication skills and the authors do not recommend that computers take the place of contact with people. Diversity is a complex issue–it requires that people have interactions and contact with people unlike themselves. Experiencing diversity through the use of computers is only a fragment of the total diversity experience.

Social workers must consider how to make technology social work friendly, which inadvertently means making technology people friendly. The use of video phones, for example, could be a way in which computer use could become more personable.

CONCLUSIONS AND RECOMMENDATIONS

In conclusion, this paper has discussed two assignments that take advantage of information technology, for potential use in social work education. The advantages and disadvantages of such application have been discussed. The authors caution that Internet information should not replace printed materials. As Miller (1997) comments, "it is far better to adopt a realistic perspective: All information is not yet electronic and probably will never be" (p. A44). Certainly, information technology alone cannot meet the goals and objectives of a course on human diversity.

Information technology can be used, however, to enhance the materials presented to students in the human diversity course. Students gain access to a variety of viewpoints, current information, and information that is global. Students are also able to contact individuals or agencies directly through email or newsgroups. The authors hope that this paper serves as a launching pad for integrating information technology into social work education, particularly in the human diversity course. Further, the authors hope that the ideas brought forth in this paper will be expanded on in the future by other social work educators struggling with the issue of integrating the new technologies into the classroom. In order to get started, the authors recommend the following:

- Incorporate at least one small assignment that involves the use of information technology.
- Provide students with the necessary computer skills (including how to use email or how to subscribe to newsgroups or mailing lists).
- Teach students how to properly use the available search engines and how to sharpen their searches.
- Teach students how to ensure the accuracy of their Internet sources and to cross-validate all information used in their papers.

- Ensure that students understand that the Internet often provides the user with one side of a story or parts of a story–they must attempt to find 'whole pictures' by seeking out original sources or cross-validating with printed sources.
- Always have students consider the role of social work and technology as well as the pros and cons of the application of technology in social work practice.

It is imperative that social work students obtain the necessary computer skills as well as have the access to the electronic resources available to them. As the use of information technology increases, social workers must also carefully consider the applications of such technology, especially its impact on individual clients. How information is controlled and to whom information is made available is a critical issue. Ensuring that all clients and communities have access to computers is also important. As Butterfield (1986) remarks, "It remains the responsibility of social workers to become informed about computer technology, confront the moral and ethical issues it raises for us and our clients, and take a strong hand in directing its inevitable application to social work" (p. 3). It is time for educators to consider the many uses of information technology to enhance the learning experiences of social work students.

REFERENCES

Beckett, J. & Johnson, H. (1995). Human Development. In *Encyclopedia of Social Work 19th Ed.* Washington, D.C.: NASW Press.

Butterfield, W.H. (1986). Computers changing social work practice. *NASW NEWS, 3* (10), 3.

Devore, W. & Fletcher, B. (1997). *Human diversity content in social work education.* Alexandria, VA: Council on Social Work Education.

The Feminist Majority Foundation Online (n.d. 1997). [WWW document]. URL http://www.feminist.org/

Furchgott, R. (1997, June 8). Surfing for satisfaction: Consumer complaints go on line. *New York Times*, p. 8F.

Halpern, D. & Associates. (1994). *Changing college classroom: New teaching and learning strategies for an increasingly complex world.* San Francisco: Jossey-Bass.

Karger, H. & Stoesz, D. (1998). *The internet and social welfare policy.* NY: Longman Publisher USA.

Li, X. & Crane, N.B. (1996). *Electronic styles: A handbook for citing electronic information* (Revised edition). Medford, NJ: Information Today.

Miller, W. (1997, August 1). Troubling myths about on-line information. *The Chronicle of Higher Education*, p. A44.

Patterson, D. & Maple, F. (1996). An electronic social work knowledge base: A strategy for global information sharing. *International Social Work, 39*, 149-161.

Race, Poverty & Environment (n.d. 1997). [WWW document]. URL gopher://gopher. igc.apc.org:70/0./orgs/urbanhab/.RPE/Subscribe

U.S. Census Bureau (1997, March 4). [WWW document]. URL http://www.census. gov/stat_abstract/

Wadsworth Publishing Company (1997, March 10). Wadsworth Sociology Resource Center–Surfing Lessons [WWW document]. URL http://www.thomson,com/rcenters/ sociology/lessons.html

Web Extensions to American Psychological Association Style (WEAPAS) (Rev. 1.4) (1996, November 25). [WWW document] URL http://www.psycho.uni-osnabrueck. de/www.pages/APAWEB.HTML

APPENDIX

Evaluation of the Internet Assignments

1. Use of the Internet provided me with access to information about different cultures.

1	2	3	4	5
Strongly Disagree	Disagree	No Opinion	Agree	Strongly Agree

2. Use of the Internet exposed me to individuals/groups with different views.

1	2	3	4	5
Strongly Disagree	Disagree	No Opinion	Agree	Strongly Agree

3. Use of the Internet provided me with more current information (for example: policy legislation).

1	2	3	4	5
Strongly Disagree	Disagree	No Opinion	Agree	Strongly Agree

4. Use of the Internet provided me with the opportunity to sharpen my computer skills.

1	2	3	4	5
Strongly Disagree	Disagree	No Opinion	Agree	Strongly Agree

5. Use of the Internet allowed me to gain access to international/global perspectives and make cross-cultural comparisons on diversity.

1	2	3	4	5
Strongly Disagree	Disagree	No Opinion	Agree	Strongly Agree

6. Use of the Internet enhanced my knowledge in this class.

1	2	3	4	5
Strongly Disagree	Disagree	No Opinion	Agree	Strongly Agree

7. I feel I had the necessary computer skills to complete the Internet assignments for this class.

1	2	3	4	5
Strongly Disagree	Disagree	No Opinion	Agree	Strongly Agree

8. I feel I was given adequate assistance to complete the Internet assignments for this class.

1	2	3	4	5
Strongly Disagree	Disagree	No Opinion	Agree	Strongly Agree

Your comments about additional ways to improve this class and expand or revise the Internet assignments will provide us useful knowledge for future classes. (Please use the back of this sheet if needed.)

SECTION 2:

TEACHING TO USE

Macro Practice and Policy in Cyberspace: Teaching with Computer Simulation and the Internet at the Baccalaureate Level

Colleen Galambos
Charles Edward Neal

SUMMARY. The integration of computer training within social work education is necessary for social workers to keep abreast of technological changes occurring within human service agencies. This article presents several techniques to integrate computer simulations and Internet research within the baccalaureate curriculum. Emphasis is placed on the use of these techniques to teach policy and macro practice. *[Article copies available for a fee from The Haworth Document Delivery Service: 1-800-342-9678. E-mail address: getinfo@haworthpressinc.com]*

KEYWORDS. Internet, computer simulations, macro practice, policy, computer skills, interactive learning

INTRODUCTION

The use of computers in social work practice has increased as the human services attempt to keep pace with an ever-growing technological world

Colleen Galambos, DSW, ACSW, LCSW-C, is Chairperson, Department of Social Work and Charles Edward Neal, PhD, is Professor, Department of Political Science, Western Maryland College.

Address correspondence to: Dr. Colleen Galambos, Western Maryland College, 2 College Hill, Westminster, MD 21157. E-mail: galambos@wmdc.edu

[Haworth co-indexing entry note]: "Macro Practice and Policy in Cyberspace: Teaching with Computer Simulation and the Internet at the Baccalaureate Level." Galambos, Colleen, and Charles Edward Neal. Co-published simultaneously in *Computers in Human Services* (The Haworth Press, Inc.) Vol. 15, No. 2/3, 1998, pp. 111-120; and: *Information Technologies: Teaching to Use–Using to Teach* (ed: Frank B. Raymond III, Leon Ginsberg, and Debra Gohagan) The Haworth Press, Inc., 1998, pp. 111-120. Single or multiple copies of this article are available for a fee from The Haworth Document Delivery Service [1-800-342-9678, 9:00 a.m. - 5:00 p.m. (EST). E-mail address: getinfo@haworthpressinc.com]

(Butterfield, 1986, Miller, 1986, Nurius, Hooyman, & Nicoll, 1988, Nurius & Hudson, 1988). In response to this increase in the use of computers in the delivery of social services, social workers need to learn how to use computers to enhance their practice and to meet organizational goals. Recognizing the necessity for education in this area, the Council on Social Work Education has identified computer training as an essential inclusion in the millennium project. Several authors in the past have recommended the integration of computer training within social work education (Cnaan, 1989, Patterson & Yaffe, 1994, Reinoehl & Shapiro, 1986, Seabury & Maple, 1993, Woodarski, Bricout, & Smokowski, 1996). However, the application of information technology and skill development in this area tends to focus on the micro practice arena (Reinoehl & Shapiro, 1986, Seabury & Maple, 1993, Woodarski, Bricout, & Smokowski, 1996). Only recently has the literature identified the importance of computer training and usage in policy and macro practice (Bynum, 1991, Chaiklin, 1991, Cordero, 1991, Patterson & Yaffe, 1994).

This article discusses how computer simulations and internet linkages may be used in baccalaureate programs to teach students policy and macro skills while simultaneously increasing their ability to work with computer technology. The use of two online political simulation games and the use of the Internet to access information will be highlighted.

COMPUTER SIMULATIONS AND INTERACTIVE LEARNING

The experiential use of computers within the classroom is based on the androgogical theory of adult education. Androgogical theory refers to methods and processes for educating adult learners and emphasizes learner control. This theory views the student as a self-directed and independent individual who will respond to the environment. The student's life experience is acknowledged, emphasized, and used. It is expected that the student comes ready to learn, and is motivated by immediate application of skills and knowledge. Using this model, the educational emphasis of course work is on presentation of problems and activities centered around the resolution of these problems (Knowles, 1980). Androgogical theory emphasizes interactive, participatory learning (Knowles, 1980).

The use of interactive, participatory exercises and projects in the classroom has been documented to be an effective teaching tool within schools and programs of social work (O'Neal, 1996, Powell & Causby, 1994, Sherraden, 1993, Slaught, 1991). The employment of an interactive approach, particularly in the areas of macro practice and policy, enhances student learning of community practice, advocacy skills, planning, and policy change (Powell & Causby, 1994, Sherraden, 1993, Slaught, 1991).

Using simulations to teach macro practice has been successfully applied to the classroom setting in MSW programs (Lowe, 1996). In simulation exercises, students are exposed to real-life problems and situations often encountered in the practice environment. Additionally, simulations allow students to work on specific tasks in small groups. The simulation format has been well received by both faculty and students (Lowe, 1996).

Simulation experiences in macro practice and policy can also be replicated using computer technology and software. O'Neal (1996) recognizes the value of computer simulations as an excellent learning opportunity for blending theory and practice in the classroom, and a method to increase classroom participation. Computer simulations fulfill a two-fold purpose. The first purpose is to provide an educational opportunity for students to gain "hands-on" experience in working with macro practice and policy issues. The second purpose is to increase student's comfort level, skill, and experience in working with computer technology. Students are able to integrate practice and technology in a structured learning environment.

COMPUTER SIMULATIONS
AND THE TEACHING OF COMPUTER TECHNOLOGY

In discussing the teaching of computer technology as it relates to the mission of social work education, Cnaan (1989) recommends that social work education focus on training students in information technology applications, rather than programming. Another recommendation is that graduates obtain broad-based knowledge that can be built upon to meet employer requirements. Using a combination of computer simulations and Internet linkages exposes students to the basics of on-line research, programming, and dialogue. These skills may be easily transferred to a variety of practice settings and issue areas.

Cnaan (1989) also recommends the incorporation of information technology into core courses, rather than developing separate technical courses. The use of computer simulations and Internet technology are two methods that can be easily integrated into existing courses for several reasons. First, computer simulation exercises can be adapted to meet time constraints of individual courses. Some exercises can be completed within one to two classroom periods, others can be more extensive. Both simulation exercises and use of the internet may be conducted out of the classroom environment, and can be designed as independent solo assignments. In addition, the use of on-line resources may be connected to preexisting assignments that require collecting information from a variety of sources. Finally, these techniques are time limited, and can be designed to fit into pre-existing course requirements.

The use of computer simulations and Internet technology also enhances critical thinking. In simulation exercises, students are exposed to life-like situations and they are asked to make choices based on presented information. On-line simulation experiences expose students to a variety of viewpoints, opinions, and information, which must be processed before drawing conclusions on the presented issues. Students are challenged to follow logical steps to obtain results.

USING SIMULATIONS

A simulation is a replication of the real-life policy making and macro environment in which participants interact with each other using computer technology as the medium. Software for this purpose is available on CD-ROM, disks, or downloadable from the Internet.

One example of an on-line simulation is Executive Decision (The Atlantic Monthly, 1997) in which the participant assumes the role of the President of the United States. In this simulation, the President's Chief of Staff and selected advisors present a policy dilemma. These dilemmas are fictitious, but may be based on issues that President Clinton has had to face, or may be based on choices a president may need to make in the future.

The participant must choose between two or more policy options. The primary consideration for choosing an option should be based on public good or which alternative is best for the country. Policy choices are explained to the participant in a short memo written by a policy advisor who strongly advocates for that course of action.

Each scenario is posted for two weeks, after which the final results are announced with a breakdown of how many people chose each option. Decisions are recorded by the completion of a formatted memo which is sent to a central location to be tallied. Participants also have the opportunity to discuss the decision with other participants in an interactive forum called The Body Politic (The Atlantic Monthly, 1997). Welfare reform and the financing of public education are two examples of former Executive Decision scenarios.

Equipment needed to use this simulation is a computer equipped with Windows 95 and Netscape 2.0 or comparable browser. This exercise can be incorporated into the classroom instruction period, using computer labs, or students may participate in the simulation outside of the classroom. The authors have conducted the simulation in a computer lab environment and received positive feedback from students on the exercise.

Concepts and skills learned using this simulation include the development of a greater sensitivity to the many variables and political considerations encountered in the policy-making process. Students begin to appreciate the conflict between policy planning and the politics of implementation. Additionally, students acquire experience in the development of policy positions on an issue and articulation of their opinion using computer technology as their communication medium. This technology provides the opportunity for immediate feedback from other participants. Students enjoy the interaction within the simulation, the ability to communicate with participants from a variety of geographical areas and diverse backgrounds, and receiving timely responses from concerned observers.

The major disadvantage of this resource is that one is dependent upon the availability of the connection. The ability to access this program is restricted to those people who have pre-registered. Furthermore, the simulation is run on a limited basis which may or may not coincide with course time frames. Students have expressed disappointment when the simulation is not in operation. Ideally, continuous access to this simulation would enhance its utility as a learning resource. In the absence of access to this simulation during a given semester, the instructor may encourage a visit to this site independent from the parameters of the course.

The second simulation, Reinventing America (Crossover Technologies & The John and Mary Markle Foundation, 1995, 1996), is a simulation game where the participants plot the course of America though voting on fictitious issues of national importance. The main action is to submit a Congressional ballot. Participants also have access to the in-game newspaper News of the Nation, a JAVA version of the Federal Budget spreadsheet, and background information on the issues before Congress. Participants have the opportunity to join debate groups and chat rooms. The simulation offered special guest chats which were pre-announced. Participants could leave questions for the special guests on Bulletin Boards. Reinventing America was in effect from January 1, 1996–January 1, 1997. While the simulation is currently not in operation, debate groups can still be accessed.

Equipment needed to participate in the simulation include a computer equipped with Windows 95 and a web browser with a news server, such as Netscape 2.0. This exercise may be initiated in the classroom. However, due to the extensive on-going nature of the simulation, using out-of-class time to participate in the simulation should also be the expectation.

Students find the opportunity to interact with well-known politicians and policy makers, within chat rooms and debate groups, interesting and insightful. This medium is particularly helpful to use in rural areas, where students have limited opportunity and access to outside resources. One identified problem the authors have found with this simulation is that students often will use information obtained in chat rooms and debate groups as formal policy, rather than recognizing it as no more than the respondent's personal opinion on the topic. Prior to the use of this exercise, students should be instructed on the type of information that will be obtained and how they can apply it to their knowledge of the policy making process.

Learning Objectives

The use of simulation in the classroom environment serves to enhance the learning experience. To this end, the exercise contributes to the following overall course objectives: (a) to acquire knowledge of the political process and how it impacts on social policy; (b) to develop an appreciation and respect for diversity in race, gender, sexual orientation, and ethnic populations; (c) to develop an ability to obtain and organize social policy information; and (d) to develop an ability to evaluate options and consequences of social welfare policy.

In evaluating whether these objectives have been achieved, the instructors measure student interaction with the simulation, and their responses to questions posed in small group discussion. Students who have achieved these objectives will exhibit a higher level of interaction with both the simulation and within the classroom discussion. Additionally, students will apply this learning experience to other activities in and outside of the classroom.

Teaching Approach in Using Simulations

The instructor's approach to using computer simulation exercises in the classroom should incorporate a three step process. The first step is to brief students with respect to requirements of the simulation: how it works, its purpose, and use of technology. In essence, the instructor sets the stage for the interactions prompted by the simulation. An important goal of the briefing should be to cultivate an intellectual fair-mindedness in the student. That is, the ability to consider evidence and reasons for positions with which students agree and disagree.

The second stage is engagement in the simulation itself which is earmarked by the scenario and the roles assigned to the students. The goal is to assist students in problem solving within a diverse setting while using computer technology. The simulation may peak student interest in the use of the computer since students focus on the virtual environment, and become engaged in the exercise. Students interact with each other, adding another dimension to the group process.

The final and most important stage is debriefing which provides the instructor the forum to integrate various aspects of the exercise. Experience has demonstrated that equal time should be spent discussing and playing the simulation. A useful model for debriefing is to answer the questions "what," "so what," and "now what." Debriefing begins with feedback on what happened during the process. Then a discussion should ensue regarding the major issues that arose during the game and how they relate to real life situations. Finally, how one might apply gained insights to one's life is an important component of the debriefing discussion. In other words, debriefing is designed to stimulate critical thinking.

A caution offered in the use of simulation is that it should not be used as an end in itself. It is valuable as an effective and innovative way to help students discover the powerful resources of their minds. Simulation enables the integration of thinking, feeling, and acting that promotes student development of the professional self.

USING THE INTERNET

The Internet is defined as "a group of worldwide information resources (Hahn & Stout, 1994, p. 2). It provides file transfer, remote login, electronic mail, news, and other services (Krol, 1994). The Internet employs a network of networks as the medium that carries information.

The Internet contains a wide variety of research options. Students may retrieve full text government documents, access policy oriented search engines such as Brookings Institution, and the Civil Rights Commission, and obtain information about advocacy groups. Students may obtain information on social policy issues such as rape, capital punishment, gay rights, and domestic violence. Access to legal policy, and legislative documents can be obtained through the Internet Legal Resource Guide.

Students may be encouraged to conduct research related to policy and macro practice issues using Internet resources. Research may be obtained on specific proposed legislation at state and federal levels, public opinion on issues, Supreme Court decisions, etc. Internet research may be connected to a preexisting term paper assignment, or may be designed to be a separate assignment in itself. This activity may be done outside of the classroom, although it's the authors' experience that some classroom lab time, in which students may work with instructors and fellow students, increases the comfort level in accessing on-line resources. Equipment needed for this activity includes microcomputers equipped with Windows 95, and access to Internet servers and browsers.

The Internet and the Instructor's Role

In introducing students to resources available on the Internet, it is important to provide students with an environment which is conducive to interaction with instructors and other students, and provides immediate access to the computer. A computer laboratory which has multiple computers connected to the web provides this type of environment.

Caution should be applied when conducting research using on-line resources. The Internet is replete with information based on poor research design, misleading data, incomplete references, and non-credential sources. It is therefore important for instructors to brief students on the use of the Internet, and provide them with workable web site options. Initially, instructors should use an interactive teaching approach to the presentation of Internet research material. Immediate availability of instructors for reference is important since they act as Internet guides. Both the instructor and student work toward the goal of student independence in the use of the Internet. Eventually, students should be able to apply critical thinking to the evaluation of materials found on-line.

Practical Application

It is the authors' observation that each course is comprised of students who have a wide variety of experiences in using computer technology. To accommodate this diversity in experience, the authors found it beneficial to structure the exercise to provide varying levels of support. For instance, our experience has demonstrated that for a lab of 20 students, at least 3 resource persons should be available to assist students with the lab exercise. These resource people could be professors, librarians, staff from the information technology department, or students who have expertise in computer technology. In addition, printed materials designed to guide the student through the lab should be distributed at the beginning of the session. Students with higher computer skill levels will use these materials independently, while the novice will require more guidance and direction. Allowing students to proceed at their own pace reduces frustration and increases their willingness to participate in the lab.

The computer laboratory environment permits multiple interactions among participants. It enhances students' interactions with each other, with instructors, and with the computer. Students sharing similar interests will often pair up and search the web together. The student with novice skills will often ask the resource people for assistance. In this environment, assistance can be provided almost immediately.

In visiting legislative web sites, students expressed a high level of interest in researching their own state activities. Some students discovered, for the first time, information about their own elected officials such as policy positions, interest areas, and voting record. Some students became so involved in the issues that they signed on-line petitions, e-mailed their representatives, and joined special interest listservs.

One caveat offered, related to introducing students to the forum of the Internet, is that sometimes, in their enthusiasm to use Internet resources for research purposes, students will focus too heavily on use of the Internet, and too lightly on the use of traditional academic resources such as journals, manuscripts, monographs, and other scholarly references. In an effort to curtail this behavior, workshops are offered on the use of library reference materials. These workshops are conducted by library staff and introduce students to the wide variety of resources available to assist in research efforts. Students are required to attend these workshops, and they are integrated into course requirements.

CONCLUSIONS

A challenge faced by many schools and programs in social work is the integration of training in computer technology within the existing curricula. Research indicates that computers in social work education are used in separate introductory courses (Caputo & Cnaan, 1990). Information technology is also not traditionally a component of macro practice and policy courses (Caputo & Cnaan, 1990). This article presents two reasonable, inexpensive techniques to integrate information technology related to policy and macro practice within baccalaureate programs in social work. In using these proposed methods and other techniques, baccalaureate programs may better prepare students to meet the demands of a more technologically advanced professional arena.

REFERENCES

Butterfield, W. (1986). Computers changing social work practice. *NASW News* (November), 3.

Bynum, P. (1991). Marketing social service programs using political campaign technology. *Computers in Human Services, 8*, (1), 67-72.

Chaiklin, S. (1991). Using computers in community educational programs. *Computers in Human Services, 8*, (1), 9-18.

Cordero, A. (1991). Computers and community organizing: Issues and examples from New York City. *Computers in Human Services, 8*, (1), 89-103.

Caputo, R.K. & Cnaan, R.A. (1990). Information technology availability in schools of social work. *Journal of Social Work Education, 26*, (2), 187-198.

Cnaan, R. (1989). Social work education and direct practice in the computer age. *Journal of Social Work Education, 25*, (3), 235-243.

Hahn, H. & Stout, R. (1994). *The internet complete reference.* Berkeley, CA: Osborne McGraw-Hill.

Knowles, M.S. (1980). *The Modern Practice of Adult Education.* Chicago: Associated Press.

Krol, E. (1994). *The whole internet. User's guide and catalog.* Sebastopol, CA: O'Reilly & Associates, Inc.

Lowe, J.I. (1996). The simulation of a neighborhood family service center for teaching macro practice. *Journal of Teaching in Social Work, 13*, (1/2), 27-41.

Miller, H. (1986). The use of computers in social work practice: An assessment. *Journal of Social Work Education, 22,* (3), 52–59.

Nurius, P. & Cnaan, R. (1991). Classifying software to better support social work practice. *Social Work, 36,* (6), 536-541.

Nurius, P., Hooyman, N., & Nicoll, A. (1988). The changing face of computer utilization in social work settings. *Journal of Social Work Education, 24,* (2), 186-197.

Nurius, P. & Hudson, W. (1988). Computer based practice: Future dream or current technology? *Social Work, 33,* (4), 357-362.

O'Neal, G. (1996). Enhancing undergraduate student participation through active learning. *Journal of Teaching in Social Work, 13,* (1/2), 141-155.

Patterson, D. & Jaffe, J. (1994). Hypermedia computer-based education in social work education. *Journal of Social Work Education, 30,* (2), 267-277.

Powell, J.Y. & Causby, V.D. (1994). From the classroom to the capitol–from MSW students to advocates: Learning by doing. *Journal of Teaching in Social Work, 9* (1/2), 141-154.

Reinoehl, R. & Shapiro, C. (1986). Interactive videodiscs: A linkage tool for social work education. *Journal of Social Work Education, 22,* (3), 61-67.

Seabury, B. & Maple, F. (1993). Using computers to teach practice skills. *Social Work, 38,* (4), 430-439.

Sherraden, M. (1993). Community studies in the baccalaureate social work curriculum. *Journal of Teaching in Social Work, 7,* (1), 75-88.

Slaught, E.F. (1991). Focusing on domestic violence to teach community intervention strategies. *Arete, 16,* (2), 39-45.

Wodarski, J.S., Bricout, J.C., & Smokowski, P.R. (1996). Making interactive videodisc computer simulation accessible and practice relevant. *Journal of Teaching in Social Work, 13,* (1/2), 15–26.

Human Services
and the Information Economy

William H. Butterfield

SUMMARY. This article discusses the impact of the information economy on human services. The major topics discussed include: the changing nature of work, the impact of the cost of adoption of technology by the human services, the changing expectations the public has for agency use of technology, the move to electronic record keeping and data management, the need for developing a data integrity management process, and the impact of the Internet and intranets on software development. *[Article copies available for a fee from The Haworth Document Delivery Service: 1-800-342-9678. E-mail address: getinfo@haworthpressinc.com]*

KEYWORDS. Data integrity, data management, electronic record keeping, electronic funds, hotelling, information economy, Internet, intranet, smart card, telecommuting, telemedicine, work

INTRODUCTION

We are in a time of great change. Some believe we are moving into a profound restructuring of work in this country. They believe we are moving into the information economy. The basic premise driving the information economy is the belief that accurate and timely information will make it possible to produce the goods and services our country needs more efficient-

---

William H. Butterfield is Professor Emeritus, The George Warren Brown School of Social Work, Washington University in St. Louis.

[Haworth co-indexing entry note]: "Human Services and the Information Economy." Butterfield, William H. Co-published simultaneously in *Computers in Human Services* (The Haworth Press, Inc.) Vol. 15, No. 2/3, 1998, pp. 121-142; and: *Information Technologies: Teaching to Use-Using to Teach* (ed: Frank B. Raymond III, Leon Ginsberg, and Debra Gohagan) The Haworth Press, Inc., 1998, pp. 121-142. Single or multiple copies of this article are available for a fee from The Haworth Document Delivery Service [1-800-342-9678, 9:00 a.m. - 5:00 p.m. (EST). E-mail address: getinfo@haworthpressinc.com]

ly. Efficiency in this context is focused on the cost of production and the quality and quantity of goods purchased. This model is money driven. Information is not seen as an end but rather as a means to accomplish the end of the most efficient utilization of resources. McNutt (1995c, p. 2) says that the transformation to an information economy "will change the nature of work and may change the character of income and poverty." One should not assume, however, that we can fully predict what the changes will be, or for that matter, that these changes will all be bad. Nor does it mean that previously dominant economic models will disappear. We still have an agricultural economy, we still have an industrial economy, and we still have a service economy. What will happen is that the portion of a nation's gross national product that is derived from each of these other sectors will shift. These older sectors will adopt the information economy's tools to their own means and will, in that sense, become a part of the new economy. But they will take a secondary place to the production and utilization of information.

IMPACT OF THE INFORMATION ECONOMY ON HUMAN SERVICES

Knowledgeable people have made many predictions about the direction of the information economy. I will draw on these sources as I discuss the impact of the information economy on the human services. Although some of my colleagues, in their papers, focus on the longer-term impacts of technology, my focus will be on the impact of the information age during the next few years. I have chosen to do this in the hope that my projections will alert agency executives, and others, to some of the issues they should consider as they move toward adopting information technology in their organizations. So, with a short-term orientation in mind, I will discuss several trends that I believe will significantly impact on the delivery of human services. These include:

1. The changing nature of work.
2. The impact of the cost of adoption of technology by the human services.
3. The changing expectations the public has for agency use of technology.
4. The move to electronic record keeping and data management.
5. The problem of too much data.
6. The impact of the Internet and intranets.

THE CHANGING NATURE OF WORK

Changes in the workplace are occurring as a result of globalization of commerce which is leading to companies having to produce goods and services at prices that are competitive in world markets. The following quotes highlight some of the changes that are occurring:

> In the next five years, 4 out of 5 people living in industrial nations will be doing jobs differently from the way they have done them in the last 50 years. By 2000, 3 out of 4 employees will have to be trained for new jobs or taught fresh skills for their old ones. The number of women in the workforce will increase. It is estimated that 80 percent of women of child bearing age will be in the workforce. . . . People will no longer be able to complete an education, because they will have to continue to gain new knowledge and new skills to be competitive . . . By 2000, about 35 percent of the workforce will be made up of employees dialing in from remote locations." (Source unknown, 1996)

For more recent labor statistics see: URL *http://stats.bls.gov:80/emphome.htm*. Another author, from Australia, expresses concerns similar to those expressed in this country:

> The evolution to an information society is likely to involve social, economic, and political challenges far more daunting than those experienced during this century (Drucker 1994, p. 80). Some of these challenges will include: a changing employment regime (Australian Science and Technology Council 1995, pp. 5-6) which will demand greater flexibility and substitute part-time work, self employment, contract employment, and unemployment for the permanent and full-time positions enjoyed by many in the current generation; reduced involvement by government in the public sector delivery of social welfare services (Lawrence and Killon 1944, p. 18); an increasingly competitive society for all as information and knowledge becomes universally available through new technologies (Drucker 1994, p. 68); and clearly defined groups of 'information rich' and 'information poor' as market forces replace public service as the prime determinant and means for the delivery of cultural and other services. (Barlow, March, 1997, p. 4)

These changes in the workplace will have profound implications for the human services. In the next section we will briefly explore some of these implications.

IMPLICATIONS FOR THE HUMAN SERVICES

John McNutt (1995c, p. 4) writes, "The nature of information work could lead to many workers being employees on a piecework or consulting basis. Some futurists (Bridges, 1994) argue that jobs, as we know them are only relevant to an industrial economy and will be eliminated by the raise of the information sector. People will obtain work (but not permanent jobs) . . . [but] there will be no lasting relationship between people and employer." This fact coupled with the efforts to replace labor with computers will exert tremendous pressures on the social welfare system. There will be fewer jobs, and those jobs that do exist will be time limited. The rapid turnover in jobs will accelerate economic and social dislocation of ,families and bring with it increased need for social services.

Similarly, the movement of large numbers of mothers, with children at home, into the workforce, will increase the types of services needed by families and substantially reduce the availability of volunteers for human service organizations.

As human service organizations adopt technology, they will need employees with increased technical skills and knowledge. These skills and knowledge will be major factors in the types of employees that agencies will hire. Agencies will also have to develop training programs to ensure that the organization's employees will be able to perform the tasks required by the technology being utilized.

I expect there will be rapid increases in the number of workers who will work away from their agencies and communicate with their agencies via computer. These methods of working, called telecommuting and hotelling, are becoming more common. In fact, a study from Telecommute America, an organization formed to promote telecommuting, indicates that sixty-two percent of the 500 companies they surveyed have more employees working at home than they did two years ago.

Telecommuting commonly refers to people working at home and using computers to do the work assigned by their employers. Substantial amounts of the work that takes place in human service settings could just as easily be done in this fashion. Employers like telecommuting because they don't have to provide office space for the employees. Employees like it because it gives them freedom to schedule work hours, to spend more time with the family and to reduce commuting time and costs and the cost of business clothing. See *www.telecommute.org/links.html* for more information. A related means of working is hotelling. Hotelling is a newer phenomenon where workers are furnished with what amounts to a portable office. They have a laptop computer and printer, a cell phone, a fax and sometimes a company vehicle. They do most of their business out of their car or in customer's offices. When they need to meet with clients in a more formal setting, they call their home office and arrange for an office or conference room for the day. It's called hotelling because it is much like renting space in a hotel. Hotelling seems to be custom made for human service workers who are expected to visit their clients in the clients' home or who are expected to visit clients at locations away from the office. One can imagine such a worker dialing the agency in the morning to pick up e-mail and to automatically update the client records stored on his/her laptop computer. The worker would spend a substantial portion of the day visiting clients and entering case notes into the laptop computer. Late in the afternoon the worker would fill out required reports that were stored on the computer using data from client files. Those reports, along with raw data from client files, would then be transmitted to the agency where data would be stored in client and administrative files and processed by statistical programs to produce the reports needed to supervise the worker and to provide the data needed by the agency's funding sources and oversight committees. Telecommuting and hotelling will increase the number of workers who work at home rather than in an office. But just as the telephone did not eliminate the need for travel to the office, neither will telecommuting or hotelling (Mokhtarian, 1977). Telecommuting and hotelling will radically alter workers' relationships with their employers and fellow employees. Supervision and a variety of other management practices will have to change. Telecommuting and hotelling also change the nature of social interactions in the workplace. We already are seeing the development of organizations that offer specialized services for telecommuters, such as special training and local office services. For an example, see the URL: *http://www.nccn.net/~lolson/*. One can expect that a large body of literature will grow out of the social and policy implications of this type of work.

A related use of technology, telemedicine, is emerging, and similar methods will likely be adopted by other human service organizations. Telemedicine, as it is now practiced, is just the opposite of telecommuting. Professionals are located at a central facility and communicate with patients, or professionals serving patients, via telephone, video, and computer links. The State of Georgia, for example, is making extensive use of telemedicine to deliver psychiatric services to patients in rural Georgia. In this implementation of telemedicine, a psychiatrist located at the Medical College of Georgia communicates with patients via a telephone and video hookup. A video facility is located in every county in the state. Thus, patients only travel a few miles to have a therapy session with a psychiatrist or to consult about medication management. For more information see Grigsby, Adams, and Sanders, (1996) and Adams and Grigsby (1995).

Each of the uses of technology, and similar uses that will emerge, will put enormous pressures on agencies to use the tools of the information economy because they reduce costs and, in many cases, provide better services to clients.

In summary, the changes brought on by the move to an information economy will have profound implications for human service organizations. Current organizational practices and procedures will not work well. Organizational structures, job definitions, work rules, training and supervisory methods, service evaluation methods and the types and ranges of services provided to clients will all have to change for human service organizations to remain viable.

THE IMPACT OF THE COST OF ADOPTION OF TECHNOLOGY BY THE HUMAN SERVICES

Traditionally, social service agencies have been slow adopters of technology. Large agencies have used computers since the 1960s. Primarily, they used computers for business tasks such as accounting, payroll, maintaining employee records and for maintaining demographic data on clients. Other uses had to wait for the introduction of the PC by IBM, which occurred in the early 1980s. A survey of Seattle-based social service agencies found, that by 1991, 92 percent of the agencies had at least one computer. However, 78 percent had fewer than six computers and only a small portion of the agencies had either local Area Networks (LANs) or wide area networks (WANs) (Nuris, Hooyman, & Nicoll, 1991). Another survey completed in 1996 by the Lillian F. and Milford J. Harris Library of the Mandel School of Applied Social Sciences at Case Western Reserve University in Cleveland, Ohio, found that ninety-five percent of the Ohio social service agencies surveyed were using computers. Forty-eight percent said that their computers were networked and 44 percent reported that they had access to the Internet. Remarkably, only 15 percent of the direct service staff and only 33 percent of supervisory staff had access to some form of electronic communication. These figures seem confusing since it would be expected that all the agencies with Internet access and many having networked computers would be expected to have electronic mail installed. Most likely it means that computers are largely used by people who are not in supervisory positions or who are not direct service staff.

These figures compare to seventy-seven percent of small businesses owning a computer with forty percent of the computers connected to the Internet. These figures are from a poll conducted by The Gallup Organization Inc. for the National Federation of Independent Businesses (NFIB) in 1997. *Computer Reseller News* (July 14, 1997), commenting on the poll, concludes that "small businesses may be entering the digital era, but they still remain on technological backroads, far from the information superhighway." It does not seem to be too big a leap to describe the technological level, of the human service organizations polled in the two surveys reported above, as also far from the information superhighway.

Nonetheless, these figures seem to show that social service agencies are moving into the information age at about the same pace as small business but at a much slower pace than larger organizations in the business and education sectors. Many agencies polled, reported using computers that were not capable of using Windows or current Apple software. Thus, although they had computers, the computers were not usable with the current generation of software programs. Before agencies, such as these, can take advantage of the potential of the information economy, these agencies will have to make major investments in new equipment and software. At a September 1996 workshop, entitled Surviving Change/Changing to Survive: Technology and Social Work Practice, sponsored by the Mandel School of Applied Social Sciences, agency after agency reported that raising capital funds for technology purchases was difficult. Yet, all participants were unanimous in their conviction that the adoption of computerized technology was a priority for them.

Although equipment prices have dropped substantially over the past several years, the costs of human service agencies moving into the information age will be substantial. According to *CIO* magazine (1996), one estimate of current costs is that almost $12,000 per year is necessary to support a networked computer. These costs include about $2,500 for hardware, software, printers, and supplies; $2,500 for technical support; $1,300 for administrative costs; and $5,500 for worker salaries.

It is worth noting that over 75 percent of the above costs are not for computer hardware, but, rather, represent the recurring cost of ownership.

The economics of information processing is rapidly changing. First, the cost of hardware, and to some extent software, continues to decrease rapidly. For example, in 1983, a fully equipped PC cost between $3,000.00 and $5,000.00. Today, the cost is under $900.00 and is falling rapidly. *Edupage* (September 11, 1997), quoting from the September 10th issue of the *Wall Street Journal,* reports that:

> The new crop of bargain-basement PCs, priced at $1,000 or lower is germinating a new market of buyers that could change the computer industry's economic model. Packard Bell says its two, top-selling, models both fall into this category, and that the lower-priced PCs now account for 30% of its retail sales, a figure that's representative of the industry as a whole. The rush to buy the new machines has boosted home-PC sales growth, and is predicted to push PC penetration of U.S. homes to 53% by 2001, according to estimates by Forrester Research.

Since the *Wall Street Journal* article appeared, costs have plummeted. As of January 1998, Micro Center, a national computer retailer, is offering a fully loaded 166MHz Pentium computer for $499.00. Costs may even fall more. *Edupage* (September 21, 1997), reporting on an article in the *Computer News Daily,* reports that Netscape Communications CEO James Barksdale said:

His company will begin providing computers and other hardware at no cost to customers within a year. 'In various parts of the country you will be definitely seeing trials within a year from now–of these kind of distribution models for appliances, network computers and personal computers.' The company's strategy is to generate revenue through advertising, subscriptions, and a percentage of each online purchase made by subscribers. 'We learned early on, give them a phone,' he says of his earlier days at AT&T Wireless Services and McCaw Cellular. 'They might use it.'

We are also seeing advertisements for network TV that provide access to the Internet through a box that attaches to a TV set and costs a few hundred dollars. These efforts to make computers more affordable for the consumer will also lead to lower prices for hardware and software for agencies. These cost reductions will be partly offset by increased salaries for technically trained staff and by the substantial increased training costs needed to ensure that the technical systems are properly utilized.

Still, it is clear that technology is increasingly being adopted by agencies. I do not think it will be too long until most social service agencies come to accept computerization as a cost of doing business. Agencies will move toward computerization because the use of computers is a cost-effective means for agencies to collect and disseminate data. Even more importantly, the public and oversight bodies of almost all externally-funded agencies are increasing their demand for data from the agencies and are increasing their demands for agencies to use technology to provide and evaluate services.

THE CHANGING EXPECTATIONS THE PUBLIC HAS FOR AGENCY USE OF TECHNOLOGY

Agencies are increasingly being asked to account for monies they spend, report the demographics of the populations they serve, and the type, quantity and quality of services they provide clients. They are also being asked for evaluation data that demonstrate that the social service programs they provide are efficient and that they produce the expected outcomes. Once collected, it is much easier to organize the collected information and to produce reports from data that is computerized than from paper records. This factor alone will push human service agencies toward the computerization of many functions. There are also increased demands that agencies provide on-line access for clients. For example, the September 23, 1997 edition of *Edupage* reports that California has passed a law requiring that state agencies with Internet sites allow citizens to make complaints to agencies via e-mail. The law also requires the agencies to include their Web addresses in telephone directories and to let people know that they can use computers at public libraries to lodge complaints about government services. *Government Technology* (September, 1997), reported by *Edupage* (September 12, 1997), reports that Oakland, California, has adopted a policy statement requiring that future public housing projects be given computer equipment and Internet access so that welfare and low-income residents can learn job-critical skills in their homes.

Increasingly, agencies are also being required to transmit funds to clients electronically and to store client data on cards that clients keep with them in much the same way they now carry a driver's license. Electronic transfer saves agencies the enormous costs of printing and mailing checks, provides more security to clients by eliminating theft from mailboxes, and reduces costs to clients by eliminating check-cashing charges. Although precise figures were not provided, it was estimated, by a State of Missouri official at a recent meeting, that it cost over a dollar to mail a check to a client and less than ten cents to transfer the funds electronically. I expect that it will be less than five years until almost all money transfers such as AFDC, SSI, Food Stamps, and Social Security are delivered by electronic deposits. There are a number of pilot programs around the country. At the same meeting where a Missouri official discussed the costs of electronic transfers, a Missouri official revealed that some public welfare clients, even with the meager incomes they have, have been able to save small amounts of money monthly. We cannot be sure whether the clients efforts, to retain monies for future purposes, were facilitated by providing the bank accounts for the clients, or whether clients who have no accounts also save money for future purposes. It is possible that what has changed is the State's ability to monitor client behavior. On the other hand, this effort by clients to accumulate assets may well be a fortuitous demonstration of the asset building that Sherraden (1990) believes is the way to help the poor out of poverty. Whatever the reason, the findings deserve systematic investigation.

It is too early to know what impact the move to electronically based technologies, by human service agencies, will have on the typical social service client. Clients do not have much access to technology. The poor are not buying computers, let alone setting up Internet accounts. Chapman (1996, p. 26) writes that a July 1995 U.S. Department of Commerce published a survey of computer and network use in poor and rural communities, the report, "Falling Through the Net," confirmed what most people suspected: Personal computer ownership and telecommunication services are far less likely to be found in poor neighborhoods than elsewhere in the United States . . . In households with an annual income above $50,000.00, PC ownership of a computer approached 50 percent; in households with annual incomes below $10,000.00 ownership was about 7 percent. It is not clear how public access will become available for the poor and uneducated. Chapman's 1996 article provides details on some efforts to provide access. Internet access may also be mandated, as is the case in the California examples cited above. Or perhaps we will see a wider adoption of technologies that are being tested elsewhere. What is clear is that access by the poor to the "information superhighway" is still a dream. "Thus public sector CIOs [Chief Information Officers] face a paradox, increasing pressure to develop on-line systems to serve the public when an overwhelming majority of government service clients do not use on-line services or have access to them. If the information superhighway is going to be as important to each citizen's life as we think, we need to develop an analog for network access public transportation or public telephones" (Chapman, July, 1996, p. 27).

> As a way of highlighting the information rich and poor dichotomy, Reinecke (1982, p. 226) reminds how universal literacy in the United Kingdom and the United States in the 19th century contributed to democracy and a fairer society by making information accessible to a wider population. He goes on to contrast the opportunities of 'unconnected' citizens in the twenty first century with those accessing sophisticated electronic networks, suggesting a degree of inequity not dissimilar to society prior to universal literacy. (Barlow, 1997, p. 4)

In conclusion, although agencies will find that they will rely more and more on electronic record keeping to reduce costs, improve services, and meet the demands of the public, they will also have to find ways to improve access or leave unserved those clients most in need of electronic access.

THE MOVE TO ELECTRONIC RECORD KEEPING AND DATA MANAGEMENT

Electronic data storage and management data introduces a whole new set of challenges for agencies. Electronic data storage involves the storage of information, in computers, that was previously collected in printed or written form and stored in file cabinets. The major advantages of the electronic storage of information are: (1) The stored information can be accessed at any site connected to a computer; (2) The data can be reproduced at will; (3) The data can be easily analyzed and manipulated to generate all sorts of information that is useful to staff, the agency, and funding sources; (4) The space required to retain records is substantially reduced. Furthermore, the electronic storage of documents is cost effective. These factors have led to the adoption of electronic data keeping by more and more agencies. For example, the New Mexico Department of Children and Youth is transferring 60,000 case records on adults and children to a computerized client tracking system that will provide social workers with the latest information on each of their clients. Connecticut, Rhode Island and Alaska have similar programs (*CIO*, July 6, 1996). Electronic records are also being used in smaller human social service agencies. For example, I have designed several systems for agencies with as few as 20 employees. This trend will accelerate as the use of electronic signatures in case records, which is in common use in medical settings, becomes commonly used in other human service settings.

Electronic data storage is not without its problems. In the following paragraphs we will discuss several emerging issues. These include: (1) Ownership of data, (2) Maintaining data integrity, and (3) The problem of too much data.

Ownership of Data

Medical records are generally recognized to be the property of the patient, or at least open to duplication and release to the patient or to others authorized by the patient. This has not been the case for many other types of human service records. The issue of data ownership is a major issue for many agencies. Traditionally, agencies have treated client data as agency property. Client access is usually limited, and data is not routinely shared with other agencies serving the same clients. For example, the author was involved on a project designed to develop a community wide database on the homeless in St. Louis. Participating agencies were very reluctant to consider recording all client contacts in a common database open to all workers working with a client. They were even reluctant to share treatment goals and the names of agencies to which they had referred the client. In the end, about all they could agree to share was basic demographic data on clients and the names of the agencies providing services to the clients. With the advent of electronic data storage, there will be substantial pressures to share data with other human service agencies or at the very minimum make it available to staff at remote sites. The introduction of the Smart Card will put even more pressure on current data keeping policies. Smart Card technology, originally developed by ATT (Fancher, 1996), is being used to store client data on a small card kept by the client. This card, which resembles a credit card, contains a small computer that can keep information on a variety of topics. Smart Cards are being tested for electronically transferring welfare payments, and for recording medical treatment data for people who are on Medicaid and Medicare. It has also been used to store client data (Butterfield, 1995). The belief is that use of the Smart Card will make it possible for the latest client and service data to be available, to all providers of service, no matter where a client receives service. It remains to be seen if agencies will agree to such profound changes in the ownership and location of the data. If the Smart Card is used, it will be only after overcoming substantial agency resistance.

Confidentiality is also a major issue. The use of community wide or nationwide on-line client record databases radically increases the possibility that client confidentiality will be compromised. Particularly problematic will be the client's loss of the ability to control who has access to information about the client. Professionals are also concerned about such data being used to document malpractice, thus increasing their potential for exposure to malpractice charges. For this reason, some professionals want to limit access to all information they collect. For example, although I do not have a reference, colleagues at a recent national social work conference told me that they know of one statewide effort to define data collected by social workers as the social workers' personal property, thus shielding the records from clients, attorneys and others.

For an in-depth discussion of the issues of ownership and confidentiality, see Solar, Shotten and Bell, 1993.

Data Integrity

Data verification and data archiving are fundamental to competent data management. However, with a few exceptions, most Chief Executive Officers of not-for-profit human service agencies have no formal training in the area of data management. They have yet to learn the hard lesson that careless or improper data management can threaten the very existence of an agency. Therefore, it is in keeping with the future orientation of this paper to predict that many agencies that move to electronic data storage will experience major problems in data management. For a few agencies, the consequences of poor data management will be so severe that their very existence may be threatened. Data management is the Achilles' heel of the information age. My personal experience leads me to believe that, in all but the very largest human service agencies, the management of data is woefully inadequate. For example, after a national professional association implemented a new online electronic data management system, it had to shut down that part of its information system that connected remote sites to the national office when it discovered that its data system was flawed and could not provide the information its remote sites needed to operate. Units were unable to do such simple tasks as generating labels for mailings to members. Fortunately, the national database was intact and could be used to provide electronic information in a format that could be mailed to the remote units. The lesson to be learned from this and similar failures is that, as human service agencies develop all electronic data systems, vastly increased emphasis will need to be put on the development of systems that maintain the integrity of the data being stored. Integrity can only be assured when there is an overall system for data management. Here are the essentials:

Internal Data Checking

Systems must have as much built in internal data checking as possible. For example, ensuring that data is not left out, or that data is in the correct format, or that the same data item is always spelled the same way.

Adequate Training

Even the best electronic systems cannot prevent all input errors. Managers of electronic databases face enormous challenges in ensuring that data is entered accurately into the computer. The first major problem is that they often fail to adequately train staff. Agencies, in general, neglect training. In fact, training should be a major part of the budget for electronic data systems. Managers should budget, as much if not more, for training as they do for hardware and software acquisition. Few agencies provide this level of training. Although training is essential, even good training is not enough. Rigorous auditing and backup procedures must also be implemented.

Auditing

Auditing is the process of sampling data to determine if it is accurately entered. Poor auditing can be costly. A school district, with which I am familiar, lost over $300,000.00 in daily attendance funds when the State audited its attendance records. The district had a 3% error rate. That is, about 3% of the electronic records did not correlate with the paper and pencil records maintained by teachers. Three percent might seem like a low error rate. However, with millions of dollars in attendance funds at stake, such error rates were unacceptable to the State. The State where the school district was located had a permissible error standard of three tenths of one percent (.003). In order to bring its records into compliance, the school district had to spend nearly $50,000.00 and set up a full time auditing department. We can expect that there is a similar lack of attention to data verification in many human service electronic data systems. For example, even after the author warned them that auditing was an essential part of database management, a large social service agency failed to implement auditing procedures for its electronic case management system. Their rationale was that auditing was time intensive and was not essential. However, when it attempted to produce reports, the agency discovered substantial portions of nearly four months of client data was missing from the database. Because the reports were used to determine the funding levels for the next fiscal year, the agency had to suspend service delivery and other activities, to reconstruct the data from their paper case files. They were fortunate they had paper files. Had their system been wholly electronic, they would not have been able to reconstruct their records. Adequate auditing would have quickly uncovered the database error and prevented this major failure in their client management system.

Backing Up Data

Another essential part of ensuring data integrity is the backing up of data. Backing up data is the process of periodically making copies of the electronic data and storing it in a safe place. There are commercial companies whose sole purpose is to store such data. Backups ensure that a recent copy of the data on the computer will be available for reconstructing the database even if the computer holding the data fails, is destroyed, is accidentally damaged, is damaged by events of nature such as lightning, earthquake, fire, or flood, or is stolen.

When it is done correctly, backing up audited data is very effective insurance against data loss. For example, after the World Trade Center explosion, some businesses, that lost their computers in the explosion, were back in operation in less than a day after the explosion because they had been regularly transferring backup data to a safe, off-site location. Very few not-for-profit agencies have developed adequate backup procedures. For example, failure to back up its financial records caused an agency the author is familiar with to pay several thousand dollars to reconstruct its financial records after a computer hard drive failure prevented access to nearly a year's financial records. They were fortunate that the computer failure was not catastrophic and that most of the data could be retrieved from the damaged hard drive. Faithful backing up of data and the use of sophisticated procedures such as data mirroring, where the same data is kept on two computers at all times, are in common use by commercial organizations and should be in use by any agency that has converted to electronic record keeping.

The Problems of Distributed Storage

A new form of data storage, distributed storage, is beginning to emerge. This form of data storage is different from the simple electronic storage of documents in a single location. Its primary use is the publishing of electronic documents over the Internet. But, it will soon be a part of many data systems. Traditional documents published electronically are self-contained. That is, they contain information that is located in a single file on a single computer. However, electronic documents utilizing distributed storage are different in that they are not self-contained but contain links to other documents, which can be accessed from the main document. Sometimes the information appears automatically in the master document (automatic linking) and sometimes it is only referenced in the master document and can be accessed by clicking on the reference. "The electronic document is an interface to an entire information world" (Delphi Consulting Group, 1995). Information located anywhere on any computer, connected to the Internet, can be linked, and published, so that it appears to the reader as a single document. This type of storage will be extremely useful to agencies that want to provide information to clients and to professionals. For example, agencies may maintain a home page with a section devoted to the latest recommended treatment approaches. For example, they might include a link to a document discussing the best means for treating various clinical problems. An example of sort of document can be found at URL: *http://text.nlm.nih.gov/nih/cdc/www/85txt.html* which discusses the treatment of panic disorders (NIH Consensus Statement Online. 1991 Sep 25-27th 9, 2, 1-24). Another link might be to a job database. For examples, see: URL: Jobs *http://gwbweb.wustl.edu/jobs/* or URL: *http://www.ajb.dni.us/*. Another link might be to a social work site that contains links to many other resources. For example, see URL: holden *http://pages.nyu.edu/~holden/gh-w3-f.htm*. It would also be technically possible to link client records located on several different professionals' computers.

Distributed electronic document storage brings with it a whole set of new problems. Reproducibility and document durability are major concerns. Linked documents may be modified or updated without the master document's author being aware of the changes that have been made in the linked document. Thus, the author of the master document may have referenced a document considerably different from the one the reader will see when the reader accesses the linked document. For this reason, readers of documents published using distributed storage technology cannot be sure the linked documents are the same as referenced by the author of the master document. A related problem is that links to referenced documents may fail because the documents have been moved or simply removed from the referenced site. The problem of broken links is very common. So, publishers of distributed documents must systematically verify that the sites they reference are still valid. There are commercial programs that can be used to automate this task. See URL: *http://www.windows95.com/apps/htmlverify.html* for a list of verification programs. In summary, the emergence of distributed documents makes it possible to publish documents on the Internet that make remote data sources easily available to someone reading a master document. The potential benefits of this type of publishing and data management are enormous. See Brody (1966) for a more extensive discussion of electronic publishing. Because of the potential of this type of publishing, it is quite possible that this method of data management will be adopted by many human service organizations.

The Problem of Virus Protection

Data integrity can be seriously compromised by computer viruses. Viruses are a threat to data integrity. Data must be checked, by using virus-checking programs, to guarantee that all data entered into the computer or transferred from another computer is virus free. Much misinformation about computer viruses is in circulation. One prevalent rumor is that it is nearly impossible for a computer to be infected from e-mail sent to it or by using the Internet. Both methods of infection are possible. In fact, the most common virus infections are now macro virus infections which can be contained in any file attached to an e-mail message. For an excellent discussion by experts on computer viruses, see Kephart, Sorkin, Chess and White (November, 1997). Another excellent source of information is the URL: *http://www.mcafee.com/main.asp*. Although viruses are a problem, with careful management they do not have to pose a major problem to data integrity.

SUMMARY

In summary, agencies moving to electronic data storage will need to make substantial investments in procedures designed to ensure that data integrity is maintained. Most agencies will need to create a Chief Information Officer (CIO) position so that as much attention is paid to electronic data integrity as is now given to the management of agency finances.

THE PROBLEM OF TOO MUCH DATA AND ITS VERIFICATION

Another issue facing workers as they enter the information age is the vast amounts of data that are available to them. In "the 21st century the body of information in the world will double every five years" (Lick, April 16, 1996). As we have already pointed out, although there will be vast stores of information available, the accuracy of the available data depends on the efforts of the manager of the data to insure data integrity. Where the data is maintained by an agency, staff can usually make good estimates about the integrity of the data and can do statistical sampling to verify the integrity of the data. The integrity of data kept by others will often be difficult to ascertain. Users of the Internet and the World Wide Web (WEB) face major data verification issues.

All data on the Internet should be approached with skepticism since much of what is published on the WEB or in other electronic formats may not have been checked by anyone. Anyone can set up a home page or publish on the Internet, and what they publish may or may not be truthful or factual. For a discussion of how to evaluate WEB based information, see the URL: *http://www.science.widener.edu/~withers/webeval.htm*.

Because so much information is available, no single person can access all of the available information. The Delphi Group anticipates that a new industry that collects and packages information will develop as a response to the problem of too much data. I anticipate that this new industry will also develop means for certifying the accuracy of the data. Even with the data verification problems that exist, the Internet is a vast treasure trove of useful information for the human services. Whole libraries are now coming on-line. For example, the *Chronicle of Higher Education* (October 24, 1997), cited in *Edupage*, reports The University of California System will create a completely digital library, with the entire collection available online. The California Digital Library will concentrate initially on building a collection of materials related to science, technology, and industry. One goal of the digital system will be to encourage professors to publish their research online. 'We would like to change the way information is disseminated for scholarship,' says the Digital Library's first librarian (*Edupage*, October 26th, 1997).

Human service agencies will find vast sources of useful information on the Internet. In time, I would expect that many sources of data like those envisioned by The Delphi Group will be available to organize and verify information of use to human service professionals. For now, however, someone within the agency will have to search for the information they need and then determine its authenticity before using it.

THE IMPACT OF THE INTERNET AND INTRANETS

The Internet has been called a 'network of networks' (McNutt, 1995a, p. 1). Others have called it the world's largest computer network with all its subnets freely exchanging information. Part of the Internet uses relatively old technology that is better relegated to people who are highly computer literate. Another part uses newer technology called web browsers that make accessing the Internet relatively easy. It is this latter technology that is behind the rush to use the Internet for communication and data management. An intranet is also a network, but rather than interconnecting to other networks outside the organization, it operates within the confines of a single organization. With that exception, it functions in the same manner as the Internet. A large organization may have several sub-nets tied together through an intranet. But an intranet could consist of a single internal network. Looked at another way, an Internet is focused on connecting an agency or person to the universe of information that exists in the world. An intranet is focused on making available internal information to members of the organization.

Both the Internet and intranets are causing excitement because they have reduced the cost of finding and communicating information to the point where even individuals can afford to use it. It has also made access easy and the transformation of information nearly instantaneous. There is nothing magical about the Internet. It is a tool, a very powerful and versatile tool, but nevertheless a tool. The establishment of the Internet has provided a means for overcoming two of the most intractable problems of the early information age. The first is the problem of easy access to data from remote sites. The second is the use of the available software by computers of varying brands and configurations. With the advent of the Internet, data can be accessed from almost anywhere in the world at a very reasonable cost. It is now cost effective for agencies to equip their outreach workers and remote sites with Internet capable machines which can connect to the agency's database system for the purposes of client data input and retrieval as well as many other functions. In fact, any function that can be performed by printed or written communication can be performed over the Internet. For a summary of available Internet functions, see Butterfield and Schoech (1997). The uses outlined in their article are well understood, and will grow rapidly as more and more workers learn to use the Internet in school or in their homes.

Before Internet communication protocols were developed, it was an expensive and difficult problem to use software developed on one type of computer with a different type of computer. The Internet provides a way to overcome the software incompatibility problem. With the Internet, it is now possible to develop computer programs that will operate on a variety of computers. The importance of this is hard to overestimate. Johnson (December 4, 1995) predicted that, between 1995 and 1997, American corporations would spend over 500 billion dollars, on labor alone, for the development of business software. Not-for-profits that choose to develop their own software will also spend enormous sums on software development. Software development is expensive, especially when the software is custom developed for a single customer. Substantial cost savings are possible if agencies learn to take advantage of the universality of Internet software. The Internet/intranet offers a golden opportunity for reducing development costs. When software is developed for use by an Internet browser it is potentially usable on any machine connected to the Internet. Thus, if careful thought is given to the task, it should be possible to develop applications for use on the NET that can be used by multiple agencies. Such efforts are well under way in the commercial arena. For example, the January 21, 1998 issue of *Informationweek Daily* reports the adoption of the same expense reporting software by several large businesses. The program is written in Java, an Internet compliant language. Gordon Jones, the Chief Information Officer of a $2 billion mutual fund, "expects to cut its expense report processing costs in half by using [the program]. Its write once, read-anywhere capability will cut our support costs in heterogeneous environments," he said (*Informationweek*, January 21, 1998). The same process could be used in the human services. Let me give some examples. The University of Texas at Austin has developed an Internet compliant program that lets students perform on-line registration for volunteer activities in the community. They have also developed several other on-line databases for use by practicum students. Most schools of social work could use similar programs, but many do not have them. There are no technical reasons why Internet programs developed at one university could not be used by other schools. For those schools that could not afford their own Internet servers, it would even be possible for a school that developed the program to host another school's database. Similar solutions could be developed for not-for-profits that want to automate their client records. A generic client record could be developed and made available over the Internet to any agency that wanted to use it. With proper attention to confidentiality and other security issues, the records could be entered over an intranet or the Internet. Another example where this method of software development would be useful is for the development of Internet compliant software for the preparation of reports wanted by funding organizations. It would make sense, for example, for the national United Way organization to develop a set of Internet compliant forms that could be filled out by agencies over the Internet. The development cost would be enormously lower than the cost of each agency developing reporting software on their own. It would also reduce the mailing and printing costs associated with paper forms. The Federal government also requires many agencies to submit information. The government could easily create Internet compliant electronic versions of the reporting forms and, with some additional effort, electronic forms for collecting the required data. Yet, as far as I know, it has yet to develop software programs that would permit the reports to be submitted over the Internet. Another example of where this approach might well be useful is in providing a means for small professional organizations to maintain their membership lists. There are literally thousands of small organizations and professional societies that maintain membership databases. Some keep them on computers, others on cards. Almost all of them would like to have a better system for keeping their data up-to-date and accessible to members. An on-line membership database would be ideal for them. Some organizations are already using Internet compliant databases. For example, ACOSA (Association for Community Organization and Social Administration) was able to develop an on-line membership database by using a free address book that was already available on the

Internet. Readers who want to get some idea of how such an on-line address book might work can look at the eOrganizer web site used by ACOSA. This site, at URL: *http://www.eorganizer.com/*, lets users create their own on-line todo lists, appointment calendar, address book, birthday list, and to maintain notes on each entry. It even offers the ability to notify the user, by e-mail, of appointments and the pending occurrence of important events like birthdays and anniversaries. Several of the functions contained in eOrganizer could be easily used by most organizations. With some further development, such a program might well be marketable to many not-for-profit organizations.

The potential for the sharing of Internet programs is enormous. Much shareware already exists. "Indeed libraries of free software for scientific purposes are blossoming all over the Internet" (Brody, 1966, p. 48). But, as far as I know, there is no organized way to promote shared software development for human service agencies. Perhaps several professional organizations could form a consortium whose sole purpose would be the development of cost effective software for consortium members. If done well, this could increase the rapidity with which agencies begin to use the Internet to conduct their business.

CONCLUSION

The intent of this paper was to highlight some of the near future technology trends that will impact on the human services in the hope that it might provide some guidance to those who are considering updating the technology in their organizations. I have pointed out how the changing nature of work will create needs for new services and may change how human service agencies structure their own work environments. I have tried to give adopters of technology some general estimates of the costs of technology implementation and have shown that hardware costs are rapidly falling. I have also emphasized that successful implementation of technology requires that organizations budget for and carry out extensive training. I have pointed out that, in some sense, organizations will be forced into adopting technology as a means to deal with increased demands for accountability and increased expectations from the public and funders. I have emphasized that competent electronic data management cannot be left to chance. It should be approached, with the same degree of seriousness, as the maintenance of the financial records for an organization. I have also suggested that agencies that want to make intelligent use of the Internet will need to pay attention to how to manage the vast amount of available data, and that there may well be opportunities for the development of data management organizations to serve the human services. Finally, I have discussed the impact of the Internet and intranets on the information economy, and have recommended that one way to lower the substantial costs of software development is for umbrella organizations to provide software, to the agencies they fund, that can be used to meet the reporting requirements of the funding organizations. I have also suggested that forming a consortium, whose task would be to develop Internet compliant software that could be utilized by many human service organizations, could reduce the costs of software development.

REFERENCES

Adams, L. & Grigsby, K. (1995). The Georgia State Telemedicine Program: Initiation, design, and plans. *Telemedicine Journal*, 1, 3, 227-235.

Australian Science and Technology Council (1995). *Matching science and technology to future needs: Key issues for Australia to 2010*. Canberra: Australian Science and Technology Council.

Barlow, D. (March, 1977). Electronic community networks in rural Australia: A model for social development in the information society. *Australian Social Work*, 50, 1, 3-8.

Bridges, W. (1994). The end of the job. *Fortune*, 129, 62-74.

Brody, H. (October, 1996). Wired science. *Technology Review*, 7, 99, 42-51.

Butterfield, W. (1995). Computer utilization. In R. Edwards (Ed.) *Encyclopedia of Social Work*, 19, 594-613.

Butterfield, W. & Schoech, D. (1997). The Internet: Accessing the world of information. In R. Edwards (Ed.) *1997 Supplement to Encyclopedia of Social Work*, 19, 151-168.

Chapman, G. (July, 1996). No cover, no minimum. *CIO,* 9, 6, 26-28. URL: http://www.cio.com/archive/rc_gv_nocov.html

Chronicle of Higher Education (October 24, 1997). U. of California plans new online library. Cited in the October 26th edition of *Edupage*. URL: http://www.educom. edu/web/pubs/pubHomeFrame.html

CIO (July 1996). Better case scenarios. *CIO*, 9, 6, 21-23.

Computer Reseller News (July 14, 1997). Poll finds small businesses off beaten path of Internet. Issue: 745 Small Business Section. URL http://techweb.omp.com/ setechsearch.cgi?

Delphi Consulting Group (December 25, 1995). Electronic documents. *Information Week*, 1d-7d.

Drucker, P. (November, 1994). The age of social transformation. *The Atlantic Monthly*, 53-80.

Edupage (September 11, 1997). Lower-priced pcs hit the "sweet spot." URL: http://www.educom.edu/web/pubs/pubHomeFrame.html

Edupage (September 21, 1997). Netscape chief predicts pc give-away. URL: http://www.educom.edu/web/pubs/pubHomeFrame.html

Edupage (September 23, 1997). Online suggestion box in California. URL: http://www.educom.edu/web/pubs/pubHomeFrame.html

Edupage (October 12, 1997). Oakland ends welfare, as we know it, by adding the net. URL: http://www.educom.edu/web/pubs/pubHomeFrame.html

Edupage (October 26, 1997). Telecommuting on the rise. Citing *USA Today*, Oct 24, 1997. URL: http://www.educom.edu/web/pubs/pubHomeFrame.html

Edupage (October 26, 1997). 10 million kids on-line. URL: http://www.educom.edu/web/pubs/pubHomeFrame.html

Fancher, C. (1996). Smart Cards. *Scientific American*, 275, 2, 40-45.

Grigsby, K., Adams, L., and Sanders, J. (1996). Overcoming the obstacles to telemedicine. *Federal Practitioner*, 13, 3, 49-53.

Informationweek (January 21, 1998). Startup names customers for Java expense-report tool. URL: http://www.informationweek.com

Kephart, J., Sorkin, G., Chess, D., and White, S. (November, 1977). Fighting Computer Viruses. *Scientific American*, 277, 5, 88-93.

Lawrence, G. & Killion, F. (1994). Challenging the equity divide in the age of efficiency. *Proceedings of the ACOSS National Congress*, 26-28 October, 1994.

Knowles, A. (June 15, 1996). The enemy within. *CIO*, 84-90. URL: http://www.cio.com/archive/061596_security.html

Lick, D. (April 16, 1996). Ivory towers and ivy-covered walls will yield to on-line learning. *Christian Science Monitor*.

McNutt, J. (1995a). National information infrastructure policy as the social policy of the next century: An empowerment perspective. Paper presented at the 1995 CSWE Annual Program Meeting, San Diego, CA, March, 1995.

McNutt, J. (1995b). Internet Resources. *Social Welfare Policy*. The newsletter of the Social Welfare and Policy Group, July 1955, 3, 1, 1.

McNutt, J. (1995c). National information infrastructure The development of the (NII) and the fate of the American welfare state: Implications for nonprofit human service agencies. Paper presented at the 1995 Annual Conference of the Association for Research on non-profit and Voluntary Associations, Cleveland, OH, November 2-4, 1995.

Mokhtarian, P. (October, 1997). Now that travel can be virtual, will congestion virtually disappear? *Scientific American*, 277, 4, 93.

Nurius, P., Hooyman, N., & Nicoll, A. (1991). Computers in agencies: A survey baseline and planning implications. *Journal of Social Service Research*, 14, 141-155.

Reinecke, I. (1982). *Micro invaders: How the new world of technology works*. Melborne: Penguin Books.

Sherraden, M. (1990). *Assets and the Poor: A new American Welfare Policy*. Armonk, New York: M. E. Sharpe, Inc.

Solar, M., Shotten, A., and Bell, J. (March, 1993). *Glass Walls: Confidentiality, provisions, and interagency collaborations*. San Francisco CA 94104: Youth Law Center, 114 Sansone Street, Suite 950.

Wildstrom, S. (September 30, 1996). A search tool with smarts. *Business Week*, 16.

The Worker Safety Advisor:
A Performance Support System

Dick Schoech
Rebecca Bolen

SUMMARY. A performance support system (PSS) improves workplace performance by providing on-demand access to the integrated information needed to complete the task or solve the problem at hand. To test the feasibility of a human services PSS, the authors developed the Worker Safety Advisor (WSA), which presents several computer screens on which workers specify the situation they face. The WSA then searches a knowledge base and presents relevant worker safety information in an easy-to-read format. This article describes the development of the WSA, including its background, rationale, objectives, resources required, and lessons learned. The PSS concepts and experiences presented can help others develop similar applications. *[Article copies available for a fee from The Haworth Document Delivery Service: 1-800-342-9678. E-mail address: getinfo@haworthpressinc.com]*

KEYWORDS. Worker safety, performance support systems, multimedia

Dick Schoech, PhD, is Professor, University of Texas at Arlington School of Social Work, Box 19129, Arlington, TX 76019 (E-mail: schoech@uta.edu). He teaches administrative and community practice and computer applications. His research and development involve multimedia based training, performance support systems, and distance education.

Becky Bolen, PhD, is Assistant Professor, Boston University School of Social Work, Boston, MA 02215.

[Haworth co-indexing entry note]: "The Worker Safety Advisor: A Performance Support System." Schoech, Dick, and Rebecca Bolen. Co-published simultaneously in *Computers in Human Services* (The Haworth Press, Inc.) Vol. 15, No. 2/3, 1998, pp. 143-158; and: *Information Technologies: Teaching to Use–Using to Teach* (ed: Frank B. Raymond III, Leon Ginsberg, and Debra Gohagan) The Haworth Press, Inc., 1998, pp. 143-158. Single or multiple copies of this article are available for a fee from The Haworth Document Delivery Service [1-800-342-9678, 9:00 a.m. - 5:00 p.m. (EST). E-mail address: getinfo@ haworthpressinc.com]

INTRODUCTION

Agencies will implement many types of computer applications as they use information technology to produce more efficient, effective, and accountable services. Most initial applications focus on efficiency and accountability, for example, budget software or management information systems. These applications do little to support the tasks of front line practitioners as they interact with clients. Agency-wide systems, which support worker/client interactions, have proven complex to build and difficult to implement (Miller, 1993). To avoid these problems, agencies often try to develop small applications that are relatively easy to build and that support a critical worker task, for example, treatment planning and matching clients with services. This article describes the development of one such application, a worker safety performance support system.

A performance support system (PSS) improves workplace performance by providing on-demand access to the integrated information needed to complete the task or solve the problem at hand. A PSS uses technology to provide supportive information when it is needed, where it is needed, and in the format in which it is needed (Grey, 1991; Reynolds & Araya, 1995). To test the feasibility of PSS software in the human services, the authors have been developing a PSS since September 1994 in the area of worker safety. Worker safety concerns the ability to recognize, prevent, assess, handle, and recover from situations that endanger one's physical and emotional well-being.

Our PSS, named the Worker Safety Advisor (WSA), presents workers with several computer screens on which they specify the situation they face. The module then searches a knowledge base of worker safety information and presents relevant information in an easy-to-read format. A variety of experts developed and reviewed the WSA knowledge base.

This article describes the development of the WSA. It begins with its background and rationale, followed by its goals and objectives. Next the hardware, software, and human resources are presented along with the development process, and lessons learned. The purpose of this article is to explain PSS concepts and our experiences so that others can learn what is required to develop similar human services applications. The term "worker" in this article refers to a child protective services (CPS) worker for whom the system is designed. For simplicity, worker is used throughout rather than the more generic term of user or practitioner, although the WSA can be used by managers, volunteers and many others.

BACKGROUND AND RATIONALE OF THE WSA

The State of Texas continually looks for ways to use information technology to improve service delivery. Technology is seen as one way to control and flatten large state bureaucracies and to devote more resources to client services. The Texas Department of Protective and Regulatory Services (TDPRS), which is the state department responsible for all child protective services, has implemented several management information systems over the years. The current effort, which began in September 1996, is an ambitious statewide, client-server system that put a networked personal computer (PC) on every worker's desk. This system, called CAPS (Child and Adult Protective System), automates all forms and reports. Like previous TDPRS systems, CAPS is designed to capture information for management and casework documentation, not to support worker/client interactions. Consequently, TDPRS was eager to use the current network to build applications that support client/worker activities. However, TDPRS did not have this developmental capacity in-house.

One outside agency working with TDPRS to improve worker performance is the Child Protective Services Training Institute (CPSTI) at The University of Texas at Austin Center for Social Work Research. CPSTI was established by TDPRS to involve Texas universities in employee training. CPSTI is a consortium of Texas schools of social work that provides advanced training for TDPRS workers and supervisors.

Since its establishment in 1991, CPSTI has viewed technology as one way to accomplish its mission. A 1992 plan identified multimedia training as one promising way in which CPSTI could incorporate technology into its training efforts. CPSTI funded three multimedia training projects. Keisha, a simulation on failure to thrive, was developed and tested at the U. of Texas at Arlington School of Social Work (Satterwhite & Schoech, 1995; MacFadden, 1997). An interviewing skills training module was developed and tested by Dr. Patrick Leung at the U. of Houston School of Social Work and a cross-cultural competency module was developed by Dr. Santos Hernandez at Our Lady of the Lake School of Social Work in San Antonio, TX (Leung, 1993). At the time these multimedia projects were developed, TDPRS had little computer hardware for training, so the systems were built with future unspecified hardware in mind.

These multimedia training efforts, although well received, were never integrated into TDPRS training. The reasons involved TDPRS's immersion in the massive statewide information system and the fact that the new PCs on workers' desktops and in training areas were not multimedia ready. Given these problems, CPSTI wanted to develop training software that could be readily integrated into the worker's everyday tasks. One way CPSTI felt that it might take advantage of the worker's desktop PC was to develop "help" modules that would provide expertise and advice to workers in areas critical to worker performance. This new emphasis moved CPSTI's technology efforts from training to performance support.

The distinction between training software and performance support is subtle, but important. The goal of training is to learn for future practice, whereas the goal of a PSS is to improve performance on the task at hand. Since a PSS presents information void of any larger context, it must assume that workers have been trained on the larger context. This point can be illustrated using an analogy. If training is analogous to watching a movie, then a PSS is analogous to users selecting and viewing short clips of the same movie (Schoech, 1996). Movie clips and a PSS provide bits of information out of context to satisfy an immediate need. In contrast, a movie and training provide information within a larger context. They use setting, pace, and other techniques to get the information across in a dramatic and coherent way that maximizes impact and retention. Just as film clips are often part of movies, a PSS, or the information it contains, might be used as one part of a training session. We continually had to make the point that the WSA is not a replacement for training, nor is training its goal. Instead, the WSA is a refresher for information previously presented during training.

The WSA was developed to test whether PSS software could meet worker needs and be well received. Worker safety was selected as the subject for the PSS for several reasons.

- Child protective services workers are facing more violence today than ever before.
- Turnover often prevents workers from accumulating the knowledge needed to become "street smart" on the job.
- Worker safety is a subject, like many in the human services, that is "a mile wide and a foot deep." That is, many small, independent bits of advice are available for a large variety of situations.
- Worker safety information does not change much and the knowledge base is manageable.
- Worker safety information can be communicated using text rather than graphics, pictures, or sound.

The idea was that once the WSA was developed and tested, it would be available under the help menu on all workstations via the server. A 3 to 5 minute interaction with the WSA was seen as similar to checking about safety considerations with knowledgeable colleagues before going out on a case. The WSA was to contain advice that was available in the literature and through CPSTI training seminars. No attempt was made to develop an exhaustive and coherent body of knowledge on worker safety. If the WSA proved to be effective and was used by workers, the knowledge base could be upgraded later.

DESCRIPTION OF THE WORKER SAFETY ADVISOR

Goals and Objectives. In a previous effort to develop a multimedia training simulation, the lack of specific objectives created problems when implementation was discussed with TDPRS. Given this problem, goals and measurable objectives were considered especially important for any application that promised to improve worker performance. Without specific objectives, improved performance could not be evaluated. Before TDPRS was willing to implement any system, it required evidence that the system was effective.

The goal of the WSA is to provide advice to workers on how to perform their jobs more safely. The objectives are:

1. Workers who use the WSA will express a higher level of confidence about their knowledge and abilities regarding worker safety in CPS practice as measured by pre and post scores on a worker safety survey of module users.
2. Workers who use the WSA will be able to better recognize situations as unsafe and recommend appropriate actions to take in unsafe situations as measured by a survey of module users.
3. Workers who use the WSA will be able to better assess the physical and emotional dangers of an unsafe situation as measured by pre and post scores on a survey of module users.
4. Workers who use the WSA will have fewer "unsafe" incidents as measured by self-reports in a survey of module users.
5. Workers who use the WSA will have fewer "unsafe" incidents as measured by CPS incident reports.
6. Workers who use the WSA and experience a threatening situation will take more appropriate actions during the incident, more appropriate actions to recover from the incident, and more appropriate actions to prevent future threats, as measured by a survey of module users.

Description of the WSA. PSS ideology and the needs of workers guided the decisions concerning the flow of the WSA. Because the WSA needed to be a quick-in, quick-out system, it made maximum use of a minimum number of screens. The schematic in Figure 1 delineates the flow of content in the WSA.

As Figure 1 illustrates, the introductory credits screen leads into a screen from which the worker selects one of six pre-crisis situations about which data need to be collected. Alternately, the worker may select one of three branches rather than one of the six data collection screens. The first branch contains scenarios, written by workers in the field, concerning actual work experiences entailing some type of danger to the worker. The second branch contains a screen relating specifically to skill building, while the third branch contains a screen concerning generic (i.e., not incident specific) post-crisis information.

FIGURE 1. Flow of the Content in the Worker Safety Advisor

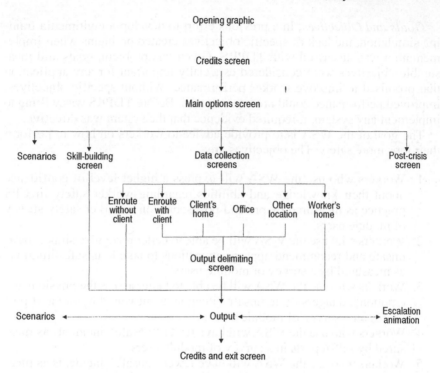

Figure 2 is a typical data collection screen. This particular screen allows the worker to delineate the circumstances of a pending visit to the client's house by checking boxes via a mouse click. Perhaps the most important checkbox is the first–whether the worker is concerned about a potentially dangerous client. When this box is checked, another screen opens that asks for the type of danger. Options include a suicidal or homicidal client, a potentially physically or verbally aggressive client, or further information on the phases of escalation.

After workers complete the data collection screen, they are usually, but not always, directed to the output delimiter screen. The output delimiter screen further clarifies the information the worker needs by refining the search and reducing the amount of information displayed. The knowledge base of safety information is so extensive that the worker could potentially be swamped by the amount of information offered. The output delimiter screen presents all choices selected on the data collection screen, with all potential output for each selection.

After completing the output delimiter screen, the worker is directed to the final output screen, shown in Figure 3. On the left side of this screen is a list

FIGURE 2. A Typical Data Collection Screen

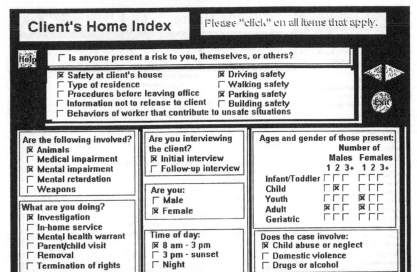

of all categories the worker previously selected, e.g., animal safety. The worker simply has to click on a specific category to view the related information. In addition, hotwords are used throughout the WSA. Hotwords are highlighted text that display a small window of additional information about that text when clicked.

Two other types of output–scenarios and an animation of the phases of client escalation–are available via the final output screen depicted in Figure 3. At the top of each page of output is a hotword that, when clicked, immediately routes the worker to the list of scenarios. On the scenarios screen, the scenarios applicable to that output page are then highlighted. The second type of output, the animation of the phases of client escalation, is page-sensitive. That is, for output pages concerning potentially dangerous clients or situations, the worker is given the option of referencing an escalation screen. This screen provides reminders on how to work with clients in various stages of escalation. After workers finish examining the output, they may choose to exit the WSA, enter a new situation, or modify the existing information.

DEVELOPMENT RESOURCES REQUIRED

Software. The WSA was developed using Authorware, a Windows based authoring package. Authorware was selected as the authoring tool because

FIGURE 3. Final Output Screen

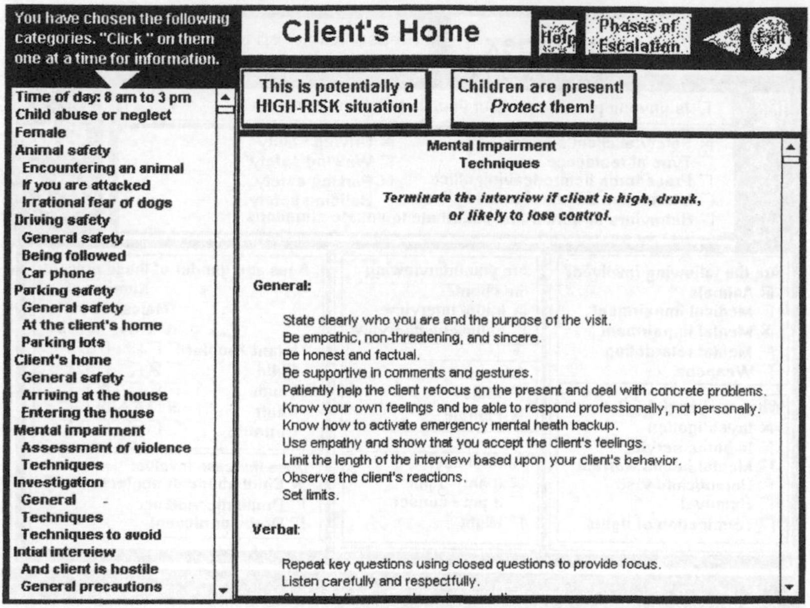

Authorware was used for the computer based training associated with the CAPS information system. The rationale was that software written in Authorware could be maintained and enhanced by TDPRS staff.

Authorware is designed for easy development of courseware by non-programmers. It works best where a seminar or course is well developed and needs to be quickly translated by non-programmers into computer screens. However, the PSS task was somewhat different. We wanted to use a minimum number of screens to capture the search criteria. Then we wanted to display selected pieces of a complex knowledge base using the search criteria selected. We were continually challenged to make Authorware do what we wanted.

One advantage of selecting Authorware is that it is well supported and problems we experience are often solved by new versions. In addition, Authorware is aggressively targeting the Internet and intranets as delivery mechanisms. The Internet version of the WSA is helpful in demonstrating the WSA in and outside TDPRS. Using the Internet also allows easy updates and distribution of these updates. In the future, Internet/intranet access may be the prime delivery mode for the WSA. The Internet has the additional advantage of making the WSA accessible anywhere in the world. The Internet version can be run from http://www.uta.edu/cussn/wsa/wsa.html.

Hardware and networking. The WSA will run on any Windows based PC. A version that runs on a local area network (LAN) is also available. However, older PCs may be slower than desired and older monitors may display colors and text unsatisfactorily. The WSA runs well on a Pentium computer. It requires approximately 2.5MB of disk space. The Internet version requires that the Authorware Shockwave plug-in be downloaded (free) and installed on the user's browser. A link to Shockwave is available through the WSA web site. The speed of the Internet version depends on the speed of the user's connection. Modem access is satisfactory for demonstration purposes, but on-the-job workers using the Internet version will benefit by a direct link to the Internet with an ISDN or faster line.

Human resources. Expertise to develop the WSA can be categorized into technical, content area, and project management and coordination.

Technical expertise was provided by one of the authors working 10 hours a week as a Graduate Research Assistant (GRA) for approximately 3 years. Technical tasks included designing and programming input and output screens, knowledge base design and development, programming Authorware, and developing links between the knowledge base and the input selection criteria. An expert consultant in Authorware was retained for approximately 5 hours to explore storage and indexing options and to debug major problems.

Content area expertise was obtained from various sources. GRAs (.50 FTE) were used for approximately three semesters to find worker safety information and to help organize it into a knowledge base. This initial knowledge base resulted in a 300-page manual that was circulated to nine "experts" consisting of TDPRS and CPSTI staff, university experts, and national experts.

Management and coordination were provided by the senior author (approximately 4 hours per week for 3 years) and a statewide Technology Advisory Committee that combines TDPRS and CPSTI staff. Management and coordination tasks include acquiring software, hiring and supervising staff, developing overall design, coordinating activities, presenting prototypes for feedback, web site design and uploads, and reporting to CPSTI and TDPRS staff.

Considerable secretarial support was used in developing and updating the written manual that was used for review and documentation purposes.

THE DEVELOPMENT PROCESS

Figure 4 presents three important features in the development of the WSA. First, from its inception, WSA development encompassed (a) the creation of a worker safety knowledge base, formatted for multimedia display, and (b) the development of the computer program. The second development feature involved the periodic demonstration of a prototype system to potential users.

FIGURE 4. Three Important Features in the Development of the Worker Safety Advisor

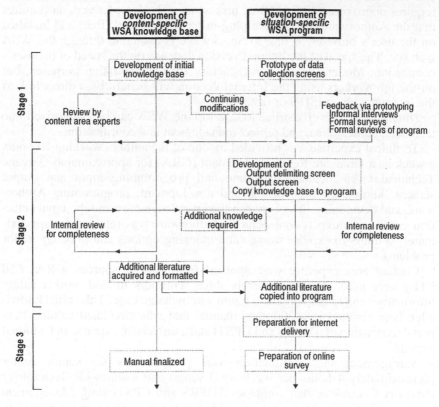

Using this process, workers, training experts, and TDPRS/CPSTI policy makers insured that the WSA screens and knowledge base met their needs. Therefore, instead of allowing the information available to dictate the limits of the program, the needs of all users influenced the available options, which in turn dictated the breadth of the knowledge base. The final important feature is that the knowledge base, of necessity, is content-specific, while the WSA program, by the request of workers, is situation-specific. The knowledge base derives directly from the available literature, which is largely categorized by topic, while workers are most concerned about how to maintain safety in specific situations.

Development of the knowledge base. Because the WSA had to contain a substantial amount of information, the development of the knowledge base was emphasized. The first step of its development was to review the published and unpublished literature on worker safety. This literature was developed into an initial manual, grouped by content. Because the knowledge base was to be accessed via a computer screen, the information was then reformatted into succinct bulleted text. After the manual was fully edited, it was given for review to a group of nine experts on safety issues for workers. After their recommended changes were made, the manual was copied into the WSA computer program and linked to the applicable screens. Upon completion of this task, it became apparent that no or minimal information was currently available for many situations that workers might enter into the WSA. For example, approximately 55 of the 160 pages of text were missing or had minimal information, along with approximately 70 of the 170 hotwords. Thus, a further search of the published and Internet literature was made to obtain additional information.

The final manual, comprising approximately 400 pages, is divided into three sections. First is the 13 scenarios written by workers. The second section contains approximately 160 different categories of information, such as how to assess a client for suicidality or what to do when a worker encounters an aggressive client. The third section consists of definitions, explanations, and examples for the approximately 170 hotwords, many of which are technical words or jargon. All categories are appropriately referenced. Even though the manual was a necessary part of the development of the WSA, it is ancillary. Its purpose is simply to provide a hard copy of what resides in the WSA.

Development of computer program. An equally important task was to develop a computer program that quickly accessed the pertinent information in the knowledge base. Authorware does not contain a database module that easily stores, retrieves, and queries information. Therefore, this part of the development proved to be more challenging than the development of the knowledge base. First, preliminary data collection screens that naturally derived from the available knowledge base were developed. Because this knowledge base was content-specific, the content of these preliminary screens was also somewhat, but not exclusively, content-specific. When various workers reviewed the initial prototype for these screens, however, it became apparent that workers wanted situation-specific screens. The challenge was to develop situation-specific screens from a content-specific knowledge base. Through an ongoing feedback procedure with workers, these initial screens were finalized.

The next critical step was to link the content-specific text to the situation-specific program. This was done, rather tediously, by linking each available option in the program to the applicable information in the knowledge base. First, the knowledge base was reduced to its smallest possible units, eventually including hundreds of sets of information. Next, the sets of information relevant to each checkbox on the data collection screens were grouped. For many checkboxes, the relevant sets often encompassed multiple pages of text. These larger topic areas were then further subdivided into smaller categories, again with the relevant sets of information grouped within category. For example, the multiple sets of information applicable to mental impairment were categorized into assessment of violence potential, delusional clients, and techniques. The end product was 160 different categories of information.

Once the physical knowledge base had all relevant links established, these then had to be integrated into the WSA program. Because of the large number of categories, to prevent the worker from being overwhelmed with text, the output delimiter screen was necessitated to narrow the choices of the user. This screen made available all options checked on the previous data collection screen, as well as all categories available for each option. Because multiple screens fed into the output delimiter screen, it had to be programmed to display from one to over 100 checkboxes in any combination. Designing a screen that could contain so many checkboxes and then programming it for the infinite number of combinations proved challenging. It soon became apparent that Authorware was not developed for such complex programming tasks.

The final important stage was to develop the output page. This screen not only had to display the choices selected on the previous screen, but also had to provide on-demand access to the appropriate pages of output, along with their applicable hotword, scenario, and escalation screen links. First, the 160 categories of possible output were copied individually from the manual into the program. Because .rtf text files converted so poorly into Authorware Ver. 3.5, what should have been easy was tedious and time-consuming. (This problem is less apparent in Authorware 4.0.) To access these categories of information on the final output screen, 160 corresponding headers (hidden unless the applicable box on the data collection screen was checked) were created. Links between these headers and the relevant categories of text were then established. Next, all 160 categories of text were scrutinized for three possible linkages. First, scenarios had to be linked to each relevant category of text. Second, a link to the escalation animation was created for all text referring to a potentially escalating client. Third, text was reviewed for jargon or other words not commonly understood. Approximately 170 words that needed greater clarification were found. For these "hotwords," a brief definition, example, and other relevant information were written and then copied, individually, into the WSA program. Finally, all hotwords on all output pages were linked to their applicable text.

The linking of the hotwords to the pages of output and of the output to the applicable checkboxes were easily the most arduous and time-consuming programming tasks. While much of this process was necessitated due to the design of the program (i.e., maximum utilization of a minimum number of screens), it was made more difficult because data collection screens were situation-specific.

Throughout this development process, formal methods of assessing the functionality of the WSA program were employed. Formal assessment occurred in four ways. First, the WSA was demonstrated to several workers individually. Second, a prototype was demonstrated to a group of 30 workers for feedback. A brief post session questionnaire using both open- and close-ended questions was also administered. Next, the WSA screens were presented to the staff at CPSTI and TDPRS for their comments and approval. Finally, students in a technology course reviewed and evaluated the WSA. Feedback gathered from all processes was used to modify the program so that it was more "user-friendly" and more specific to workers' needs. This process was extremely important for screen design. For example, we found that workers preferred fewer, more complex screens rather than many simpler, linked screens.

LESSONS LEARNED

Perhaps the biggest surprise in the development of the WSA was the amount and proportion of time spent in converting content-specific information into a situation-specific program. Probably 65% to 75% of the actual development time was spent in preparing the knowledge base and then linking it to the program. Having a previously developed manual that could be reformatted for multimedia presentation would surely cut developmental time somewhat, although linking the knowledge base to the program will remain an imposing task. Those developing similar applications should do a thorough assessment of the completeness and quality of the information and how difficult it will be to convert the information into a format the PSS can use. They should make their sponsors realize how time consuming knowledge base development can be. Codifying available information into a PSS knowledge base is a critical task because a PSS is only as good as the knowledge it contains.

Another surprise was the difficulty in working with Authorware (see Bolen, 1997 for a formal review of Authorware). While certain of its features enhanced the developmental process, its limitations continued to require complicated work-arounds for the roadblocks encountered.

The most challenging aspect of development was designing and programming the PSS. The necessity of providing quick on-demand access to a large knowledge base increased the complexity of the project geometrically. We had to access a large knowledge base with a limited number of screens while maximizing the usability of each screen. This programming challenge is best typified by the final output screen and the output delimiter screen. The output delimiter screen had to display up to 100 checkboxes in an infinite number of combinations. The final output screen had to link approximately 330 individual pieces of output to their applicable headers.

Several other lessons deserve to be mentioned.

- Expect resistance from trainers who rightly fear that management will be tempted to cut the training budget after several PSS modules are developed.
- Take time to investigate your choice of software. You will have to live with it for years to come. Our criteria, future agency support and enhancements, was probably not the best reason to select the software. The agency currently is not using Authorware and does not have the capacity to support Authorware applications.
- Select software that keeps up with the latest developments, such as use of the Internet.
- Use a prototyping development process. That is, develop a "quick and dirty" prototype that is presented to management and end users for feedback.
- Set up mechanisms to quickly obtain clarification on issues from top-level decision makers and users throughout the organization. We continually faced development and implementation issues that required decisions that cut across departments and levels of staff, e.g., allowing worker intranet access or testing of the PSS module in one region. These crosscutting issues are the most difficult to resolve, e.g., how and when to test the module in an actual work environment.
- Continue to get feedback to insure that the system meets the needs of the end user.
- Be careful when budgeting resources. PSS efforts grow as those involved understand the nature of the supporting information needed. Being locked into a rigid contract can result in an unsatisfactory product.

Our project evolved and escalated because workers liked the prototype and requested further development. Most further developments involved enhancing the knowledge base rather than screen redesign. However, we still have not formally tested the program or knowledge base in a real work setting. Future efforts involve testing the WSA in a work environment to determine who uses it, what type of situations workers seek advice on, and what type of information is most useful or missing. We are especially interested to know whether the WSA will be used by both new and experienced workers.

CONCLUSION

The WSA is a complex program housed in simplicity. With only a small number of screens, workers can quickly obtain a selection, from over 400 pages of information, that is customized to their situation. They are also a mouse click away from relevant help, scenarios, and other useful information. From this respect, the WSA achieved the PSS goal of providing on-demand access to a knowledge base when it is needed, where it is needed, and in the format in which it is needed.

Perhaps the biggest conclusion is that putting specialized human services expertise and advice into a computer program is powerful. With today's technology, that advice can be customized and delivered around the world in minutes. However, automating meaningful advice in a substantive human service area is a difficult task that is best approached as a long term reiterative process of development, demonstration, and evaluation. Not surprisingly, the most substantial task is collecting and categorizing the human services advice rather than putting the advice into technology.

AUTHOR NOTE

The Worker Safety Advisor was developed through a contract between the U. of Texas at Arlington (UTA), Judith Granger Birmingham Center for Child Welfare and the Children's Protective Services Training Institute (CPSTI), Center for Social Work Research at the University of Texas at Austin. The Texas Department of Protective and Regulatory Services (TDPRS), Child Protective Services Program funded the project. Those providing assistance include Carol Kahler, Sheila Kendricks, Eric Hendricks, Russel Louer, and Jerry Toops (UTA). The worker safety knowledge base was reviewed by Joan Rycraft, Jo Ann Coe, Pat Newlin (UTA), Anna Rae Rozell, Paul McClean (TDPRS), Joan Richardson, Sondera Malry (U. of Houston), Doug O'Dell, and Diane Irwin, Safe and Sound program, New York.

REFERENCES

Bolen, R. M. (1997). Macromedia Authorware. *Computers in Human Services, 14*(1), 77-84.

Grey, G. J. (1991). Electronic performance support systems. Boston: Weingarten.

Leung, P. (1993). Interviewing strategies for child protective service workers: A multimedia computer-based training program. Austin, TX: Children's Protective Training Institute.

MacFadden, R. (1997). Software review: Keisha. *Computers in Human Services, 14*(2), 51-56.

Miller, L. S. (1993). The optimum allocation of in-home supportive-type services in the multipurpose senior services program. *Computers in Human Services, 9*(1/2), 111-135.

Reynolds, A. & Araya, R. (1995). Building multimedia performance support systems. New York: McGraw Hill.

Satterwhite, R., & Schoech, D. (1995). Multimedia training for Child Protective Service Workers: Results of initial development and testing. *Computers in Human Services, 12*(1/2), 81-97.

Schoech, D. (1996). Performance support systems: Integrating information technology under practitioner control. *Computers in Human Services, 13*(3), 1-18.

Changing to Learn:
Learning to Change

Jackie Rafferty

SUMMARY. This paper provides an overview of the use of 'communication and information technologies' (C&IT) in social work education in Britain. It outlines the development of the use of 'learning technologies' generally, and focuses specifically, on the impact of 'learning technology' in social work education and training. It looks at various factors influential in achieving, or blocking, cultural change in higher education, which may be of interest to social work educators in other countries. *[Article copies available for a fee from The Haworth Document Delivery Service: 1-800-342-9678. E-mail address: getinfo@haworthpressinc.com]*

KEYWORDS. Social work education, communication and information technology, cultural change, organisational change

INTRODUCTION

This paper describes how communication and information technology (C&IT) is being promoted and used within British social work education and

---

Jackie Rafferty is Senior Research Fellow, University of Southampton, UK. She is the Director of the Centre for Human Service Technology which hosts a range of communication and information technology projects within the human services.

Address correspondence to: Jackie Rafferty, Centre for Human Service Technology, Department of Social Work Studies, University of Southampton, Southampton SO17 1BJ. E-mail: jr@chst.soton.ac.uk

[Haworth co-indexing entry note]: "Changing to Learn: Learning to Change." Rafferty, Jackie. Co-published simultaneously in *Computers in Human Services* (The Haworth Press, Inc.) Vol. 15, No. 2/3, 1998, pp. 159-169; and: *Information Technologies: Teaching to Use–Using to Teach* (ed: Frank B. Raymond III, Leon Ginsberg, and Debra Gohagan) The Haworth Press, Inc., 1998, pp. 159-169. Single or multiple copies of this article are available for a fee from The Haworth Document Delivery Service [1-800-342-9678, 9:00 a.m. - 5:00 p.m. (EST). E-mail address: getinfo@haworthpressinc.com]

training. It begins by looking at the role of centralised developments across disciplines in higher education.

BACKGROUND TO UK HIGHER EDUCATION USE OF 'LEARNING TECHNOLOGY'

In Britain, in 1982, the Universities Funding Council commissioned the Nelson report on 'Computer facilities for teaching in universities' (Nelson, 1983). The report dealt with the hardware infrastructure issues which would ensure that British universities were prepared for an increasingly information rich technology environment. The report identified: "serious shortages in the provision of workstations for use in teaching in universities, and in the support of those workstations with software and skilled staff. Countries such as the USA, Japan and Germany were at that time apparently doing much better." (Gershuny & Slater, 1989). At this stage the introduction of computers in higher education was seen as necessary by senior managers in higher education to remain competitive but there was no clearly elucidated pedagogical rationale. The 'Nelson' report led to funding being made available for the Computers in Teaching Initiative (CTI). This in turn led to the first phase of CTI funded projects (139 in all) whose remit was fourfold:

1. To promote greater awareness amongst academics, administrators and students in all disciplines and at all universities of the potential of information technology to enhance the teaching and learning process.
2. To facilitate development within universities of skills in the use of computers in the teaching process.
3. Encourage the development of . . . using computers to assist the learning process by the provision or production of appropriate courseware.
4. Finally, to evaluate the potential of, and subsequently to assess the hardware, software and organisational requirements for the successful introduction of information technology.

The programme of initiatives was carried out between 1985 and 1987 and a summary of the programme identified achievements and challenges (Information Systems Committee Courseware Development Working Party, 1992). The emphasis throughout the programme was on finding or developing teaching applications for computers and 63% of the projects produced software. A major finding was that single institution developments, although significant in themselves, had limited transferability.

A follow-up initiative was funded to address the transferability issue. Social work did not feature in Phase 1 of CTI and there was only one social science project. It was not until Phase 2 of CTI that social work and related disciplines were included when Bryan Glastonbury from the University of Southampton bid for the CTI Centre for Human Services. The bid was successful and the centre was set up in 1989 as one of 21 discipline based centres.[1]

The Phase 2 centres had two main aims. Firstly, the dissemination of information on the software and services available. Second, the development of national subject communities with common interests in sharing their computing experience to achieve economies of scale and ownership of innovation (Gershuny & Slater, 1989). The second phase of CTI was expressly excluded from developing software for teaching and learning.

LEARNING TECHNOLOGY AND SOCIAL WORK EDUCATION 1989–1996

A survey carried out by the CTI Centre for Human Services in 1989 revealed social work teachers were using computers to word-process and undertake statistical analysis for research purposes, and a handful were teaching students how to use office tools such as word-processors, databases and spreadsheets. A few were, however, making imaginative teaching use of software developed for social work agencies, such as welfare benefit calculation programs.

The mission of the CTI Centre for Human Services is to maintain and enhance the quality of learning, and increase the effectiveness of teaching, through the application of appropriate learning technologies and by providing a national information and development service.

CTI Human Services does this by:

- seeking and disseminating good practice;
- answering individual enquiries;
- providing workshops, visits and conferences;
- publishing electronic and paper based material;
- supporting change agents;
- building good relationships with teachers and developers; and
- being aware of and involved in national & international developments.

In 1989, before the growth of communications technologies and the Internet, an anomaly between the mission statement and the reality soon became apparent. The vision of senior managers in higher education had been of a large range of computerised teaching materials available. All CTI Phase 2 projects needed to do was to let their education communities know about its availability. The anomaly was that there was hardly any computerised teaching materials available within the human services. There were programs developed for practice to support practitioners, but they rapidly became out-dated as they had been developed on computers such as the Sinclair ZX, BBC Microcomputer, Acorn, etc. The programs were not updated, and as MS-DOS became the norm within higher education, there was little software information for the centre to disseminate. There was also only a handful of social work academics interested in information technology. The CTI Centres were funded to employ one full time co-ordinator and this was thought to be sufficient to meet the dissemination aims. With hindsight it is apparent that one worker would have some difficulty achieving change within the teaching culture of a subject community across England, Scotland, Wales and Northern Ireland.

Nevertheless, with the support of motivated teachers the Centre began to develop a workshop programme and information dissemination network that has become a major factor in helping the social work teachers to integrate the use of learning technology within their courses. The methods used were borrowed from community development practices. Teachers who were potential 'change agents' were identified and provided with the support required to enable them to gain ground within their department.

For example, a motivated teacher would invite the centre to provide a day's workshop and, with their Head of Department's support, ensure that the majority of the department attended. The facilitators would arrive the day before and load relevant software onto the network and make sure the technology worked, a task which should not be underestimated in terms of time and negotiation skills to achieve. The workshop would provide a safe opportunity for those without either the skill or the interest in learning technology to perceive the added value that the technology could provide. The workshop would also look at the institutional support, how the teaching was structured, and work together to produce a set of short-term and longer-term goals for integrating learning technology. This role of convincing the unconvinced that learning technology is relevant to them has become much easier as the World Wide Web has developed. It is now possible for teachers to search for their own subject specialism and find useful sources on the subject in a way that was impossible only two years ago. The Centre has developed a set of web pages called 'Social Work on the Web'[2] expressly for this purpose and it has become an important gateway to information for both teachers and students.

The workshop programme is backed up by newsletters, the journal *New Technology in the Human Services*[3] and a frequently used e-mail and telephone enquiry service. The web pages also hold the Centre's *Resource Guide*[4] that is a listing of all the software currently relevant to British social work education and training.

The CTI mission statement has remained constant since 1989 yet debate continues over what is meant by the phrases 'enhance the quality of learning' or 'increase the effectiveness of teaching.' Initially it was clear that senior managers expected 'effectiveness' to involve financial savings and this is still a longer-term goal. A comparison problem remains. Measuring the effectiveness of learning technology requires measurement of the effectiveness of traditional teaching and learning methods such as lectures and seminars. This can be done with some difficulty using a cost benefit analysis but it is proving much more difficult to measure 'learning' in higher education.

DEVELOPING LEARNING MATERIALS

In 1992, a further national higher education initiative was announced, inviting bids for courseware development, and CTI Human Services was obviously keen to see projects within social work funded (UFC, 1992). Applications were made but none succeeded until the second round of bids in 1993. One of the criteria for success in the bidding process was a large undergraduate student body. It was clear that the numbers of social work students were not enough to support a successful bid so a link was made with the nursing disciplines. An application led by Bournemouth University was submitted for development of courseware across both nursing and social work. During the course of bid preparation, research was undertaken into which elements of the curricula were common across the disciplines. The research identified the curriculum areas of interpersonal skills development and research methods. Thus Procare was born, a joint project between CTI Human Services' parent centre–the Centre for Human Service Technology (CHST) at the University of Southampton–and the Institute for Health and Community Studies, Bournemouth University (Hopkins, 1997). During this period CHST also undertook the development of a *Social Work & Information Technology* courseware module to fill the perceived gap of materials to support social work lecturers teaching the use of information technology in practice.

During the development period of the materials described above (1994-1996), further technology-based materials became available from the Social Service and Research Development Unit (SSRADU) based at the University of Bath. These materials covered the UK Children's Act of 1989 and child protection research (*Child Care Information System*). Also significant was the development of on-line and CD-ROM based resources such as *Child Data* and *Caredata* and other social science abstracting services.

As access to suitable hardware became easier for social work teachers and students, e-mail achieved the critical mass to allow discussion groups and bulletin boards to become useful tools for the exchange and sharing of information. Literature on learning technology also became more plentiful with its focus on pedagogy, technology and implementation and integration issues (Laurillard, 1993, Martin & Beetham, 1997).

SOCIAL WORK EDUCATION, HIGHER EDUCATION AND LEARNING TECHNOLOGY IN 1997

There has been a massive shift in the use of information technology in all forms of organisations during the lifetime of the CTIs. Therefore, although a simple cause and effect could be hypothesised with the CTI Human Services work as the only variable in terms of the changes in teaching practice from 1989 to 1997, this would be extremely misleading. CTI's role has been in supporting and guiding changes that have there own impetus and agenda. A range of factors have come together to support changes in teaching and learning methodologies and the process of change has still a long way to go. Availability of suitable hardware and software and support services are not enough in itself to change the culture of higher education. This section of the paper looks at current practice, the lessons learned, and at some of the challenges still facing higher education social work in Britain.

Social work education and training is undergoing transition, as is higher education. Qualifying courses for probation officers (US Correction/Parole Officers) have already been separated from the traditional link with the social work qualifying body, the Central Council for Education and Training in Social Work (CCETSW). In 1996 the Conservative government, which was then in power, removed probation and offender qualifying training from higher education and placed responsibility with the Probation Services. The Labour Government, which took office in May 1997, is reviewing the provision of Probation training again but meanwhile has also instigated reviews of CCETSW and social work.

CCETSW has been in the forefront of developing and implementing a system of National Vocational Qualifications (NVQs) for social work, which is based on a 'competence' approach at different levels (CCETSW, 1993). Levels 1 and 2 equate to a social care qualification aimed at front-line care staff such as residential home workers and social work support staff such as home care workers. A Level 4 NVQ is being developed which would equate with the Diploma in Social Work, the qualifying award for professional social workers. The Diploma can already be obtained with or without a first degree and all the awards pose alternative routes to that preferred by academics, i.e., the Masters of Social Science award with the Diploma in Social Work. The NVQ curricula are seen by some academics as mechanistic and undermining of the theoretical discipline of social work. This scenario surrounding social work education and training supports many academics' perceptions of learning technology as equally mechanistic and threatening to the academic base of social work. The

CTI role is important in challenging those perceptions and demonstrating how learning technology can support both skill and theoretical learning.

Meanwhile, higher education has also experienced considerable change with more accountability within the structures. In addition, there is the need for a broadening of access to higher education, with fewer resources having to meet the requirements of a growing student body. The past 20 years have seen a doubling of student numbers, with a 40% reduction in the unit of public funding per student. New management practices have become familiar to higher education and rest uneasily alongside the traditional autonomy of academics. Despite the pressure on academics to find ways of coping with their teaching load, the one 'driver' for a successful university department remains their research productivity and quality ratings. Whilst this remains the case, there are no 'carrots' to encourage teachers to adopt new teaching methodologies.

Managers of higher education have seen learning technology as an important element in delivering education to the increased number of students without raising the staff teaching resource. Understandably, teachers were less than enthusiastic to embrace measures that were seen to support cost cutting measures without being convinced that quality and learning effectiveness would not be impaired. It has become clear that 'throwing' learning technology at higher education is not the answer and a range of innovation and change has to be implemented and managed.

> Institutions of higher education have often adopted what Hammond and Trapp (1992) call a 'minimalist approach' when implementing new technology and subsequently, rather than re-evaluating or re-structuring practices and procedures, educational managers have tended to simply place such technology over existing organisational structures. (Henry & Rafferty, 1995)

It is therefore a signal of the strength of the new learning technologies that there have nevertheless been substantial developments within social work education in Britain. In 1997, social work teachers are using communication and information technology for:

- Courseware to support the curriculum.
- CMC–computer mediated communication.
- Library searches and bookings.
- Bulletin boards–or 'Intranets' to post course timetables, notices, etc.
- Student registration and information systems.
- Practice placement databases + on-line support.
- Video-conferencing.
- Teaching using the WWW and 'MANs' (Metropolitan Area Networks).

Students meanwhile are not subject to the dilemmas affecting academics and the last 5 years has seen a substantial change in the IT skill level of social work students. In 1992, approximately 80% of a course's intake would have little or no computer experience. Now 70% do have familiarity with at least word-processing and they are quick to take opportunities to use communication and information technology for:

- Using courseware at home, on site, or in the workplace.
- Word-processing assignments.
- Searching libraries and bibliographic databases.
- E-mail to keep in touch with peers, tutors, friends and family.
- WWW–as a means of information and resource exploration.
- Discussion lists and bulletin boards.
- Job searches and self promotion through the WWW.

Social work educators are generally using learning technology as an adjunct to their normal teaching methods, since to fully integrate the technology requires a much more radical approach to restructuring the timetable and curriculum. Such changes impact on the role of educators to as they move from being ". . . 'directors of learning' (or information deliverers) to that of 'facilitator of learning' (or curriculum designer)" (McCaffery, 1997).

A framework for learning technology use within the social work curriculum may be helpful. It is possible to differentiate between:

- learning information technology skills;
- learning about the use of information technology in social work practice (social informatics); and
- using learning technology to learn social work skills and knowledge (Steyaert et al., 1996).

Equally, a framework for learning technology use within social work education and training, as well as elsewhere, should promote social work 'values.' There is an agenda that includes concerns about the potential for misuse and promotes a commitment to ethical use of personal data and empowering modes of working. This agenda would include an appreciation of differing learning styles, user control and anti-oppressive practice. The agenda is much broader than learning technology within social work and there is a role for social work to influence both their own practice and the IT industry. Glastonbury and LaMendola's book, *Integrity of Intelligence* (1993), set out a 'Bill of Rights' which remains apposite.

THE DEARING REPORT

In the 15 years since the first phase of CTI, the learning technology community has become clearer about the elements needed to integrate learning technology effectively into higher education. These have been confirmed and defined in what is known as the 'Dearing Report' (The National Committee of Inquiry into Higher Education Report *'Higher Education in the Learning Society'* http://www.ncl.ac.uk/ncihe/natrep.htm).

In summary, the elements can be categorised as requiring:

- clarity about the role and function of learning technology within HE;
- a critical mass of learning technology resources (WWW, courseware, videoconferencing, etc.);
- technical infrastructure and support;
- staff development, training and, newly on the agenda, accreditation; and
- management of the process of innovation and change, both institutionally and within the discipline.

There have been a range of short-term projects that have addressed elements of the above to a limited extent. CTI itself was seen as a short term initiative. The 'Dearing Report' sees the need to integrate these issues into the context of whole organisational change. The report also states that there is a continuing role for discipline-related support within a 'learning society.' Unless most of the report's recommendations are implemented, the following areas will continue to be problematic in terms of reaching the aim of integrating learning technology into higher education.

The recurrent themes for higher education are:

- the cost of providing up-to-date computers, networks and support;
- integration into the curriculum (including practice elements for social work);
- technical advice and support;
- facilitative change agents;
- incentives to change;
- staff training and development;
- avoiding a piecemeal approach to development;
- research into learning effectiveness; and
- issues of collaboration, co-operation and competitiveness.

CONCLUSION

Most social work courses in higher education in Britain now include elements of learning technology but development is still piecemeal and dependent upon 'champions' within faculties. What is taking place is evolution not revolution, with learning technology being placed over existing frameworks and structures. There are signs that a more radical re-appraisal of teaching and learning within higher education will need to be taken or learning technology will remain an adjunct to traditional teaching methods. What is required is a range of innovative teaching and learning styles that can support students' learning in an effective way. The 'Dearing Report' is important, as it provides influential evidence backing the CTI message. The report also emphasised future developments and there are already experiments in the global university being conducted by higher education institutions that offer distance learning over the Internet. Modularised open and distance learning, alongside lifelong learning, give weight to the credit accumulation and transfer systems which the NVQ competency based approach favours. It will be interesting to see whether traditional social work education based on a theoretical academic platform survives into the next century.

NOTES

1. Three other centres represent neighbouring disciplines to social work: CTI Centre for Sociology, Social Policy and the Policy Sciences, CTI Centre for Psychology and CTI Centre for Nursing and Midwifery.
2. 'Social Work on the Web'–http://www.soton.ac.uk/~chst
3. 'New Technology in the Human Services'–http://www.soton.ac.uk/~chst/
4. 'Resource Guide'–http://www.soton.ac.uk/~chst/ctiinf.htm

REFERENCES

CCETSW, (1993) *National Vocational Qualifications: Awards in Criminal Justice Service at Level 4*, London.

Gershuny J., and Slater J., (1989) *Computers in Teaching Initiative Report*, CTISS.

Glastonbury, B., & LaMendola, W., (1992) *Integrity of Intelligence: A Bill of Rights for the Information Age*, St. Martins Press.

Henry, M.S., & Rafferty, J., (1995) Equality and CAL in Higher Education, *Journal of Computer Assisted Learning*, No. 11.

Hammond, N., & Trapp, A., (1992) CAL as a Trojan Horse for Educational Change: The case of Psychology, *Computers and Education*, 19, 1/2.

Hopkins, T., (1997) *Developing competence through technology: Computer assisted learning for professional practice*, Paper presented at Using to Teach–Teaching to Use, Information Technologies for Social Work Education Conference, South Carolina. September 1997.

Information Systems Committee Courseware Development Working Party, (1992) *Beyond Lectures*, CTISS Publications, Oxford, UK.

Laurillard, D., (1993) *Rethinking University Teaching: A framework for the effective use of educational technology*, Routledge.

McCafferty, P., (October, 1997) University Challenge, *People Management*, Institute of Personnel and Development, Personnel Publications Ltd., London.

Martin, J., & Beetham, H., (Eds.) (July, 1997) Embedding Technology into teaching: Achieving institutional change, *Active Learning*, No. 6, CTISS Publications, Oxford, UK.

National Committee of Inquiry into Higher Education Report, (1997) *Higher Education in the Learning Society.* (The Dearing Report). Full report available at http://www.leeds.ac.uk/educol/ncihe/

Nelson, D., (Chair) (1983) Report of a Working Party on Computer Facilities for Teaching in Universities, Computer Board for Universities and Research Councils, UK.

Steyaert, J., Colombi, D.P.C. and Rafferty, J., (1996) *Human Services and Information Technology: An International Perspective*, Arena.

Universities Funding Council, (March, 1992) *Teaching and learning technology programme.* Circular 8/92, UFC, Bristol.

APPENDIX

CTI Centres

CTI Centre for Human Service Technology
WWW: http://www.soton.ac.uk/~chst

CTI Centre for Sociology, Social Policy and the Policy Sciences
WWW: http://www.stir.ac.uk/socinfo/

CTI Centre for Psychology
WWW: http://www.york.ac.uk/inst/ctipsych/

CTI Centre for Nursing and Midwifery
WWW: http://www.shef.ac.uk/uni/projects/ctinm/

Courseware

Details of all the courseware mentioned in the paper can be found in the CTI Human Services Resource Guide at http://www.soton.ac.uk/~chst/direct.htm

Journal

Subscription and author information for the international, refereed journal *New Technology in the Human Services* can be obtained from: Mary Busby, Centre for Human Service Technology, Department of Social Work Studies, University of Southampton, Southampton SO17 1BJ, UK. E-mail: mary@chst.soton.ac.uk

Information Technology
and Social Work Education in Malaysia:
Challenges and Prospects

Gabriel Chong

SUMMARY. Given the current stage of development of social work in Malaysia, the potential of harnessing the advancements in information technology (IT) for the development of social work education in Malaysia is immense. However, there are multiple barriers to cross before reaching this potential. *[Article copies available for a fee from The Haworth Document Delivery Service: 1-800-342-9678. E-mail address: getinfo@ haworthpressinc.com]*

KEYWORDS. Malaysia, social work education, information technology

INTRODUCTION

The development of Malaysia in the last decade has brought about many changes. Modernization, affluence and materialism have affected the lives

Gabriel Chong, MSW, is Social Work Lecturer, Faculty of Social Sciences, University Malaysia, Sarawak, 94300 Kota Samarahan, Sarawak, Malaysia (E-mail: gchong@mailhost.unnimas.my).

The author would like to thank Dr. Leon Ginsberg for encouraging him to submit an abstract and to write this paper for the conference. The author also thanks Professor Allan Wicker and Gill Raja for their comments and feedback on the paper, and Janice Kaur-Munster for proofreading the final draft. The author would also like to express his gratitude to Universiti Malaysia Sarawak for financial assistance and support.

[Haworth co-indexing entry note]: "Information Technology and Social Work Education in Malaysia: Challenges and Prospects." Chong, Gabriel. Co-published simultaneously in *Computers in Human Services* (The Haworth Press, Inc.) Vol. 15, No. 2/3, 1998, pp. 171-184; and: *Information Technologies: Teaching to Use–Using to Teach* (ed: Frank B. Raymond III, Leon Ginsberg, and Debra Gohagan) The Haworth Press, Inc., 1998, pp. 171-184. Single or multiple copies of this article are available for a fee from The Haworth Document Delivery Service [1-800-342-9678, 9:00 a.m. - 5:00 p.m. (EST). E-mail address: getinfo@ haworthpressinc.com]

171

and values of its people. While the benefits have been evident, societal problems have also increasingly come into the spotlight and are being addressed by government and community groups. Though there is still the question of accuracy of reporting, there has been a rise in the number of reported cases of child abuse, abandoned babies, domestic violence, drug abuses and sexual offenses. This awareness of social problems has created an opportunity for social workers to play a more central role in assisting in the development of the country. However, as will be noted, social, cultural and political factors have adversely affected the development of the profession.

In contrast, Information Technology (IT) has been at the forefront of the country's agenda in the recent years. This paper presents an argument that IT can be used as a catalyst to develop and enhance the social work profession in Malaysia.

MALAYSIA

Malaya declared its independence from its British Colonial ruler on August 31, 1957 and became Malaysia six years later with the inclusion of Singapore (which became independent in 1965), Sabah and Sarawak. In the last several years it has exploded onto the international scene as a country to be recognised. Led by a dynamic Prime Minister with an aggressive plan for Malaysia to achieve the status of an industrialized country by the year 2020, the country has gone from a primarily agrarian society to one of the fastest growing and most economically successful countries in Asia.

Malaysia has a population estimated at just over 20.56 million in 1996 (Star, 1997), spread over a land area of 330,434 sq. km. It is a multiracial society with the majority being Bumiputras. Bumiputra literally means 'sons of the soil' and is comprised of Malays and indigenous people such as the Ibans, Bidayuhs and Kadazans. Together, this group makes up 56% of the population. Chinese and Indians comprise 26% and 8% respectively. Islam is the national religion, though other religions are allowed to be freely practiced. It is governed by a coalition of component parties, with the Malay UMNO party in control of the coalition. Opposition parties exist but have little influence or impact. The ruling coalition has not lost its two thirds majority since Independence. This multiethnic coalition has been the political answer to maintaining racial harmony since the race riots of October 13, 1969.

For eight uninterrupted years, the economy has grown at 8% per annum. Malaysia's current annual per capita GDP is estimated at USD2076,[1] with a projected annual growth rate of 5.5% to the year 2000. Mean monthly income between 1990-1995 grew at a rate of 9.5% from USD416 to USD716 (Malaysia, 1996). Programmes targeted at reducing the number of people living in poverty have been aggressively introduced and have shown successful results. The poverty rate has rapidly declined since Independence from 16.5% in 1957 to 8.9% for 1990-1995. Poverty eradication efforts have come in the form of positive discrimination and income-generating agricultural projects aimed at the rural poor. However, critics charge that these programmes, deliberately targeting poor Bumiputras to address structural racial inequalities, have neglected poverty among the Chinese and Indians (Featured Article, 1989). Today, the policy of income redistribution among the races has been substantially achieved.[2] However, the disparity between the ratio of haves and have nots has become greater. A study by the United Nations Development Programme indicated that Malaysia has the largest disparity between the rich and the poor among Asian countries (Loh, 1996).[3]

The country has embarked on several development agendas closely linked to social work. Vision 2020 is the Prime Minister's master plan to propel Malaysia into becoming an internationally recognised industrialized nation and a caring society. According to this plan, the development of Malaysia into an industrialized country will be holistic, taking into account the development of strong moral and ethical values: the strengthening of a democratic society that is liberal, tolerant, civic, caring, economically just and equitable. The New Development Policy (NDP) which is the government's plan for 1990-2000, seeks to build upon poverty eradication and the restructuring of society by correcting the remaining racial economic imbalances through generating income and creating wealth among the Bumiputras.

Malaysia hopes to develop into a "Caring Society" by developing a caring attitude amongst its citizens towards the "less fortunate" and to minimize the negative consequences of industrialization. Though expounded by politicians, this theme has been more political rhetoric than substance. The existence of professionals in developing effective caring services and programmes in a variety of sectors, such as for people in drug rehabilitation, people living with AIDS, children and adults with special needs and the elderly, are still very much wanting. The role of the family is greatly emphasized, yet infrastructural support by government to family is minimal. Disparities in the allocation of the federal budget is reflected by Jaysooria (1992) who cited the work of Sushama (1985) to affirm this point. Between 1974-1984, although the allocation of the federal budget increased three-fold, it still only accounted for 0.23% of the total federal budget.

SOCIAL WORK IN MALAYSIA

Though social work has been practiced in Malaysia since colonial days, the profession has yet to gain recognition or status. The term "social worker" is still used loosely in the community to apply to anyone who spends time doing charitable work for those who are considered marginalised in profession terms, or "less fortunate" by the public. Ismail Baba (1995) summarizes the history of the profession as starting from 1912, when a special department was created to attend to the well being of migrant laborers. Abandoned in the 1930s, this department was resurrected again in 1937 as the Social Service Department within the Colonial Office. The Department of Social Welfare was established in 1946, and later became the Ministry of Social Welfare in 1964. The Ministry of Health also developed medical social workers as early as 1952.

Currently there are three universities in Malaysia offering Bachelors in Social Sciences with specialization in social work. The oldest, and the only one which is accredited by the International Association of Schools of Social Work (IASSW), is Universiti Sains Malaysia (USM) located in Penang. It was first established in 1975 and was originally known as the Department of Social Development and Administration. The other universities started offering social work courses much later. Universiti Malaysia Sarawak (UNIMAS) established its programme in 1993 and had its first graduating class of 12 in August, 1997. Universiti Utara Malaysia (UUM) has just started its programme in 1998 with an enrolment of 60 students, the majority of which are probation officers. Two other universities in the country are in the planning stages of offering social work programmes.

The government is the largest employer of social workers. However, funding and proper training for human resources development have not kept up with the needs of the profession and society. Between 1976-1977, almost 70% of welfare personnel were not fully trained in social work (Siti Hawa, 1985). A more recent assessment of the situation indicates that only 50% of professional and 20% of semi-professional staff have had any formal social work or human development based training (Jeshurun, 1995).[4] A vicious circle therefore exists. As social workers are perceived as bureaucrats having minimal effective impact on social problems, there is no momentum to increase their numbers and quality. The professionals within the government sector are left to grapple with tasks beyond their resources. In Jeshurun's review, there were 125 managers and 295 semi-professional staff covering a population of 18.2 million in Peninsular Malaysia, and 2.4 million in Sabah and Sarawak where only a few federal staff are employed to augment state employees (Malaysia, 1996). It is therefore not surprising that this has caused an image crisis for the social work profession, which has stunted its development in Malaysia.

Non-Governmental Organisations (NGOs), which are comparable to non-profit groups in the United States, play a very important role in providing services to marginalised communities. NGOs are divided into basically two groups in Malaysia, service provision groups and social justice/advocate groups. Though we are moving towards a new century, NGOs involved in social work provision in Malaysia continue to operate with an institutional and charity mindset. The number of trained social workers in NGOs is unknown, but it is quite certain to be low. The low remuneration and minimal or no benefits, are major barriers for NGOs to attract trained social workers to this important area.

Social workers, who are also referred to as welfare officers *(Pegawai Kebajikan)*, are seen as people who give money and material goods to the poor, aged, disabled and marginalised groups. Unlike social workers in developed countries, in Malaysia social workers have rarely led the way in addressing policy issues or social problems despite the renaming of the Ministry of Welfare to the Ministry of Social Development and National Unity. This can be partly due to four factors:

1. The Malaysian Association of Social Workers (MASW) was established in 1973, but was not registered as an organisation till March 28, 1974. It is an affiliated member of the International Federation of Social Workers (IFSW) but it has not been active in advocating for more humane, progressive legislation and agendas. The direction of the professional association is also very unclear.
2. There is a small number of professional social workers in the country. Currently, the Malaysian Association of Social Workers has only about 60 members scattered across the country. It is therefore not surprising that its activities are limited.
3. There is a lack of transparency within the Malaysian political system. This prevents people from being part of the democratic process. An example is the current effort to privatize health care in Malaysia: the Malaysian Medical Association, despite its size and status, has not been able to access any of the consultative reports, estimated to be at least 5 in number, that were written for the government, despite repeated requests (Chan, 1997).
4. Culturally and politically, a social action agenda is not the traditional Malaysian way of addressing issues, especially contentious ones. Dialogue behind closed doors is the norm which accounts in part for the lack of transparency. To play an effective role in such dialogues, social workers need more professional credibility and public recognition.

SOCIAL WORK EDUCATION AND POTENTIAL USES OF IT

Given the large number of untrained social workers, as noted by Siti and Jeshurun earlier, it is imperative that social work education in Malaysia includes current workers in the field. In the current thrust of Malaysia's development, IT is a tool that can play a significant role.

In Malaysia, IT has been identified as the key ingredient needed to propel the country into the status of a developed nation by the year 2020. Currently ranked 35th in a new "information society index" of 55 countries by the International Data Corporation, the country is considered less developed as a technology center compared to its regional neighbors such as Singapore, Taiwan, Japan and Korea (Kraar, 1997).

The 7th Malaysia Plan intends to overcome this low standing by developing an IT infrastructure in order to create a strong foundation for building a knowledge-based industrial economy and information-rich society. The Multimedia Super Corridor (MSC) project, launched August 1, 1996, is a key part of that solution. A US$15 billion megavision project of the Prime Minister, it will be located 15 miles south of Kuala Lumpur and will be spread over a 290-square-mile area, larger than the size of Singapore. Dubbed the Asian Silicon Valley, the area will not only boast a 2.5-10 gigabit digital optical fiber backbone, but will be in the vicinity of the new administrative center of Malaysia, Putrajaya, a new international airport and an attractive living environment. Other areas that will be incorporated into the Multimedia Super Corridor are telemedicine and smart schools. Computer giant Microsoft has promised to locate its Asia Headquarters in this area. The advisory board of the Multimedia Super Corridor consists of a Who's Who in the computer industry world, including Presidents and CEOs from Microsoft, Netscape, Oracle, Hewlett-Packard and IBM.

The creation of the Multimedia Super Corridor in Malaysia will be an invaluable resource for social work to tap into. I will mention four specific types of IT development that could be adapted for the enhancement of social work education in Malaysia.

Using Training Software for Staff Development

Currently, computers are not used in the teaching of social work skills. The existing training system in the Ministry is designed to provide all new social work staff with a four week induction training programme at their training center. As individuals hired as social workers come from various fields, this training encompasses Human Development, basic social work and welfare services. Specialized training courses, lasting up to 10 days, are conducted at a later stage as new staff are assigned to their respective departments. This training includes child care, probation services, child abuse, and domestic violence. This training is insufficient to develop staff who are comfortable with and knowledgeable about the "how to" skills. Computer training software, if introduced during training courses, could help social workers to develop their "how to" skills during both formal training sessions and private study.

There is an opportunity for the social work profession to work together with software designers to construct 'learning by doing' software, such as those developed by Robert Schank and his Learning Sciences Corporation (LSC). LSC designs and develops scenarios that allow a user to self learn through guided simulations. Schank's approach asks "what should students know how to do?" and then develops software packages towards that end.

For example, one of LSC's biology simulations is called "disease outbreak." This allows students to uncover the source of a mysterious outbreak by conducting interviews of patients in a hospital, the relatives of "dead victims," conducting a press interview, and writing a press statement. On top of handling the case, the students learn about laws, interpersonal skills, decision making and risk taking. People who have experienced such a situation also give their views at critical points of the simulation. Another example is the "Sickle Cell Counselor" designed for the Museum of Science and Industry in Chicago which allows museum visitors to role play a genetic counselor giving advise to a couple about the risks of passing on the sickle cell to their offspring. Visitors can question experts who appear on the screen and give pros and cons to their advice.

For social work, a programme simulating a child abuse or domestic violence case can be developed at the current stage of technology development. A simulation programme with multiple layers of difficulties and objectives can provide new staff with many possible scenarios that they may face. To further develop a sense of professionalism rather than just doing a job, the values, principles and ethics behind the profession need to be part of this training simulation. With the current shortage of skilled staff in the department, such simulations may be cost effective and efficient. Such packages, possibly available in the western developed markets, will need to be adapted to the Malaysian scenario. An example of adaptation will be to Malaysia's dual legal system. People of the Islamic faith are under the jurisdiction of civil and religious courts. The political, cultural and resource differences are other variables that need to be taken into account when developing such a programme.

Distance Education

These simulation packages can also be incorporated into distance learning programmes. Distance education in Malaysia is set to expand during the Seventh Malaysian Plan covering the years 1996-2000. Currently, no social work programme offers distance education packages. However, with the severe shortage of trained social workers and the need for upgrading of skills and knowledge, there is a potential market for simulation packages. This is particularly true as many of those currently in the field have limited relevant training and cannot be released for full time courses because this would accentuate already chronic staff shortages. IT can play a role in helping to access distance learning packages that are currently at an early stage of planning.

Telesocial Work

Telemedicine, which is a part of the Multimedia Super Corridor, is a concept that can be duplicated in social work. The philosophy behind the concept of telemedicine is to use IT as a tool for medical and health services. Rural hospitals can be connected to medical specialists in urban settings who will assist in diagnosis and in surgical intervention. This is to help ease the shortage of medical doctors in rural areas. The doctor to population ratio in certain rural areas is as high as 1:4,000, significantly higher than the national average of 1:2,100 (Kadir, 1997).

Following on the philosophy of telemedicine, something like "telesocial work" could be developed to help practitioners in the field with complicated cases that need a trained social worker to assist in the intervention. The pressures of working on complicated cases makes immediate access to resources or professional assistance attractive to workers in the field and therefore they are more likely to take advantage of such technology where available. Telesocial work would allow a professional, using real time video links and multimedia, to assist in the intervention of a case and at the same time help develop the skills and confidence of the field social worker. Telesocial work would also allow social workers in the field to access a database of social workers and their area of expertise for assistance. Resource materials, for example journals for self learning and past case histories for references, could be obtained and organisations that may be helpful to a specific case could be contacted. Telesocial work could be incorporated into the government's aim to become a paperless government by the year 2000. This would also provide continuous training and upgrading of field practitioner skills and consequently the profession as a whole. The ratio of government and NGO social workers to the general population is not available, but can be safely assumed to be lower than that of doctors, thus it is more crucial that this new approach is extended to the social work field.

International Networking

The telesocial work concept can also be extended internationally so that trained social workers in Malaysia can access appropriate expertise outside the country, adapt the knowledge to the local context and, through the exchange of views, broaden the knowledge base of both parties. However, another more pressing need is for international exchange for Malaysian students.

Social work, being still relatively undeveloped in Malaysia, has been a difficult profession for university students to grasp. There is no general knowledge of the profession to draw upon and no role models in the community to help the student identify what a social worker is, the worker's role, the profession's history, values, essential skills and knowledge. Without such a background, it is difficult to inculcate social work values and principles into young students. Information technology and the borderless world provide students with a potential arena to discover the ethos of the profession. IT allows students to visit webpages and social work cafes to read about social work, to email other people around the world and be involved in discussion, and use listservs such as the National Institute of Social Work (NISW). These sources provide knowledge, an exchange of ideas and, more importantly, the discovery of values that lie behind the social work profession. Of course, social work values need to be culturally sensitive. In exchanging ideas with professionals and students in neighboring countries, social work students in Malaysia may learn solutions to problems that are more applicable than those of industrialized countries. Less developed countries may share a similar stage of development in social services or hold similar cultural and value systems that can be drawn upon. Also, industrialized countries can benefit from approaches devised in developing countries where innovative approaches are developed in light of limited resources.

For educators, IT has brought access to abundant resources that can be tapped into by pressing the send button. When I first started teaching, I discovered the NISW listgroup and got answers to every question I sent out. I also used the NISW listserv to get comments and statements from social workers all over the world about what social work meant to them or what they did as a social worker in their country. These statements were then used as part of an exhibition to expose students to the breadth and depth of social work.

Text and resource books across subjects are sometimes limited in Malaysia. Access to books relating to social work are even more limited and very expensive to buy. At my new university, our bookstore has yet to open. Students very rarely buy books and mostly depend on photocopying or handouts from lecturers. The scope and variety of academic journals are limited. Access to the Internet is a great resource for students to gain valuable information which they may not otherwise have access to. These include documents, data and general information.

CHALLENGES OF IT IN SOCIAL WORK EDUCATION

The combination of IT and social work in Malaysia could be an ideal marriage. The use of IT can enhance the social work profession, while social work can help widen the application of IT. However, there are barriers and challenges that need to be overcome. Many of these issues lie beyond the realm of social work, as they arise from government policies, past and present, that have affected education in Malaysia.

The socioeconomic awakening of Asia has seen countries in the region playing catch up with the West. The installation of telecommunication infrastructures, increase in PC and IT literacy, and the drive to develop and adopt cutting edge technology to reduce the technology gap has made Asia the fastest growing IT market in the world. Malaysia was recently ranked the sixth most wired country in Asia, after Japan, Hong Kong, Singapore, Korea and Taiwan. Although, compared to America, there are still vast disparities.

The desire for Malaysia to be an industrialized country has made it necessary to "leap frog" from being a primarily agrarian society to an IT society. IT literacy, however, has not kept up with the quantum leap of development. In a recent study by the National Library of Malaysia on 22,000 people, only 20% of those 15-24 years old were computer literate, the highest of all age brackets. In age brackets from 25-55, the figure was no more than 10% (Bernama, 1997). To increase IT literacy, the government plans to develop "smart schools" in conjunction with the MSC. It can therefore be assumed that many people working in the social work field are not IT literate.

If programmes such as telesocial work are targeted to people working with marginalized communities, accessibility will be an issue due to the lack of access of supporting IT infrastructures, such as phone lines, electricity and proper maintenance. With pockets of areas unable to access such programmes, a disparity between areas served by trained and non trained personnel will be created. The scale of these constraining factors are evident from the following statistics:

1. only 17 per 100 people in Malaysia have access to phone lines, compared to 63 for the US, and
2. just 56% of schools in Sarawak, the state where UNIMAS, a leading IT university, is based, have electricity.[5]

Another practical point when thinking of IT use in social work education is accessibility to computer hardware by students. In Malaysia, the ratio is 3.2 computers per 100 people compared to 21.2 computers per 100 people in the United States. This will have implications for distance learning programmes. At the university, few students have access to their own personal computers and those that do usually do not have Internet access. Internet in Malaysia costs approximately US$20-US$40 per month, compared to US$15-US$23 in the United States (Krar, 1997). Students access the Internet by booking time slots in the university's libraries or computer labs. As the semester progresses, time slots for computer usage become more limited as the demand increases.

English is the second language used in Malaysia, the national language being Malay. Goh (1997) relates how the rise in nationalistic spirit and the importance of national unity influenced the rise of Malay as the main medium in schools. Since the 1970s, educational policy dictates that, in all government schools, Malay is used for all subjects except English classes.[6] Simultaneously, there have been sustained efforts to develop the Malay language and to increase publications in the national language. However, part of globalization and the IT revolution is that the mastering of the old colonial language is necessary if Malaysians are to excel globally in academic studies or international business. In recognition of this reality, the government now emphasizes bi-lingualism. However, the inheritance of past policies has meant that a substantial student population struggles to read and comprehend English text and lacks confidence in expressing themselves in English. UNIMAS is one of the few universities which insists that students take generic courses which include IT and English. As the Internet is heavily English based, the lack of language skills can cause difficulties in fully utilizing search engines.

The Malaysian education system has long been criticized within the country as one that does not adequately encourage critical and creative thinking (Silverman, 1996). The practice of spoon-feeding information and subsequent regurgitation of facts during examinations begins at the primary level and continues through to university level. Memorization and conformity to the "right" answers, including values, are part and parcel of schooling. Although the authorities are trying to change this approach, these issues are still evident. With IT, an evolution of the university needs to occur as students need to absorb more information, synthesize and be more critical of the body of knowledge they will be exposed to. IT also places Malaysian education and society in a paradox. IT has opened up access to information in a society that has traditionally followed an autocratic style of leadership. It will be interesting to see how this sense of open access to information will affect society and vice versa.

The IT skill level of social work educators is another barrier to maximizing the potentials of IT in teaching social work. Computers are used by social work educators for primarily word processing, email and Internet access. Many see little correlation between the use of computers, IT's potential for developing a more enriching social work curriculum for students, the further evolution of the profession. A very poignant example of the level of IT comfort was when I sent a questionnaire as an attached document to a lecturer at another university to distribute to her colleagues. Instead of forwarding the attachment, she printed, photocopied and placed it in their pigeon holes. An email that followed further confirmed the level of IT knowledge and attitude.

It stated "Do you still want your questionnaires back? I can tell you frankly, there is nothing in them. My colleagues felt that it is not relevant to them as they don't use IT in the program."

FUTURE DIRECTIONS

The commitment of the Malaysian government to be a major global IT player provides social workers with an opportunity that has yet to be recognised by social work educators in Malaysia. With such a strong mantra on information technology in Malaysia, there is abundant technical expertise available to develop interactive and simulation programmes that can further enrich the quality of education of future social workers. The current lack of professionally trained social workers also allows room for IT to be used in a continuous self learning approach. Here, I would like to make it clear that IT should only complement and enhance, rather than replace, the need for inter-personal learning in a field which has interpersonal relationships at its core.

On another level, if the profession can capitalize on this medium, IT can be used as a catalyst to improve and enhance the credibility and status of social work in Malaysia. With the profession currently holding low status in the country, the embracing of IT in a very technologically driven society allows the profession, by association, to increase its position and to have a medium in common with leading policy makers in society. Through this commonality, the profession of social work, its importance and its important role in society can be further established.

The teaching of social work in Malaysia is complicated with the underde-veloped state of the profession in the country and the limited access to materials. Alternative methods and approaches need to be utilized to over-come these inequities. The desperate need to train current field workers to deal with increasingly complex issues and situations makes it necessary to use whatever means are available to enhance their skills. In the Malaysian context, where the government is deeply committed to funding IT develop-ment and usage, social work educators must see IT as an additional tool to assist in the development of future social workers. We cannot allow ourselves to miss an opportunity that has so much potential, but one that has yet to be recognised by the profession.

ADDENDUM

Since the writing of this paper, Malaysia and neighboring countries have suffered a major economic and currency crisis. At its lowest level, the Malaysian stock market lost 50% of its values and the ringgit depreciated 45% of its value against the dollar. Projected growth rates for the country are now below the initial projections of 7%, to between 4% and 5%.

As a consequence of the economic crisis, the government has implemented a 21% cut in budgets for all agencies and frozen the hiring of new staff. Several national projects have been placed on hold; however, the Multimedia Super Corridor project is ahead of schedule. Those who have been hardest hit are people who speculated on the stock market and property sectors. Rises in food prices across the board has affected all Malaysians who now have to pay higher prices for basic household products and goods. Pay cuts as high as 30% have been implemented in several sectors. The Government claims that the country still has full employment as there are jobs available in manufacturing and plantation sectors.

The implication of the current crisis on information technology and social work has yet to be seen. However, it can be assumed that with the major cuts in government budgets, new programmes will not be implemented while the focus would be on maintaining and maximizing existing programmes. Cuts in budgets of healthcare and social services would affect the poor and vulnerable at a time when such services will be needed most. Though basic services will remain, the focus on IT and staff development in the field of social services will be scaled back as finances are channeled to other areas. The purchase of computers and other high ticket items would be put on hold for schools and families as they concentrate their resources on meeting basic needs. This would widen the information access gap between those who can and those who cannot afford the necessary technology.

NOTES

1. At the current exchange rate of buying USD at RM2.80.

2. Bumiputra average income increased from RM940 to RM1600 between 1990-1995. However, average income of Chinese and Indians is still higher, at RM2,895 and RM2,153 respectively, in 1995. Government efforts are also aimed at increasing the number of Bumiputras in the professional sector. Bumiputras in the professional sector grew at a rate of 10.5% between 1990-1995.

3. The lowest 40% of households have only 12.9% of the total income share, the least in Asia. The ratio of income share between the highest 20% and the lowest 20% of the population for the period 1981-1993 is 11.7 to 1, the highest in Asia. The income of the bottom 40% rose only 8.1% compared to 10% and 9.2% for the top 20% and the middle 40%.

4. Jeshurun refers to people in management as the professional group, and to field workers as the semi-professional group.

5. There is a total of 1,406 schools in Sarawak, inclusive of grade and high schools. Six-hundred two grade schools and 16 secondary schools are not supplied with elec-

tricity, but are provided with generators. Information was gathered from the *Unit Maklumat* or Information Department of the State Education Department on September 2, 1997. This data is based on figures from a July 1997 report.

6. Non government schools teach in either Mandarin or Tamil, except for the few international schools that operate in English for foreign students only.

REFERENCES

Baba, Ismail (1992). Social work–An effort towards building a caring society. In: Cho Kah Sin & Ismail Muhd Salleh (1992) *Caring Society. Emerging issues and future directions.* ISIS: Malaysia.

Bernama (1997). Study: Computer literacy rate still low. *Sarawak Tribune,* July 13. p. 4.

Chan Chee Koon (1997). *Towards a citizens health manifesto.* Proceedings of the First International Malaysian Studies Conference. Universiti Malaya, Kuala Lumpur. August 11-13.

Featured Article (1989). Poverty amid plenty: People of all races slip through the NEP net. *Far Eastern Economic Review.* January 22, Vol. 144, p. 32.

Goh Pek Chen (1997). *The problems of science and technological development in Malaysia.* Proceedings of the First International Malaysian Studies Conference. Kuala Lumpur. August 11-13.

Hawa, Siti (1988). *Social work education in Malaysia.* Proceedings of Seminar on Social Work Education in the Asia Pacific Region.

Jayasooria, Dennison. (1992). Disabled persons, the caring society and policy recommendations for the 1990s and beyond. In: Cho Kah Sin & Ismail Muhd Salleh. *Caring Society. Emerging issues and future directions.* ISIS: Malaysia.

Jeshurun, Peter (1995). *Training needs for social work education: End user perspectives.* Proceedings of Southeast Asian Conference on Emerging Trends in Social Work Education: Challenges for the 21st Century. Kuching. August 28-30.

Kadir, Abdul Hamid Abdul (1997). *How many doctors do we need?* Proceedings of The National Conference on Privatization and Health Care. Emerging issues and concerns. Universiti Sains Malaysia, Penang. April 5-6 1997.

Kraar, Louis (1997). Malaysia. Building a field of dreams. *Fortune.* August 18 (16), pp. 52-56.

Loh Foon Fong (1996). A gap too wide for comfort. *The Star,* August 20. Section 2, pp. 11.

Malaysia (1996). *Seventh Malaysia Plan.* 1996-2000.

Silverman, G. (1996). Silence of the lambs. *Far Eastern Economic Review.* November 14, pp. 24-26.

Star (1997). Malaysia Population. *The Star,* August 11. p. 4.

Sushama P.C. (1985). Malaysia. In John Dixon and Hyung Shik Kim (eds). *Social Welfare in Asia.* London: Croom Helm.

Multi-Media Computer Technology in the Classroom

Jim Stafford
Michael V. Namorato

SUMMARY. This article recounts the experiences of the authors as participants in the quest of their university to bring multi-media computer based technology into the classroom. The authors discuss the method of the university's approach to this task, review the process leading to the development of their own project, and then review some of the lessons they learned in the process. They conclude by discussing the outcomes and presenting a number of recommendations for other campuses that might be considering similar endeavors. *[Article copies available for a fee from The Haworth Document Delivery Service: 1-800-342-9678. E-mail address: getinfo@haworthpressinc.com]*

KEYWORDS. Computer-based multi-media classroom presentations

INTRODUCTION

About four years ago, the University of Mississippi committed itself to bringing technology into the classroom on all levels, undergraduate and

Jim Stafford, DSW, ACSW, LCSW, is Assistant Professor and Coordinator of Field Instruction, Department of Social Work, University of Mississippi, 225 Hume Hall, University, MS 38677 (E- mail: swjames@olemiss.edu).

Michael V. Namorato, PhD, is Professor, Department of History, University of Mississippi, 318 Bishop Hall, University, MS 38677 (E-mail: hsmvn@olemiss.edu).

[Haworth co-indexing entry note]: "Multi-Media Computer Technology in the Classroom." Stafford, Jim, and Michael V. Namorato. Co-published simultaneously in *Computers in Human Services* (The Haworth Press, Inc.) Vol. 15, No. 2/3, 1998, pp. 185-191; and: *Information Technologies: Teaching to Use– Using to Teach* (ed: Frank B. Raymond III, Leon Ginsberg, and Debra Gohagan) The Haworth Press, Inc., 1998, pp. 185-191. Single or multiple copies of this article are available for a fee from The Haworth Document Delivery Service [1-800-342-9678, 9:00 a.m. - 5:00 p.m. (EST). E-mail address: getinfo@ haworthpressinc.com]

graduate. To facilitate this, the University, supported by state legislative funds, awarded each full-time tenure-track faculty member a grant of $1500 to purchase computer equipment which would enable them to bring computer technology into the classroom. The University also decided to establish a technology lab in the library for the use of faculty. As a third step, the University provided the means for faculty to learn the skills needed to develop computer based multi-media presentations for classroom use.

In the spring of 1995, faculty were asked to submit proposals for a faculty technology Development Institute to be held in the first summer term. Interested faculty had to commit themselves to spending one full summer semester, working every day from 1 p.m. to 5 p.m., learning about hardware and software. As extra incentive, faculty selected to participate were to be paid the equivalent of teaching one three-hour course. Dr. Namorato and I were selected for the first summer institute.

THE METHOD–FACULTY SUMMER INSTITUTE

The method of training faculty selected by the University was to have the institute run by other faculty. By doing this, the University was attempting to insure that the training would be consistent with faculty needs, and would be easily accepted by the faculty. This idea worked reasonably well. A fairly comfortable, give and take atmosphere developed in which faculty were introduced to hardware and software by several other faculty who had prior experience with the process. The 20 members of the group were paired up and assigned three separate projects which they were expected to develop using the skills and materials they were learning about. Each faculty team was seated behind a pair of PCs or Macs, according to their preference. Instructors used projection devices as they walked (or ran) faculty through the program. On presentation days, University administrators were invited to watch the presentations. A surprising number did show up, and on those days it was hard to find a seat if you arrived late.

THE NUTS AND BOLTS

Faculty were introduced to a lot of hardware and software in a very short period of time. The hardware included flat-bed scanners, slide scanners, video capture devices, and digital cameras, as well as machines which allowed the user to digitize sound. Most of this equipment was unfamiliar, and required a considerable investment of time. The software was equally daunting. Programs like Persuasion (Adobe), Authorware (Macromedia), and HyperStudio (Roger Wagner Publishing, Inc.) constituted the core programs around which the presentations were built. Other, more specific software was used in the process of capturing, cropping, and refining images scanned in from a variety of sources. One constant source of frustration for faculty was that so much material had to be introduced in such a short period of time. One never had the luxury of feeling any sense of mastery, which was aggravated by the fact that the software was not initially available for the faculty to install on computers in their offices or at home. The lab became a very crowded place, as faculty worked nights and weekends on their creations.

THE AUTHOR'S PROJECT–
A BRIEF OUTLINE HISTORY OF SOCIAL WELFARE
IN THE UNITED STATES

The major project for the authors was a brief outline of the social welfare history of the United States from the mid 1800s to modern times. I teach a course which includes this content, and Dr. Namorato specializes in 19th and 20th century American history, so this represented a good collaboration for us. The initial program we developed within the class consisted of forty computer slides. We are currently in the process of expanding this initial effort into a larger program for extended use in classes taught in both of our respective departments.

Beginning with Copeland's "Appalachian Spring" as a background, the program first introduces its creators and asks the student to identify him/herself. The program then proceeds to give a short history of social welfare, utilizing both slides and text. As they go through the program, students read text and look at photos and graphics illustrating the themes. As the modern era approaches, the student is introduced to individuals such as Horace Mann, Dorothea Dix, and Progressive Era leaders like Jane Addams, each with corresponding text and photos. As the 20th century unfolds, the student is taken through the 1920s, the Depression, and the New Deal. Here, the student listens to a popular Depression song "All's Gone," watches and listens to Franklin Roosevelt's "All we have to fear is fear itself" inaugural address, and sees prominent examples of New Deal programs and personalities like Harry Hopkins, Frances Perkins, the National Recovery Administration, TVA, and especially Social Security. The student also views two video clips (about 15 seconds each) dealing with Hoovervilles and the CCC.

Moving through World War II, the student is then briefly introduced to all the post-war presidents, but especially Kennedy, Johnson (and his Great Society), and Jimmy Carter. Ronald Reagan's attacks on the social welfare philosophy are noted and emphasized as the program draws to a close with vivid and telling photographs of orphaned children with Copeland's fanfare again in the background. The final slides present an interactive test, written in Authorware, which the student initiates by pressing the mouse button. Once the test is completed, the program returns to the Persuasion program where the credits are presented.

LESSONS LEARNED

As already indicated, this program is being expanded into a full-length interactive program on the history of social welfare in the United States. Nevertheless, while we are enthusiastic about the use of multi-media computer technology in classroom teaching, both of us, and the other faculty involved in this process, have learned some cautionary lessons. Creating multimedia presentations can be a very frustrating endeavor. The learning curve for the technology required is fairly steep and very specific. Learning how to operate one machine does not ensure that you will know how to work one from a different manufacturer. There are many short cuts and "do's and don'ts" to learn, and unless you are using the machines and the software on a very regular basis, you find yourself constantly having to re-learn operating skills. Creating the presentations themselves requires a major commitment of time, as well as the previously mentioned high frustration tolerance to deal with the inevitable glitches and snags encountered.

One of the major frustrations we encountered was that our office computers would not support several of the programs we learned, and our hard drives were inadequate to store the programs we created. This was caused by purchasing computers before we knew exactly what would be required of them. Storing the programs on "zip" drives or other similar devices is a partial solution, but beware of the fact that some media, especially video, coming in from an external storage device simply does not come in fast enough to prevent break-up. Be sure you have enough muscle in your hardware before attempting to build anything with imported video or audio. Large programs (just our brief overview was 60+ MB) can be stored on CD-ROM, but once done this way, cannot be changed. Large gigabyte size hard drives and speedy processors are a must. In order to have true mobility, a full-featured large capacity laptop/notebook computer with onboard CD-ROM is essential. Wheeling desktops around on carts is a difficult proposition, at best. Unless you are fortunate enough to have a very generous budget, you may find yourself in a situation similar to ours in regard to equipment. Neither of our departments have scanners or other importing devices mentioned above, so we must make a lot of trips over to the technology lab. This again requires time investment, and the equipment and technical support is not always available when we need it.

In terms of bringing the completed presentation into the classroom, again we found many frustrations. While there has been a lot of discussion on our campus about making every classroom "technology-ready," the fact remains that very few classrooms have built-in projectors, or are even set up in such a way that using a built-in or portable projection device would be at all practical. If we could advise other colleges and universities that are contemplating training their faculties in these skills, one item of advice would be simply this–do not train faculty in these skills until your classrooms are equipped to accept this technology. The alternative is to have many frustrated faculty trained to use technology that they are unable to bring to the classroom. Dr. Namorato and I have both experienced this frustration. While the cost of projection devices, like the cost of virtually all other computer hardware, is coming down, buying a projection device still represents a significant cost for academic departments, especially during this time when so many departments are experiencing cutbacks. Less expensive alternatives, like computer to TV converters, which hook the computer directly to a TV, cannot work with all TVs, especially older ones.

If you are able to clear the technology hurdles and can display your presentation on a large screen in your classroom, you must allot extra time to set up (and take down). We've found that it often works better to work from the back or side of the classroom as the material is presented on the screen, rather than standing right next to it, so a laser pointer is most helpful, as would be a remote cordless mouse.

Having set forth the many frustrations and pitfalls, we now must acknowledge the considerable benefit we have noticed from using our presentation. Simply put, we teach a generation used to video and graphics. We've observed that graphics that astound us are merely taken as part of the show by our students. They're used to information being presented in the most eye catching ways, and they're geared toward this, even if many of us are not. We've noticed that students pay more attention to material presented via graphics on a screen accompanied by lecture, than they do to lecture alone. While many teachers lament the fact that they must now "entertain" in order to be heard, adding multi-media to the lecture material does seem to enhance attention. Especially in the area of history, the addition of pictures and graphics seems to enhance class discussion and overall interest in the material. We've also found that multi-media presentations are very easy to adapt to an instructor's particular style of teaching. For example, some instructors we've talked to use their presentations to free up valuable class time by assigning students to view the presentation independently outside of class. Presentations can also be designed to be interactive to allow students to proceed at their own pace. Overall, we're happy with what we've developed, and the way it has been received, but frustrated that the settings in which we teach often make using it impossible.

One issue needing discussion relates to scanning in pictures from textbooks, or using other copyrighted materials in the development of presentations. We have been told that as long as the presentation is developed for classroom use and is not commercially marketed or distributed, simply giving credit within the presentation to the source is sufficient, and specific permission from the author or artist is not required. Classroom use falls under what is referred to as the "fair use" part of the law, as we understand it. Once the use involves profit, or large scale distribution, the situation changes, and specific permission is required.

OUTCOMES AND RECOMMENDATIONS

There has not yet been a formal study of how well the University has achieved its objectives to this point through the approach it has used. Any good study addressing this, it seems to us, would have to find out how many of the trained faculty are using multi-media in their classrooms, and if not, why not. It would also be interesting to know how faculty who are using these presentations incorporate them into their teaching of the course material. We do have some anecdotal data gathered from faculty we have talked to informally about this. From these accounts, it seems that most of the faculty who have been trained in the use of this media have used it at least occasionally in their classrooms, even if they have had to overcome hardware problems in order to do so. The extent to which they have used it as a regular part of their teaching seems to be a function of the readiness of their classroom facilities to accept this technology, and the way that they teach. We have talked to several trained faculty who, even though possessing multi-media classroom facilities, have decided after using their presentations that this just did not fit their spontaneous style of teaching. We have also heard from faculty who, while initially quite enthusiastic about this approach, found themselves turned off by several bad experiences with hardware or software problems. Other faculty who have the necessary resources have successfully adapted multi-media to their courses and use it on a very regular basis as just a regular tool of the trade.

In sum, from our experience with the University of Mississippi's efforts to bring multi-media technology into the classroom, we would make several recommendations for other campuses considering this endeavor.

1. Faculty should be trained by other faculty, with grants and/or equipment or software to serve as incentives for those who make the commitment to learn this technology.
2. Software which will be used in the training should be made available to faculty to put on computers in their offices at the start of the training. This will provide more time for learning, and prevent the lab facilities from becoming so crowded.

3. There should be on-going training for previously trained faculty to keep skills sharp.
4. Emphasis should be placed on faculty developing materials to fit into their current teaching style.
5. The classroom hardware (wiring, projection devices, screens, etc.) to support the technology should be in place before the faculty is trained.
6. Every academic unit intending to make fairly regular use of multi-media in courses should have at least one full featured, large capacity laptop/notebook computer with on board CD-ROM for every two faculty members in the unit.
7. Specialized equipment needed for developing multi-media presentations should be centrally located, open regular hours, and staffed by a technical person who can assist as problems come up.
8. Development of multi-media presentations should be recognized by the university as a credible faculty activity, worthy of support and recognition.

There is one additional note of caution. This area of technology is developing faster than most faculty's abilities to keep up. Consult an expert in this area before buying anything, explain what you need, and the purposes for which you will use it, and take their advice about what to buy. You can easily spend way more than you should have, and still not have what you need. Then, roll up your sleeves, open your mind, and dive in. You're in for quite an adventure.

Computer-Assisted Instruction in the Classroom: Using a Web Shell

Wendy P. Crook
Myriah Jayne Brady

SUMMARY. This article provides an overview of the development of computer-assisted instruction and the history of related theories. It discusses the integration of an Internet-based shell program into traditional social work courses at Florida State University. A description of the shell program itself is also provided. The results of student surveys from two courses indicated that the majority of students felt that the computer work enhanced their educational experience and increased their comfort using computers. The primary difficulties that students had centered on technical problems or problems related to having access to computers. *[Article copies available for a fee from The Haworth Document Delivery Service: 1-800-342-9678. E-mail address: getinfo@haworthpressinc.com]*

Wendy P. Crook, PhD, is Assistant Professor, School of Social Work, Florida State University. She teaches and conducts research in the areas of administration, policy and community organization. Dr. Crook uses computer-based instruction in all of her courses.

Myriah Jayne Brady, MSW, LCSW, is a doctoral student, Florida State University. She is a Research and Training Specialist with the Florida Department of Corrections. Ms. Brady directs an innovative program designed to teach emergency management skills using computer-based instruction.

Address correspondence to: Wendy P. Crook, PhD, School of Social Work, 2511 UCC, Florida State University, Tallahassee, FL 32306-2570 (E-mail: wcrook@mailer.fsu.edu).

The authors would like to express their appreciation to Dr. Walter Wager for his work on the Construe shell program in cooperation with NCR Corporation.

[Haworth co-indexing entry note]: "Computer-Assisted Instruction in the Classroom: Using a Web Shell." Crook, Wendy P., and Myriah Jayne Brady. Co-published simultaneously in *Computers in Human Services* (The Haworth Press, Inc.) Vol. 15, No. 2/3, 1998, pp. 193-208; and: *Information Technologies: Teaching to Use–Using to Teach* (ed: Frank B. Raymond III, Leon Ginsberg, and Debra Gohagan) The Haworth Press, Inc., 1998, pp. 193-208. Single or multiple copies of this article are available for a fee from The Haworth Document Delivery Service [1-800-342-9678, 9:00 a.m. - 5:00 p.m. (EST). E-mail address: getinfo@haworthpressinc.com]

KEYWORDS. Computer-based instruction, technology and teaching, social work education, web-based instruction, computer-assisted learning

INTRODUCTION

Social work has begun to move into the computer age using clinically oriented social work-based software, expert systems, statistical programs and a variety of case management programs. Although many schools of social work integrate computer technology with traditional classroom approaches, little empirical data exists on the effectiveness of this technique. The empirical data is absent due in part to the rapid growth of technology over the past several years.

This article provides an overview of the development of computer-assisted instruction and the history of related theories. It discusses the integration of an Internet-based shell program into traditional social work courses at Florida State University. The application of the shell program with one social work course and description of the shell program itself are also provided. Finally, the article presents an analysis of responses to student surveys evaluating their satisfaction with the use of the shell program and computer-assisted learning as an adjunct to classroom education.

DEVELOPMENT OF COMPUTER-ASSISTED AND WEB-BASED INSTRUCTION

Computer-assisted instruction (CAI) and web-based instruction (WBI) are rapidly expanding fields of knowledge that extend across the boundaries of many disciplines and professions. Since 1958, when Roth and Anderson developed the first CAI on the IBM mainframe to teach binary arithmetic, CAI was dependent on expensive and inaccessible mainframe or mini computers. As a result of the proliferation of the personal computer, there was a phenomenal growth in the use of CAI at all levels of education in the 1980's (Alessi & Trollip, 1985; Hudson, 1985).

The World Wide Web (WWW) has grown rapidly and is described as a "wide-area hypermedia information retrieval initiative aiming to give universal access to a large universe of documents" (Crossman, 1997). Web-based instruction (WBI) can be defined as "the application of a repertoire of cognitively oriented instructional strategies implemented within a constructivist and collaborative learning environment, utilizing the attributes and resources of the World Wide Web" (Relan & Gillani, 1997). A WBI learning environment should include many resources, support collaboration, implement Web-based activities as part of the learning framework, and be accessible to both novices and experts (Sherry & Wilson, 1997).

According to Relan and Gillani (1997), WBI has contextual assumptions different from those found in the traditional classroom.

> First, it is assumed that the learner has access to the World Wide Web at all times and is allowed to explore it in a self-determined or guided sequence. Second, WBI would function best in a constructivist environment. Third, the teacher 'dethrones' him/herself as the disseminator of information, and becomes a facilitator for finding, assessing and making meaning from the information discovered from a variety of media. Fourth, learning occurs in an interdisciplinary fashion without regard to the attainment of learning objectives within a fixed time. (p. 44)

The nature of the relationship between teacher and learner changes as developments in technology allow them to communicate in various ways and access and generate a wide range of resources.

HISTORY OF THEORY DEVELOPMENT

Early conceptualizations of cognition related to hypertext were supported by theories of cognitive knowledge representation (Jonassen, 1988) where information and knowledge are held in networks composed of ideas, concepts, or bits of information and their associative connections (Bobrow & Norman, 1975). Learning is seen as the process of acquiring new ideas, concepts or bits of information linked to networks already present in the learner (Jonassen, 1988). Comprehension is enhanced when the number of associative links from the existing informational network to the new ideas, concepts or bits of information are maximized. These informational networks can be conceived of as "webs of information" (Jonassen, 1988).

Teaching principles were derived from the concept of webs of learning (Jonassen, 1988; Norman, 1973). Reigeluth (1983) proposed an elaboration theory of instruction, which states that instruction should be a process of moving from simple to complex, allowing for the establishment of a strong contextual base on which to build detail and conceptual linkage. In this model, learner control over selection and exploration of the components of the material that are of greatest personal interest is emphasized.

The notion of learner control is central to andragogical theory. Knowles (1984) identified four basic andragogical assumptions about learners. First, the learner is self-directed and independent in his or her pursuit of information. Second, the learner's life experience should be acknowledged, emphasized, and built upon. Third, the learner comes with a readiness to learn, and is driven by his/her social occupational roles. Finally, the learner is motivated by the potential for immediate application of skills and knowledge.

Andragogical assumptions about learner characteristics are consistent with the social work education model that promotes student integration of theory and practice through field placements. Assuming that social work students, especially those at the graduate level, tend to have characteristics consistent with andragogical theory, hypermedia programs, which have the potential to maximize user-directed exploration, present a powerful means for social work education (Patterson, 1994).

Unfortunately little empirical evidence exists about the effectiveness of either computer-assisted instruction or web-based instruction in social work education. Two studies found positive outcomes for social work students who used computerized tutorials or study guides for statistics and research courses (Collis, Oberg & Shera, 1988-89; Flynn & MacDonald, 1991). Two studies concluded that social work practice skills could be taught via computer or interactive videodisk programs (Patterson & Yaffe, 1993; Seabury & Maple, 1993). However, Patterson, Pullen, Evers, Champlin and Ralson's (1997) study failed to demonstrate a difference in knowledge or skills between experimental and control groups of social work students learning substance abuse assessment, diagnosis and treatment. Finally, van den Berg and Watt (1991) studied the effects of educational settings on student responses to structured hypertext documents and concluded that educational settings affected users' perceptions of how much they thought they had learned, as well as their acceptance of the technology. Clearly there is a need for additional empirical research on the efficacy of computer-assisted instruction.

Absent from the literature are studies that examine the WWW as an instructional tool. The research reported in this article focuses on a software program created and delivered via the WWW. In an effort to integrate the computer into the classroom, a pilot study was conducted using three graduate social work courses at Florida State University. The goal was to determine if the WWW in general, and *Construe* specifically, could support and enhance learning for social work students. *Construe* is a software shell developed for the purpose of facilitating the development and management of learning environments on the World Wide Web. It is the result of a collaborative effort between Florida State University and the NCR Corporation, and is considered to be cutting edge technology in interactive asynchronous tools for instruction and collaborative learning via the World Wide Web.

USE OF CONSTRUE AS A SUPPLEMENT TO CLASSROOM LEARNING

Construe was used as a course supplement with three social work courses during 1997: Psychopathology in Clinical Practice (PCP); Social Work with

Task Groups, Organizations and Communities (TOC); and Evaluation Research (ER). This section will discuss its application as a learning adjunct to the classroom experience using examples from the ER course.

ER presented students with didactic and field experiences for the development of research skills related to the evaluation of social programs. Students conducted an actual evaluation of a community transitional housing program for homeless families, culminating with the production of a monograph that presented a literature review, research plan, findings and recommendations. Construe was used as an adjunct to the classroom and field experience. The instructor's goals for use of Construe were to facilitate cognitive knowledge representation, enhance communication, encourage self-directed learning, acknowledge the learners' life experiences, and provide opportunities for immediate application of skills and knowledge.

At the first class session, students received training in its use. Consistent with andragogical theory, learning to use Construe proceeded from the simple to the complex. The students were instructed how to locate a welcome message that the instructor had previously posted on Construe and to E-mail a code word found in the message to the instructor.

The next assignment that students tackled was somewhat more complex. Students were required to locate a function on Construe that enabled them to follow links to course-related documents on the WWW that had been previously developed by the instructor. Then, students read the documents and posted their reactions to them on Construe. Finally, students used Construe to communicate with each other via E-mail and posting the results of their individual assignments related to the accomplishment of the program evaluation. They used Construe to arrange site visits, post preliminary research results, pose questions to each other and/or the entire class, develop meeting agendas, and track progress on the overall program evaluation.

Although a formal evaluation of their experience was not conducted, at the end of the course, all of the students (n = 6) expressed the belief that the experience of using Construe as a supplement to their classroom and field learning opportunities was very positive. They were delighted with their new computer skills, especially learning how to "surf" the World Wide Web. They found it very convenient to communicate with each other and the instructor via the E-mail function embedded in Construe. The class was also very pleased to have a repository of information where the complex and interwoven data generated by the program evaluation could be accessed. The instructor believed that her goals were met:

1. cognitive knowledge representation: students built networks of knowledge based on their exploration of the World Wide Web, classroom learning, their field experience, and course readings. For example, students read each others' reactions to articles posted on Construe, re-

sponded with their own reactions, and integrated this virtual dialog with their traditional course experiences, thus creating a collaborative learning environment;

2. communication among students and between students and the instructor was enhanced via the E-mail capabilities embedded in Construe. For example, when a student had a question related to a course activity or reading assignment, s/he could receive a response from the instructor or another student without waiting for the following class;

3. self-directed learning was facilitated on two levels: individualized exploration of the WWW and skill development in the use of Construe;

4. the learners' life experiences were acknowledged via immediate feedback from the instructor and other learners, especially regarding the reporting and interpretation of data derived from the program evaluation; and

5. students were able to immediately apply their new skills and knowledge in both course content and the use of a computerized application.

NAVIGATING CONSTRUE

The main screen on Construe provides links to its individual components: Articles, Concepts, Reports, People, Groups, Resources, Personal Info, Home and Admin. This discussion will present the features of two key components (Articles and People) in detail and a brief description of the remaining components.

1. *Articles:* The first screen in Articles (see Figure 1) provides the ability to sort and select from pre-posted links to categories of readings. The user clicks on the arrow next to "topic" and a list of categories appears. The user clicks on "create index" to see all categories.

The next screen in Articles shows all the categories of links and postings available for access (see Figure 2). By clicking on the link, the user moves to a screen with a list of documents; from there the user links directly to the desired article. The screen shown in Figure 2 also allows users to post reactions to articles and the instructor to track and access students' reactions. Once the user has read an article item, the ± sign can be clicked to gain access to a form used to post reactions. The instructor can see, from the bracketed number next to the link category, how many students have posted reactions to an item in the list. The instructor can click on the bracketed number to identify users who have posted reactions, then click on the name to read the reaction. A sample reaction posted by a student can be found in Figure 3.

2. *People:* The People function provides several options: viewing the user's home page (click on the name); immediately sending an E-mail to a

FIGURE 1

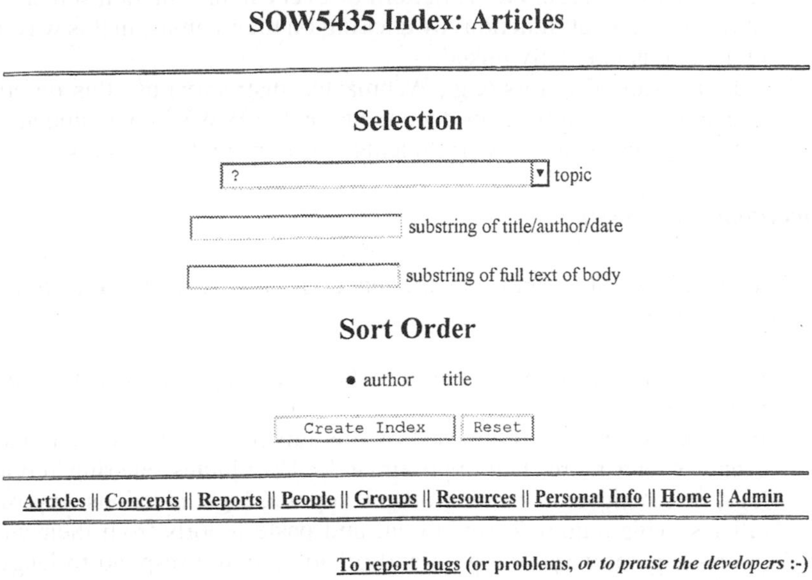

SOW5435 Index: Articles

Selection

| ? | ▼ | topic |

[_____] substring of title/author/date

[_____] substring of full text of body

Sort Order

● author   title

[Create Index] [Reset]

Articles || **Concepts** || **Reports** || **People** || **Groups** || **Resources** || **Personal Info** || **Home** || **Admin**

To report bugs (or problems, *or to praise the developers* :-)

user (click on the E-mail address); and viewing reactions and/or reports generated by individuals (click on reactions, bp, or pp). This function is particularly useful for the instructor as it allows immediate viewing of individuals' work for grading purposes. Users can also send an E-mail to everyone in the class from this screen by clicking on "mail to all the above" (see Figure 4).

Other Construe Components

1. Concepts: This function can be used to post course concepts, theories and/or definitions.
2. Reports: Two types of reports can be posted: Best Practices (bp) and Project Plans (pp).
3. Groups: The Groups function allows the instructor to assign class members to groups that conform to course-related assignments.
4. Resources: This function allows the student to access links to resources on the WWW, such as Internet help and search sites, software download sites, online journals, and copyright information.
5. Personal Info: This function is used to enter information for the user's home page, manage data files, upload data files, and change her/his password.

6. Home: By clicking on Home, the user is immediately linked to the initial Construe screen. At the bottom of every main function screen, the user can access all functions by clicking on their names; in this way, the entire site is internally linked.
7. Admin: Administrators (e.g., Webmaster, instructor) use this function to create links to articles or documents on the WWW, enter students as authorized users, and assign students to groups and/or clusters.

Limitations of Construe

There were several limitations experienced by the instructor and students in using Construe:

1. Users cannot edit their own reports once they are downloaded to Construe.
2. Because of time limits imposed by the university server system, users cannot spend more than approximately 15 minutes entering reports, logs, or reactions, or reading others' reports, logs, reactions or posted articles. This required users to cut and paste reports from their word processing software or log on and off to read and respond to lengthy articles. This process was awkward and frustrating for students.
3. Students were advised at the beginning of the course that they would need access to computers with specific hardware and software capabilities. This created problems with new computers that some chose to purchase and with various commercial Internet providers (e.g., Compuserve or AOL) or WWW software (e.g., Internet Explorer).

Support and Resource Requirements

In order to use the Construe website, the instructor worked closely with two individuals: the School of Social Work's Webmaster and an Instructional Designer who was an expert in WWW educational applications and is the co-author of this article. The Webmaster's role was to accomplish the initial set-up of Construe for the course and create links to Internet articles identified by the instructor. The Instructional Designer's role was to provide the initial training for students, entering all students as authorized users and providing technical support to students throughout the course. In addition, a Teaching Assistant was helpful for monitoring reports and logs when Construe was used with a much larger class the previous semester.

The initial use of Construe required significant resources in terms of the instructor's time and the support personnel identified above. The instructor's time decreased in subsequent semesters as she became adept with Construe,

FIGURE 2

SOW5435 Index: Articles

{ all } by author

link97a **Dr. Wendy Crook [5] +**
    Purposes and Use of PE links page
link97b **Dr. Wendy Crook [1] +**
    Program Evaluation Reports links page
link97c **Dr. Wendy Crook [2] +**
    Legislative Mandates links page
link97d **Dr. Wendy Crook [1] +**
    Notice of Funding links page
Croo97a **Dr. Wendy Crook**
    Course syllabus for SOW 5435
link97e **Dr. Wendy Crook [5] +**
    Types of Sampling
0033 **Kim Tocco and Lisa Bretz**
    Checklist for Records Review
croo97j **Wendy Crook [2] +**
    Final Report Draft

Articles || **Concepts** || **Reports** || **People** || **Groups** || **Resources** || **Personal Info** || **Home** || **Admin**

To report bugs (or problems, *or to praise the developers* :-)

---

which also resulted in decreased dependency on support personnel. Support personnel had various responsibilities within the School of Social Work, which relieved the financial impact on the Construe project. Another factor, which served to decrease the use of instructor's time and support personnel, was the completion of the School of Social Work's new computer laboratory. By holding an early class session in the laboratory and providing hands-on training for students in the use of Construe, the instructor was able to minimize class time and out-of-class communication regarding the mechanics of Construe. Finally, some students struggled initially with the use of the computer in general, and the following year, the School of Social Work required all entering graduate students to have access to a computer, with specifications listed in graduate admissions materials. This resulted in a cohort of students who were prepared for the use of computerized applications in their graduate education, with the outcome of reduced instructor and support personnel time.

In summary, although substantial resources are required to implement the use of Construe in initial semesters, the dependency on these resources decreases over time. The instructor continues to communicate more often with

FIGURE 3

SOW5435 Reaction to `link97a`
"Purposes and Use of PE links page"
Dr. Wendy Crook

by <u>Sharon Traxler</u> *<<u>sst0593@garnet.acns.fsu.edu</u>>*

Gut Reactions

First reaction: This is a sales pitch for his rating system!

This is my quote from the article: "Policy makers need to be taught how to interpret the research that can be done and how much weight to give it in their decision-making." Who is going to do the teaching?

Big Ideas

none at the moment!

Implications for Teaching and Learning

This speech brings up three issues: "1- foundations, agencies & officials need to invest more resources in quality evaluation. 2- need for program directors to embrace evaluation as an essential part of good management practice. 3- relative lack of influence that even good evaluations have on the decisions made by policy makers and administrators."

Nagging Questions

Are the only people who feel evaluation is important the evaluators themselves? Can't research be made 'user friendly'?

Usefulness of This Article: *good*

<u>Articles</u> || <u>Concepts</u> || <u>Reports</u> || <u>People</u> || <u>Groups</u> || <u>Resources</u> || <u>Personal Info</u> || <u>Home</u> || <u>Admin</u>

<u>To report bugs</u> (or problems, *or to praise the developers* :-)

students via E-mail than she normally would, but this means of communication is efficient and results in an improved ability to monitor students' work and provide them with feedback. Both the instructor and students believed that the outcomes associated with using Construe were well worth the effort and time required. Finally, the School of Social Work's commitment to providing a graduate education that will result in community-based practice is supported by providing students with critical computer skills that will aid them in their future careers.

FIGURE 4

SOW5435 Index: People

{ all } by last name

* Jane Allgood<jallgood@ix.netcom.com> admin - *(FSU)* Reactions[]
* Jayne Brady<mjb1845@garnet.acns.fsu.edu> admin - *(FSU)* Reactions[]
* Lisa Bretz<llb9119@garnet.acns.fsu.edu> TA - *cl* () Reactions[2] pp
* Louis Brooks<lfb8809@mailer.fsu.edu> admin - *(FSU)* Reactions[]
* Wendy Crook<wcrook@mailer.fsu.edu> admin - *(FSU)* Reactions[2] pp
* Glenn Ford<gfl1446@garnet.acns.fsu.edu> TA - *cl* () Reactions[1] bp pp
* Karen Joseph<klj7685@garnet.acns.fsu.edu> TA - *cl* () Reactions[3] bp pp
* Kim Tocco<kmt3422@garnet.acns.fsu.edu> TA - *cl* () Reactions[4] pp
* Sharon Traxler<sst0593@garnet.acns.fsu.edu> TA - *cl* () Reactions[2] pp
* Terry Trent<tlt2302@garnet.acns.fsu.edu> TA - *cl* () Reactions[1] pp
* Walt Wager<wagerw@edres.fsu.edu> admin - *(FSU)* Reactions[1]

---

* Mail to all the above *(warning: Mac browsers truncate a long list back to about 10 addresses)*

Articles || Concepts || Reports || People || Groups || Resources || Personal Info || Home || Admin

---

To report bugs (or problems, *or to praise the developers* :-)

WBI ALTERNATIVES

Instructors can implement web-based instruction in its most basic form by assigning readings related to course concepts that are found on the WWW. However, a shell program can provide the benefits of centralized availability and integration of the various components of a course, such as the syllabus, reading assignments, calendar of activities, etc. In addition, a shell program will integrate E-mail features and most provide real-time chat rooms. These offer opportunities for collaborative learning and enhanced communication among students and between students and the instructor.

There are two primary categories of shell programs available for web-based instruction. The first is university-developed, of which Construe is an example. California State University at Sacramento has made a shell program available at no cost to universities which integrates eighteen screens of information including syllabus, calendar, assignments, etc. Other universities are in the process of developing similar shell programs. University-developed shell programs can benefit from the addition of web conferencing software, of which Webboard from O'Reilly Software (http://webboard.oreilly.com) is a leader. Webboard can be purchased for under $500 and offers asynchronous, threaded discussions and real-time chat features. The second category is commercially-developed, with LearningSpace from Lotus Notes/Domino (http://www.lotus.com) and TopClass from WBT Systems (http://www.wbtsystems.com) two with which the authors are familiar. University-developed shell programs are costly to develop (in terms of time and technical expertise), but inexpensive to implement. Commercially-developed shell programs are costly to implement: LearningSpace would cost $15,000 per year for a university with 10,000 full-time equivalent faculty, staff and students. Moreover, Learning-Space requires Lotus Notes (intranet software) to operate, which has an additional cost.

DOCUMENT AND COPYRIGHT ISSUES

While students were encouraged to locate course-related documents on the WWW, primary reading assignments were for documents identified by the instructor, with links provided. The availability of full-text documents on the WWW is staggering, and instructors at the School of Social Work have had no problem locating reading materials appropriate for their courses. Documents may be found on commercial sites (e.g., an article on task group leadership prepared by a management consulting company), on lecture notes posted by other universities, or on government sites (e.g., the Census Bureau prepares many reports based on its demographic data).

Copyright issues related to WWW documents are currently the subject of intense controversy. Those documents that are considered in the public domain (e.g., government documents) are available for viewing and downloading and not subject to copyright laws. In general, "there appears to be a doctrine of implied public access on the Web" (O'Mahoney, 1995), where WWW authors give implied permission to link to their pages. However, if an instructor wants to download a copyrighted WWW document to be displayed on a course shell program, permission should be sought. Similarly, copyrighting their documents can protect instructors who include their own original material (including syllabi, lecture notes and lists of links) in their course shell programs. The courses discussed in this article all used links to WWW documents, therefore, copyright permission was neither needed nor sought.

RESEARCH METHODOLOGY

The remainder of this article presents the results of an evaluation conducted for two courses presented in the Spring, 1997 semester: Psychopathology in Clinical Practice (PCP) and Social Work with Task Groups, Organizations and Communities (TOC). Both were graduate-level courses required of all first-year students.

The Instructional Designer developed pretest and posttest surveys. Both surveys contained questions about the students' knowledge of and comfort with computers, their belief about the importance of computers in social work practice, their preference for working in small groups, and their beliefs about communicating with students via E-mail. The questions were formatted as forced-choice responses using a five-point Likert-type scale and responses were analyzed quantitatively. The pretest also contained open-ended questions regarding students' fears and expectations about the course. The posttest survey contained open-ended questions about students' reactions to the use of the computer in the course. Students were also asked if they would recommend the course to a friend. All open-ended questions were analyzed qualitatively.

There were a total of 70 students in the two courses: 32 in PCP and 38 in TOC. Of these, 18 students completed surveys in PCP and 22 in TOC (N = 40). This was a convenience sample and completion of surveys was voluntary. Subjects ranged in age from 22 to 57 years; there were 33 females and seven males. The subjects in PCP were volunteers who elected to use Construe in lieu of a class paper. The students in TOC were required to use Construe as an integral part of their course work. The students in both groups had a range of previous computer experience from none to those who had some programming background. There were no significant differences between the groups in terms of computer experience or age.

PROCEDURE

On the first day of class the students were given the *Participant's Guide for Construe*, a detailed manual explaining the navigation and use of the shell program. Written tutorials were also provided on the use of Netscape and how to obtain E-mail. Students in each class were provided on-line technical support. The students in TOC were required to use Construe as an integral part of the class, communicating with each other in groups and completing on-line assignments. Students in PCP volunteered for the project; those who participated were required to read twelve articles contained in Construe, select a diagnosis and search the web for the best treatment sites available, prepare a report documenting the findings and then read and comment on the reports of classmates. Construe was not integrated into regular class discussions but acted as a stand-alone assignment.

The Instructional Designer reviewed the evaluation procedure with each class and requested that students complete a survey, which they would receive via E-mail within one week. Students were assured that the surveys would be reported to the instructor in aggregate form only to encourage complete and honest responses. Both pretest and posttest surveys were administered and returned via E-mail.

RESULTS

Quantitative Analysis

Of the 40 students who returned pretest surveys, 75% reported that they were "comfortable" with computer use; 12% reported that they were "adept" with the use of computers; 13% reported that they were unfamiliar with the use of computers. The two courses had similar proportions of students who were either adept at or unfamiliar with computers. Fifteen students in the PCP course who elected not to participate in the study returned the pretest survey. Of those students, 10 (75%) reported that they were unfamiliar with the use of computers and the remaining 5 students (25%) reported that they were comfortable with the use of computers.

Analysis of the posttest surveys indicated that fifty-seven percent of the students believed that the computer experience with Construe enhanced their course work; 33% of the students believed that the computer work had no impact on the course and 10% felt the computer work was of little value. The students had generally positive remarks to make about their instructors; 100% of the students reported that their instructors were responsive and helpful, and at the end of the semester, 90% reported that they were very comfortable communicating with their professors via E-mail. Eighty-eight percent of the students believed that the majority of their difficulties centered on server difficulties or problems accessing a computer.

The Wilcoxon-Mann-Whitney nonparametric test was performed on posttest data and no significant differences were found between the two groups on any items except the variable which asked if the subject would recommend the course to a friend. Students in PCP were significantly more likely to recommend the course to a friend than those in TOC (p = .004). This difference could be attributed to the course content or because the PCP students were allowed to generate their own knowledge acquisition through the assignments. Furthermore, students in the PCP class were not required to use Construe, indicating that those students who elected to participate in the project might have been more motivated or interested in acquiring computer knowledge. Conversely, students in the TOC class were required to use Construe, regardless of their motivation or interest in acquiring computer skills, which may have affected their overall assessment of the course.

The Wilcoxon-Matched Pairs Sign Ranks test was performed on survey questions common to both pre- and posttests. There were no significant differences between pre- and posttest responses on any common questions except students' reports of their comfort with using computers. The analysis showed that the mean comfort level increased by 1.60 (n = 40, p = .0000). This finding indicates that the computer-assisted learning experience had a positive impact on students' comfort with computer usage.

Qualitative Analysis

A qualitative analysis was performed on posttest survey questions related to students' reactions to the class. Students were also asked to state what they liked most and least about the use of computer-assisted learning. Difficulties with the computer program, lack of computer access, and server difficulties were identified most often. Students liked the ability to communicate with each other and the professor via E-mail, the convenience the computer provided for group work, and becoming computer proficient. In addition, many students believed that the computer work made the class more interesting.

DISCUSSION

With the advent of the information age, social workers will be required to become increasingly knowledgeable about computers. This study was conducted to examine the effectiveness of using a software web shell as an adjunct to classroom learning. The results indicated that the majority of students felt that the computer work enhanced their educational experience and increased their comfort using computers. Students were comfortable communicating with their professors via E-mail. The primary difficulties that students had centered on technical problems or problems related to having access to computers.

For both courses, the data analyses indicated that students felt positive about their experience with computer assisted learning as a supplement to the traditional classroom environment. Although Construe provided an opportunity to integrate learning theory with computer-centric objectives, the software shell itself had limitations. Therefore the authors recommend that research and web shell development continue in order to create optimal applications and demonstrate the efficacy of web-based instruction for social work education.

REFERENCES

Alessi, S. M., & Trolip, S. R. (1985). *Computer-based instruction: Methods and development*. Englewood Cliffs, NJ: Prentice-Hall.

Bobrow, D. G., & Norman, D. A. (1975). *Representation and understanding: Studies in cognitive science*. New York: Academic Press.

Collis, B., Oberg, A., & Shera, W. (1988-1989). An evaluation of computer-based instruction in statistical techniques for education and social work students. *Journal of Educational Technology Systems, 17*, 59-70.

Crossman, D. M. (1997). The Evolution of the World Wide Web as an emerging instructional technology tool. In B. H. Kahn (Ed.), *Web-based instruction* (pp. 19-23). Englewood Cliffs, NJ: Educational Technology Publications, Inc.

Flynn, J., & MacDonald, F. (1991). Waterslides and landmines in computer-based education. *Journal of Teaching in Social Work, 5*, 101-105.

Hudson, W. W. (1985). Computer managed instruction: An application in teaching introductory statistics. *Computers in Human Services, 1*, 117-123.

Jonassen, D. H. (1988). Hypertext principles for text and courseware design. *Educational Psychologist, 21*, 269-292.

Knowles, M. (1984). *The adult learner: A neglected species*, 3rd Edition. Houston, TX: Gulf Publishing.

Norman, D. A. (1973). *Cognitive organization and learning*. ERIC Document ED083543. San Diego, CA: University of California Center for Human Information Processing.

O'Mahoney, P. J. (1995). *Copyright fundamentals*. [Online]. Available: http://www.benedict.com [1998, January 17].

Patterson, D. (1994). Hypermedia in social work education. *Journal of Social Work Education, 30*, 267-277.

Patterson, D., & Yaffe, J. (1993). Using computer-assisted instruction to teach Axis-II of the DSM-III-R to social work students. *Research on Social Work Practice, 3*, 343-357.

Patterson, D., Pullen, L., Evers, E., Champlin, D., & Ralson, R. (1997). An experimental evaluation of HyperCDTX: Multimedia substance abuse treatment education software. *Computers in Human Services, 14*, 21-38.

Reigeluth, C. M. (Ed.). (1983). *Instructional design theories and models: An overview of their current status*. Hillsdale, NJ: Lawrence Erlbaum Associates.

_____ . (1995). Educational systems development and its relationship to ISC. In G. J. Anglin (Ed.), *Instructional technology* (pp. 84-93). Englewood, CO: Libraries Unlimited.

Relan, A., & Gillani, B. (1997). Web-based instruction and the traditional classroom: Similarities and Differences. In B. H. Kahn (Ed.), *Web-based instruction* (pp. 41-65). Englewood Cliffs, NJ: Educational Technology Publications, Inc.

Seabury, B., & Maple, F. (1993). Using computers to teach practice skills. *Social Work, 38*, 430-439.

Sherry, L., & Wilson, B. (1997). Transformative communication as a stimulus to web innovations. In B. H. Kahn (Ed.), *Web-based instruction* (pp. 67-73). Englewood Cliffs, NJ: Educational Technology Publications, Inc.

van den Berg, S., & Watt, J. (1991). Effects of educational settings on student responses to structured hypertext. *Journal of Computer-Based Instruction, 18*, 118-124.

Geographic Information Systems (GIS): Implications for Promoting Social and Economic Justice

Paige L. Tompkins
Linda H. Southward

SUMMARY. This article is a consideration of the implications for the use of Geographic Information Systems (GIS) technology in social work practice as a tool for improved visualization of social and economic inequalities. Along with a brief, general introduction to GIS, overviews are included of the historical uses of geographic mapping, as well as current applications of GIS technology in social work practice, education, and research. Specific illustrative examples of GIS-generated maps are presented. *[Article copies available for a fee from The Haworth Document Delivery Service: 1-800-342-9678. E-mail address: getinfo@ haworthpressinc.com]*

KEYWORDS. Geographic information systems (GIS), social work, social inequality, social justice

This article highlights the early uses of geographic mapping in social work practice and presents an overview of current technology using GIS to im-

Paige L. Tompkins, PhD, is Research Scientist, Social Science Research Center, and Adjunct Professor, College of Education, Mississippi State University, 100 Research Park, P.O. Box 5287, Mississippi State, MS 39762.

Linda H. Southward, PhD, is Research Scientist, Social Science Research Center, and Associate Professor, Sociology, Anthropology, and Social Work, Mississippi State University, 100 Research Park, P.O. Box 5287, Mississippi State, MS 39762.

[Haworth co-indexing entry note]: "Geographic Information Systems (GIS): Implications for Promoting Social and Economic Justice." Tompkins, Paige L., and Linda H. Southward. Co-published simultaneously in *Computers in Human Services* (The Haworth Press, Inc.) Vol. 15, No. 2/3, 1998, pp. 209-226; and: *Information Technologies: Teaching to Use–Using to Teach* (ed: Frank B. Raymond III, Leon Ginsberg, and Debra Gohagan) The Haworth Press, Inc., 1998, pp. 209-226. Single or multiple copies of this article are available for a fee from The Haworth Document Delivery Service [1-800-342-9678, 9:00 a.m. - 5:00 p.m. (EST). E-mail address: getinfo@haworthpressinc.com]

prove social work research and development activities. These research and development activities are important technological tools for social work in visualizing disparities as an impetus to promoting social and economic justice. Specific applications and examples of social work research incorporating GIS technology are included.

HISTORICAL ROOTS OF GIS

The founders of Hull-House, one of the earliest Settlement Houses in the United States, established in 1889, noted the importance of geographic mapping as a way to assess communities on a variety of social and economic indicators. Hull-House workers used mapping as an assessment tool in response to social and economic injustices related to child labor in the 19th ward of Chicago, the same area of town in which Hull-House was located. These settlement house workers had the insight to obtain information about social and economic injustices through an "extensive investigation in their neighborhood" and used community mapping as a primary data source. A compilation of these maps and essays by Hull-House residents in 1895 was entitled: *Hull-House Maps and Papers: A Presentation of Nationalities and Wages in a Congested District of Chicago, Together with Comments and Essays on Problems Growing Out of the Social Conditions.* Davis and McCree (1969) noted that a compilation of Hull-House investigations (e.g., door-to-door surveys, wage maps, studies of the Chicago ghetto and essays by Jane Addams and Ellen Starr), included multi-colored maps. Holbrook (1895) noted how these early community maps were used in describing neighborhood demographics:

> The Italians, the Russian and Polish, Jews, and the Bohemians lead in numbers and importance . . . The Irish control the pools; while the Germans, although they make up more than a third of Chicago's population, are not very numerous in this neighborhood; and the Scandinavians, who fill northwest Chicago, are a mere handful. Several Chinese in basement laundries, a dozen Arabians, about as many Greeks, a few Syrians, and seven Turks engaged in various occupations at the World's Fair give a cosmopolitan flavor to the region, but are comparatively inconsiderable in interest. (p. 17)

An assessment of wages by dwelling in this same geographic area was conducted, with six different income categories noted, ranging from $5.00 per week to "over twenty" [dollars] per week (Davis & McCree, 1969). In addition to the mapping of the neighborhoods by ethnicity and income, the *Hull-House Maps and Papers* included documentation of the sweatshops and working conditions of children in Chicago.

Geographic mapping has also been used as a tool in a wide array of epidemiological studies throughout the early part of this century with public health agencies (Haug, 1995). However, it has only been at the end of this century that technology has significantly improved upon the early ideas of community mapping.

CONTEMPORARY MAPPING APPLICATIONS

Technological advances in the last twenty years have improved upon earlier mediums of geographic mapping, resulting in an extremely useful tool with untold applications. This tool, GIS, is a branch of information sciences somewhat unique in that it holds not only the capacity to communicate to a broad audience including both professionals and nonprofessionals, but also has the power to explain and even persuade. Computer-based GIS technology is a tool that evolved from the need to integrate graphical data with tabular data. Using GIS to combine digital maps with tabular database information allows for the creation of thematic, "intelligent" maps (Hutchinson & Scott, 1995). These data maps provide viewers the opportunity to "visualize" the data, the results of which include a more efficient and more meaningful interpretation of data.

A simple, but limited (due to the formatting restrictions of a journal article) example of the visualization benefits of GIS technology can be seen by comparing Table 1 and Figure 1. Using a common demographic variable, population dispersion in the U.S., data are shown first in traditional tabular format (see Table 1) and then as a data map (see Figure 1). It is important to note that in Table 1, only a very small portion of the data (17 of 3,141 U.S. counties) has actually been included. In its entirety, Table 1 would occupy about 185 pages.

A second method of presenting the 1996 population data for the U.S. is presented in Figure 1. As noted previously, the benefits of this example of GIS technology is greatly limited by the lack of color, as well as size restrictions. In a full-scale GIS demonstration, these limitations would not exist, and a number of enhancements (e.g., zoom, interactive queries, etc.) would be available. However, regardless of the limitations, Figure 1 allows for a quicker and easier understanding of how the population of the U.S. was distributed in 1996 than does Table 1.

INCREASED UTILIZATION OF GIS TECHNOLOGY

The first GIS was created by the Canadian government in the 1960s (Goodchild, 1995). Other agencies designed similar systems, but it was not

TABLE 1. 1996 Population, by County, USA

State	County	Population
Alabama	Autauga	40113
Alabama	Baldwin	122654
Alabama	Barbour	25538
Alabama	Bibb	17938
Alabama	Blount	42553
Alabama	Bullock	11337
Alabama	Butler	22130
Alabama	Calhoun	119065
Alabama	Chambers	37481
Alabama	Cherokee	20952
Alabama	Chilton	34893
Alabama	Choctaw	16152
Alabama	Clarke	28476
Alabama	Clay	13620
Alabama	Cleburne	13511
Alabama	Coffee	42900
⋮	⋮	⋮
Wyoming	Weston	6632

Note: Data to be used for illustration purposes only.

until the late 1970s and early 1980s that improved technology and lower costs paved the way for widespread use of GIS technology. By the late 1980s, affordable personal computers, user-friendly GIS software, available GIS data, and powerful technological breakthroughs allowed governments and businesses, both public and private, to turn GIS into a multi-billion-dollar-a year industry (Hutchinson & Scott, 1995).

As a major thrust of contemporary political campaigns, politicians are also using GIS technology to target voters by geographic areas (Novotny & Jacobs, 1997). While sophisticated measures of polling electorates among various constituent groups is commonplace in political campaigns, it has only recently been coupled with GIS technology in an attempt to further distinguish differences, as opposed to similarities, of potential voters. According to

FIGURE 1. 1996 Population of the U.S. as a dot density map. Each dot represents 5,000 people. (Data to be used for illustration purposes only.)

Novotny and Jacobs (1997), this technology has increased the likelihood of candidates to "run several different simultaneous campaigns for several different constituencies, with different literature and materials for each." (p. 279). While this technology increases political candidates' ability to predict specific concerns by household, city block, neighborhood and community levels, it is cause for concern for persons who may not even be taken into account even as potential voters (Hill, 1991; Kline & Burstein, 1996). These persons, who are potentially "lost" voters, are among constituencies for whom social workers have historically advocated for in promoting social and economic justice.

SOCIAL WORK EDUCATION AND CURRICULUM

Social work educators should be at the forefront in linking research and development technologies to social work practitioners and policy makers. GIS technology is an excellent mechanism in which linkages among practice, policy, and research can occur. Social workers need to continue learning about technologies and information systems which can facilitate more accurate assessment, interventions and evaluation of services. Hoefer, Hoefer, and Tobias (1994) have been among the few writers to link social work practice, research, and education with GIS technology. The current wave of changing responsibilities from the federal to the state and local levels demands that more accurate, accessible and succinct information be made available on state, community and neighborhood levels. This devolution of government programs should also serve as a wake-up call to social work education at both the undergraduate and graduate level in returning to its historical roots of community-based practice, as established with the settlement house movement, over a century ago (Weil, 1996). Social work curriculums should be strengthened to integrate and promote the principles of century old community practice with the contemporary technologies, which together can serve to enhance social work practice and research. Hoefer et al. (1994) underscore one of the tenets of social work practice in viewing persons within their environmental context and suggest that GIS technology can assist in tracking both the physical and social aspects of these environments.

The Curriculum Policy Statement of the Council on Social Work Education (CSWE) is explicit in its charge to promote social and economic justice throughout the curriculum. Accredited social work programs must provide students with "an understanding of the dynamics and consequences of social and economic injustice, including all forms of human oppression and discrimination" (CSWE, 1992, p. 6). While policy, practice and human behavior sequences are generally considered customary venues for this content, the research sequence is a distinct arena which should not be overlooked, given increasing technological tools, such as GIS technology, in which indicators of social and economic injustices can readily be distinguished.

RESEARCH AND POLICY DIRECTIONS

Research projects which focus on various topics and components relating to social and economic justice can be sharpened by using GIS technology. Defining and redefining research question(s), formulating hypotheses, defining methodologies, analyzing data, interpreting results and disseminating reports are enhanced by visualization of the data. The following overview of the 1995 National Science Foundation (NSF) Initiative is a sound framework of social indicators of interest to social work researchers and policy-makers in which data can be visualized.

National Science Foundation Initiative

In this 1995 initiative, the NSF identified the following six areas of research to improve public policy regarding the social, economic, and cultural situations of U.S. citizens: workplace, education, families, neighborhoods, disadvantage, and poverty. Clearly, these are integral areas related to social work's historical and contemporary practice arenas. Calkins and Eagles (1995) pointed out that each of these areas has geographic components. A brief summary and practical use of these variables follow.

Workplace

In order to employ a productive workforce in a particular locale, the skills of the labor force must match the needs of the job market. Assessing the match by geographic variation can provide valuable information to policymakers. One of the cornerstones of recent federal and state welfare reform legislation is the mandate for recipients of Temporary Assistance to Needy Families (TANF) to be employed within specific time frames. GIS technology is a useful tool to visually overlay several variables of interest. For example, the geographical location of the clients can be compared with the geographical location of the jobs. Any number of variables such as transportation availability, child care sites and available slots, and educational level of clients in specific areas can all be entered to facilitate program planning for both short- and long-term initiatives. Changes in circumstances can also be tracked through virtually any time frame (i.e., weekly, monthly, yearly changes, etc.).

Education

Geographic variations between student performance and accessibility of educational opportunities exist. Both a community's and an individual's economic success depends on an educated workforce. In a recent publication, *Re-thinking the Brain: New Insights into Early Development* (1997), many of the country's foremost authorities came together for a conference to share empirical research findings and make recommendations on the importance of infant bonding as well as early childhood stimulation by families and care givers which reinforce the importance of the early years upon brain development and adult social-emotional functioning. Geographic mapping of various demographic variables coupled with the burgeoning development of brain research among children in the first three years of life could provide opportunities for more accurate assessments and appropriate interventions with children and their families.

Families

Changes in family life (e.g., more single-parent, more two-career, two-parent families) have been blamed for many social problems. These changes are often combined with locale-specific circumstances (e.g., concentrations of single-parent families residing in low-income housing projects). By mapping geographical locations to determine both positive and negative outcomes of families, social workers and other human service professionals could more accurately match services to needs of families within their own geographical area.

Neighborhoods

This area of inclusion in the NSF initiative makes explicit the importance of geography. Neighborhoods, while explicitly spatial, often function as the personal identity for their residents' families, educational, and economic status. Using GIS technology could be a relatively simple way in which researchers, community planners and citizens could better understand social, economic and political components of neighborhoods and then determine strategies to strengthen neighborhoods based upon these assessments.

Disadvantage

The nation's social diversity is structured by decisively spatial neighborhoods. The differences among neighborhood crime rates, poverty, labor markets, and property values are forces that play a role in the differentiation and segregation of U.S. social class and race. By utilizing GIS technology, not only can the differences of variables among geographic locations, but also similarities, be noted. In a recent editorial in *Social Work*, Mulroy and Ewalt (1996) note that social work practitioners in poor communities want to know the following:

> more about the characteristics of poverty neighborhoods, whether traditionally accepted indicators of housing need are still appropriate and, how to measure service needs in neighborhoods and communities that are increasingly diverse and multi-cultural. (p. 248)

Poverty

In the United States, the location of impoverished groups of people tends to be concentrated in certain geographic locations. These areas have disproportionate numbers of unskilled labor, low income families, poor schools, and reported incidences of criminal activity. In addition, it is also readily understood and accepted by practitioners and researchers in a variety of disciplines that there is a distinct difference between persons with low socioeconomic status and persons with higher socioeconomic status in terms of mortality and morbidity rates and available care (Ewalt, 1994).

GIS TECHNOLOGY RELEVANCE

With this initiative, the NSF emphasized the importance of using GIS technology to strengthen the understanding of policy-makers to assist in developing strategies to employ a productive workforce, enhance education, strengthen family functioning, build strong neighborhoods and communities, reduce factors associated with being disadvantaged, and overcome poverty. To be sure, these goals are congruent with the community-based social work practice. Utilizing GIS technology to connect social work research with macro practice yields a powerful source of advancing research, practice and policy decisions.

The community mapping begun by social workers at Hull-House has evolved from a rudimentary assessment technique to a state-of-the-art technology which has tremendous potential implications for social work practice, education, policy, and research. The use of computer technology (e.g., GIS) has become essential as an aid to understanding society and its complexities (Dribble, 1996). GIS can simplify the collection and manipulation of a wide variety of data, from a broad range of sources, for analysis within a single, coherent structure (Calkins and Eagles, 1995). Curry (1996) points out that previously, in order to obtain information associated with a particular geographic area, "one had to dig through masses of paper, during business hours, in a central location, and under the watchful eye of a suspicious bureaucrat . . ." (p. 1). The application of GIS technology is particularly useful in the areas of assessment and policy development, as well as a vast array of research and development social work activities. The following section presents an overview of practical applications of the use of this technology by Mississippi State University's Social Science Research Center (SSRC) and its use of GIS, along with specific examples of research and development activities in the areas of child welfare (e.g., family support/family preservation services (FP/FSS) and Adoption Foster Care Analysis and Reporting System (AFCARS)) and economic assistance programs (e.g., JOBS and Food Stamps).

MISSISSIPPI STATE UNIVERSITY'S
SOCIAL SCIENCE RESEARCH CENTER (SSRC) AND GIS

To meet GIS software needs, SSRC researchers use ArcView, a desktop mapping software package developed by Environmental Systems Research Institute, Inc. (ESRI), one of the leading companies in the information management industry. ArcView allows for data input, manipulation, management, analysis, and presentation. Although there are varying ways to use GIS,

SSRC researchers approach GIS as a five-component structure (as does ESRI) represented in Figure 2.

Part 1: Data

With the exception of some geographic boundary files, GIS software packages do not come stocked with data. However, most GIS software is helpful with regard to getting data into the system. SSRC researchers frequently use large databases (e.g., U.S. Census data, U.S. Department of Education data) within GIS projects. The data are converted to dBase files beforehand since ArcView handles these types of databases easily. ArcView also offers the opportunity to build databases within the system.

Part 2: Data Manipulation

There are numerous situations in which data might need to be manipulated in some manner. Examples of the types of manipulation include spatial, file-format, and numerical. At the SSRC, rarely are databases from secondary sources, such as those mentioned above, used without manipulation. Depending on the need(s), some manipulation is done within ArcView. More often, however, manipulation of databases is handled by some other software package such as Statistical Package for the Social Sciences (SPSS).

Part 3: Data Management

Good management of GIS data is crucial to the utilization of the technology. Those who manage the data must be adept at handling and manipulating

FIGURE 2. Components of a GIS

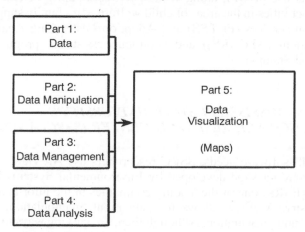

(sometimes very large) databases. SSRC researchers who use GIS maintain their own databases, but the manner in which the data are managed is similar enough that database sharing is feasible.

Part 4: Data Analysis

GIS has many more uses than simply producing static geographic maps. In a functional GIS, questions ranging from very simple to very complex can be asked and answered. SSRC mainly uses GIS technology as a way to visualize data. Examples of the types of analysis used to do this include proximity analysis, buffering, and thematic overlay analysis of related data.

Part 5: Data Visualization

SSRC researchers use GIS technology both interactively and non-interactively. ArcView offers methods of data mapping to facilitate both approaches. Additionally, SSRC researchers sometimes incorporate text, charts, graphs, photographs, and various multimedia into GIS presentations in order to extend the functionality of data visualization.

The following section and figures are examples of the areas in which researchers have used GIS technology on research projects relating to child welfare and economic assistance programs. It should be noted that the example maps are for illustration purposes only, and are limited by the same restraints as mentioned in the discussion of Figure 1 (see Contemporary Mapping Applications).

CHILD WELFARE SERVICES

Family Preservation/Family Support Services

As part of the development for Mississippi's Five Year Plan for FP/FSS, baseline data was pursued through several avenues (e.g., public forums, state-wide survey, review of previous studies). One of the most informative components was the use of thematic maps in determining quality of life indicators on county level data on a number of variables. This information was valuable to the developers of the Five year plan by facilitating an understanding of how counties within the state vary on indicators of child well-being. By using GIS technology, a profile of how similar and how different quality of life indicators varied by state could be generated. Selected indicators of thematic maps included:

1. Percent of all births to single, teenage mothers.
2. Percent of all premature births.
3. Child death rate per 100,000 youth.
4. Child suicide rate per 100,000 youth.
5. Percent of all children below poverty line.

Adoption Foster Care Analysis and Reporting System (AFCARS)

A growing body of literature suggests the increased expectations of government agencies and legislative bodies in tracking cohorts through the foster care systems and what changes occur (e.g., rates of recidivism, number and length of placements, etc.) while children are in placement (Goerge, Wulczyn & Fanshel, 1994). Integrating GIS technology with child welfare information systems becomes a powerful tool for policy- and decision-makers in child welfare in the areas of program planning, practice initiatives and resource allocations. GIS technology allows for thematic maps in assessing social workers' assessments of child welfare practice. Some examples of these questions include (see Figure 3 for a thematic map example):

1. Current number of active cases and ideal case load.
2. Current number of foster care cases vs. ideal caseloads.
3. Percent of reports by ethnicity and case types.
4. Percent of removals by categories (abuse, neglect).

While each of these categories of information can be reported in conventional forms, it does not have the power, richness or clarity as when presented in conjunction with graphic representations of the data. Moreover, the ability to see changes in cohorts over time equips social workers and policy planners with more accurate assessments of the gaps and needed changes in service delivery.

ECONOMIC ASSISTANCE

Job Opportunities and Basic Skills (JOBS)

In Fall, 1996, a qualitative research project was conducted by SSRC researchers to assess experiences of clients, service providers and case managers of the JOBS program. Although the methodology was qualitative, the importance of using thematic maps, in which demographic and project related data could be visualized, enhanced this project. Specific maps graphically displayed county level information which included information on child care, transportation and job training (see Figure 4).

FIGURE 3. Percent of removals for abuse, data for active cases by county, MS, May 1997. Thematic map example of AFCARS data. (Data to be used for illustration purposes only.) Produced by: Social Science Research Center, Mississippi State University.

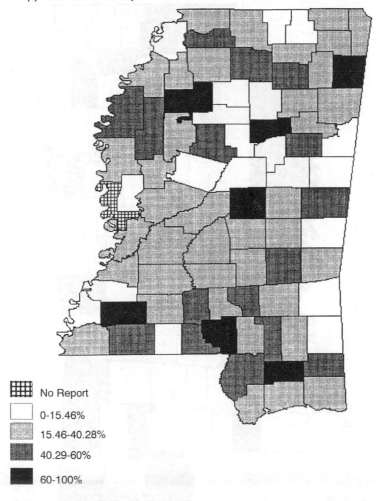

Another application of GIS technology in an economic assistance program was a feasibility study of implementing an electronic benefit transfer (EBT) for persons who receive Food Stamps. In a rural state, such as Mississippi, where not all grocery stores are equipped with electronic scanners, it was necessary to determine the proximity of clients to grocery stores that can

FIGURE 4. Number of clients receiving GED's by county, MS, 1995. Thematic map example of JOBS data. (Data to be used for illustration purposes only.) Produced by: Social Science Research Center, Mississippi State University.

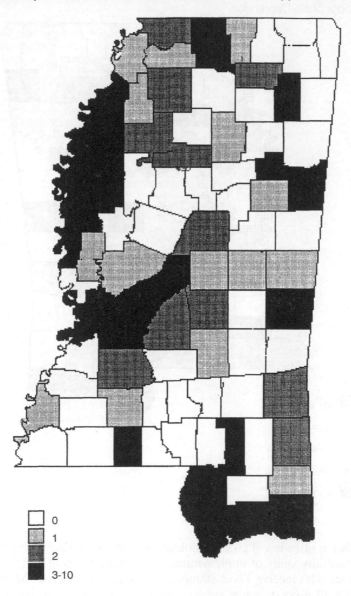

0

1

2

3-10

accept the electronic cards. By entering the client's zip code and the location of all grocery stores throughout the state, areas in which electronic cards would be plausible were readily apparent. Using this technology not only was cost effective in terms of selecting sites in which to pilot the EBT cards, it assisted agency planners to consider the access issues of clients who were geographically distant from area groceries. This is just one example of how the constraints of geographic boundaries (particularly in predominantly rural states) affect recipients' access to services. DuBois and Miley (1996) note that services in rural areas reveal "gaps in the availability and accessibility of services" (p. 96). Utilization of county-level, census track information through GIS technology allows researchers and policy-makers to determine areas of greatest need.

COST EFFECTIVENESS AND BENEFIT-COST ANALYSIS

In addition to enhancing policy-makers' ability to make more informed decisions by utilizing GIS technology in terms of promoting social justice, there is also opportunity to use GIS technology to advance both cost effectiveness and benefit-cost analysis. In cost effectiveness models, inputs are estimated in economic units and outcomes are measured by the actual impact upon populations, while cost effectiveness measures both inputs and outputs in economic units (Pecora, Fraser, Nelson, McCroskey & Meezan, 1995). Until recently there have been scant benefit-cost analyses of social service programs, particularly in many prevention-based programs (Kim, Coletti, Crutchfield, Williams & Helper, 1995). Given that many of the prevention and intervention programs social workers are involved with measure data that is not always easily quantifiable, GIS technology affords researchers and practitioners the opportunity to visualize changes in outcomes.

ADDITIONAL APPLICATIONS

Schools of social work, professional membership organizations (e.g., CSWE, NASW, BPD, etc.), and state-level licensing boards can benefit by utilizing GIS software to learn more about their students, memberships and constituents. Mapping demographics of survey data paints striking visuals that help identify groups of individuals by any number of variables. One application of this used by these researchers was to determine the number of social workers by degree, county of residence (see Figure 5) and university geographic catchment area, as a part of a feasibility study for an M.S.W. program in

FIGURE 5. Licensed social workers by county, MS, 1997. Thematic map example. (Data to be used for illustration purposes only.) Produced by: Social Science Research Center, Mississippi State University.

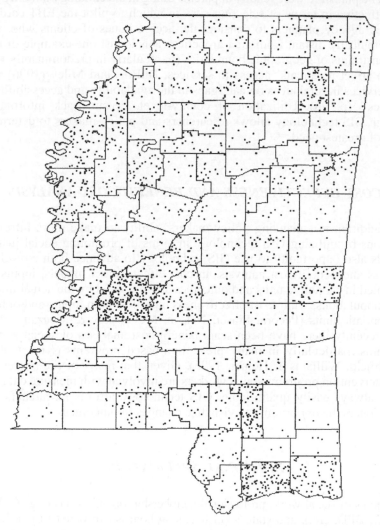

predominantly rural, under-served areas of the state to university administration and college board administration. Once again, the visual representation/display of data, generated through GIS mapping, reinforced the support and testimony from both B.S.W. alumni and area social work employers to administrators and policy-makers.

CONCLUSIONS AND RECOMMENDATIONS

Similar to Jane Addams' use of hand-drawn maps to depict Chicago residents and their needs in the late 1800s, today's social workers can use GIS as an even more powerful tool to help delineate client needs. Despite the milieu, (private practice, social work education, research, policy & planning, macro practice, etc.), social workers have unprecedented opportunities to advance social work practice by having more information about individuals, families, groups, communities, organizations and institutions and their environments through GIS technology.

The professional Code of Ethics of the National Association of Social Workers (NASW) is crystal clear on social workers' responsibilities to "critically examine and keep current with emerging knowledge relevant to social work and fully use evaluation and research evidence in their professional practice" (p. 25). As noted earlier, implications for using GIS technology with social work include: planning, policy-making, decision-making, communication, and instruction in the areas of workplace, education, families, neighborhoods, disadvantage, and poverty. Further research could develop frameworks in which to fully examine components in which GIS technology could advance social work research and thereby inform practice. The use and responsible application of these skills and other developing technologies will be useful tools to the social work profession to advance social and economic justice into the next millennium.

REFERENCES

Addams, J. (1910). *Twenty years at Hull-House.* New York: Macmillan.

ArcView GIS, version 3.0. (1996). Redmond, WA: Environmental Systems Research Institute, Inc.

Calkins, H., & Eagle, M. (1995). Geographic information analysis and human capital research: A report to the National Science Foundation and the Department of Housing and Urban Development. *Proceedings of the Geographic Information Analysis and Human Capital Research Conference.* Boulder, CA: National Center for Geographic Information and Analysis.

Council on Social Work Education. (1992). *Curriculum policy statement for the baccalaureate degree programs in social work education.* Alexandria, VA.

Curry, M. (1996). The ethics of spatial-visual representation. *Research Initiative 19: GIS and Society: The Social Implications of How People, Space, and Environment are Represented in GIS–Specialist Meeting Report.* South Haven, MN: National Center for Geographic Information and Analysis.

DuBois, B., & Miley, K. (1996). *Social work: An empowering profession.* Boston: Allyn & Bacon.

Davis, A.F., & McCree, M. (Eds.). (1969). *Eighty years at Hull-House.* Chicago: Quadrangle Books.

Dibble, C. (1996). Representing individuals and societies in GIS. *Research Initiative 19: GIS and Society: The Social Implications of How People, Space, and Environment Are Represented in GIS–Specialist Meeting Report.* South Haven, MN: National Center for Geographic Information and Analysis.

Environmental Systems Research Institute, Inc. (ESRI). (No date). ESRI Homepage [Online]. Available://www.ersi.com [1997, August 25].

Ewalt, P. (1994). Poverty matters. *Social Work, 39*(2),148-150.

George, R., Wulczyn, F., & Fanshel, D. (1994). A foster care research agenda for the 90s. *Child Welfare, 73*(5), pp. 525-537.

Goodchild, M.F. (1995). Geographic information systems. *Microsoft Encarta '95.* Redmond, WA: Microsoft (CD ROM text and images).

Haug, R. (1995). *From the group up: The institutionalization of public health administration in Mississippi.* Unpublished dissertation, Mississippi State University.

Hill, D. (1991). Strategic polling: The fine art of honing in on voter preferences. *Campaigns and Elections, 12*(3), 26-34.

Hoefer, R.A., Hoefer, R.M., & Tobias, R. (1994). Geographic information systems and human services. *Journal of Community Practice, 1*(3), 113-128.

Holbrook, A. (1985). Map notes and comments (p. 17). In *Hull House map and papers; A presentation of nationalities in a congested district of Chicago, together with comments and essay on problems growing out of the social conditions. Authors: Residents of Hull-House.* New York: Crowell.

Hutchinson, S., & Daniel, L. (1995). *Inside ArcView.* Santa Fe, NM: OnWord Press.

Kelley, F., & Stevens, A. (1969). Wage earning children. (pp. 45-50). In A.F. Davis & M. McCree (Eds.), *Eighty years at Hull-House.* Chicago: Quadrangle Books.

Kim, S., Coletti, S., Crutchfield, C., Williams, C., & Healer, N. (1995). Benefit-cost analysis of drug abuse prevention programs: A macroscopic approach. *Journal of Drug Education, 25*(2), 111-127.

Kline, D., & Burstein, D. (1996). Is government obsolete? *Wired, 4*(1), 86-104.

Mulroy, E., & Ewalt, P. (1996). Affordable housing: A basic need and a social issue. *Social Work, 41*(3), 245-249.

National Association of Social Workers. (1996). *Code of Ethics,* Washington, D.C.

National Science Foundation. (1995). *The Human Capital Initiative: Opportunities for Human Capital Research* (NSF 95-8). Arlington, VA: Division of Social, Behavioral and Economic Research.

Novotny, P., & Jacobs, R. (1997). Geographic information systems and the new political landscape of political technologies. *Social Science Computer Review, 15*(3), 264-285.

Openshaw, S. (1996). GIS and society: A lot of fuss about very little that matters and not enough about that which does! *Research Initiative 19: GIS and Society: The Social Implications of How People, Space, and Environment Are Represented in GIS-Specialist Meeting Report.* South Haven, MN: National Center for Geographic Information and Analysis.

Pecora, P., Fraser, M., Nelson, K., McCroskey, J., & Meezan, W. (1995). *Evaluating family-based services.* New York: Aldine de Gruyter.

Shore, R. (1997). *Rethinking the brain: New insights into early development.* New York: Families and Work Institute.

SPSS for Windows, version 7.5.1. (1996). Chicago: SPSS Inc.

Weil, M. (1996). Community building: Building community practice. *Social Work, 41*(5), 481-499.

Index

Note: Page numbers followed by f indicate figures; page numbers followed by t indicate tables.

227